Demopolis

MW00613608

What did democracy mean before liberalism? What are the consequences for our lives today? Combining history with political theory, this book restores the core meaning of democracy as collective and limited self-government by citizens. That, rather than majority tyranny or human rights, is what democracy meant in ancient Athens. Participatory self-government is the basis of political practice in "Demopolis," a hypothetical modern state powerfully imagined by award-winning historian and political scientist Josiah Ober. Demopolis's residents aim to establish a secure, prosperous, and nontyrannical community, where citizens govern as a collective, both directly and through representatives, and willingly assume the costs of self-government because doing so benefits them, both as a group and individually. Basic democracy, as exemplified in real Athens and imagined Demopolis, can provide a stable foundation for a liberal state. It also offers a possible way forward for religious or otherwise nonliberal societies seeking a realistic alternative to autocracy.

JOSIAH OBER is currently Professor of Classics, Political Science, and (by courtesy) Philosophy at Stanford, and he has chaired both a department of humanities (Classics at Princeton) and a department of social science (Political Science at Stanford). He has held visiting professorships in the UK, France, and Australia. His previous books have won prizes from the American Philological Association, the Society for Institutional and Organizational Economics, and the Association of Academic Publishers and have been translated into French, German, Greek, Italian, Chinese, Korean, and Turkish.

THE SEELEY LECTURES

The John Robert Seeley Lectures have been established by the University of Cambridge as a biennial lecture series in social and political studies, sponsored jointly by the Faculty of History and the University Press. The Seeley Lectures provide a unique forum for distinguished scholars of international reputation to address, in an accessible manner, topics of broad interest in social and political studies. Subsequent to their public delivery in Cambridge, the University Press publishes suitably modified versions of each set of lectures. Professor James Tully delivered the inaugural series of Seeley Lectures in 1994 on the theme of *Constitutionalism in an Age of Diversity*.

The Seeley Lectures include

(1)   Strange Multiplicity: Constitutionalism in an Age of Diversity
JAMES TULLY
ISBN 978 0 521 47694 2 (paperback)
Published 1995

(2)   The Dignity of Legislation
JEREMY WALDRON
ISBN 978 0 521 65092 2 (hardback) 978 0 521 65883 6 (paperback)
Published 1999

(3)   Women and Human Development: The Capabilities Approach
MARTHA C. NUSSBAUM
ISBN 978 0 521 66086 0 (hardback) 978 0 521 00385 8 (paperback)
Published 2000

(4)   Value, Respect, and Attachment
JOSEPH RAZ
ISBN 978 0 521 80180 5 (hardback) 978 0 521 00022 2 (paperback)
Published 2001

(5)   The Rights of Others: Aliens, Residents, and Citizens
SEYLA BENHABIB
ISBN 978 0 521 83134 5 (hardback) 978 0 521 53860 2 (paperback)
Published 2004

(6)   Laws of Fear: Beyond the Precautionary Principle
CASS R. SUNSTEIN
ISBN 978 0 521 84823 7 (hardback) 978 0 521 61512 9 (paperback)
Published 2005

(7)   Counter-Democracy: Politics in an Age of Distrust
PIERRE ROSANVALLON
ISBN 978 0 521 86622 2 (hardback) 978 0 521 71383 2 (paperback)
Published 2008

(8)   On the People's Terms: A Republican Theory and Model of Democracy
PHILIP PETTIT
ISBN 978 1 107 00511 2 (hardback) 978 0 521 18212 6 (paperback)
Published 2012

(9)   The Politics of the Human
ANNE PHILLIPS
ISBN 978 1 107 093973 (hardback) 978 1 107 475830 (paperback)
Published 2015

(10)   The Sleeping Sovereign: The Invention of Modern Democracy
RICHARD TUCK
ISBN 978 1 107 130142 (hardback) 978 1 107 570580 (paperback)
Published 2015

DEMOPOLIS

Democracy before Liberalism in Theory and Practice

JOSIAH OBER

Stanford University, California

CAMBRIDGE
UNIVERSITY PRESS

CAMBRIDGE
UNIVERSITY PRESS

University Printing House, Cambridge CB2 8BS, United Kingdom

One Liberty Plaza, 20th Floor, New York, NY 10006, USA

477 Williamstown Road, Port Melbourne, VIC 3207, Australia

4843/24, 2nd Floor, Ansari Road, Daryaganj, Delhi – 110002, India

79 Anson Road, #06–04/06, Singapore 079906

Cambridge University Press is part of the University of Cambridge.

It furthers the University's mission by disseminating knowledge in the pursuit of education, learning, and research at the highest international levels of excellence.

www.cambridge.org
Information on this title: www.cambridge.org/9781316510360
DOI: 10.1017/9781108226790

© Josiah Ober 2017

First published 2017

Printed in the United States of America by Sheridan Books, Inc.

A catalog record for this publication is available from the British Library

ISBN 978-1-316-51036-0 Hardback
ISBN 978-1-316-64983-1 Paperback

For Denise, Spike, Stella, Blanche, Bindi, and Enki.
They pounced.

Contents

Figures

Tables

Preface: Democracy before Liberalism

Imagine a country that is secure, prosperous, and ruled by its citizens. They disagree on many things, some of them very deep and important. But they agree about the high value of collective self-government, and they are willing to pay the costs of having it. The people of this country live with freedom of speech and association, political equality, and civic dignity. But they have not settled on their stance in regard to state religion. Nor have they committed to promoting universal human rights at home or abroad. Nor have they decided on a principle of social justice for distributing the benefits of social cooperation. Call that country Demopolis and its government basic democracy.

This book asks what it would mean to be a citizen of Demopolis. What will be gained and what is lost when life in Demopolis is compared to life in a liberal democracy? I answer those questions, first, from the vantage point of a worried liberal, one who hopes to shore up the political foundations of liberal values and who believes that government could be something other than a potentially intrusive threat to personal liberty combined with a potentially paternalistic provider of distributive outcomes. But I also try to answer questions about what life in Demopolis would entail from the very different perspective of a religious traditionalist residing in an autocratic state. The traditionalist I have in mind dreams of a life without autocrats but is not ready to embrace contemporary liberal values. Does a theory of democracy have anything to say to him or her?

I focus on democracy "before liberalism" because I suppose (without arguing the point) that in the twenty-first century, liberalism is the dominant value system with which democracy has been interwoven. Political liberalism is the tradition in which I was raised and to which I remain deeply attached; I have no wish to live in a society that is anything other than a liberal democracy. But, like every value system, liberalism obscures what it does not promote. I argue that the intermixture of liberalism has obscured the positive value of collective self-government, as an instrument to desired ends and as a choiceworthy end in itself. I hope to show liberals why it is a wrong to regard citizen participation in government as a cost that can or should be minimized. And that it is a mistake to view a preference for citizen self-government and a fear of government captured by self-interested elites as uniquely appropriate to populists, anarchists, or Schmittian agonists.[1]

Liberalism is not the only system of value that can be blended into democracy or that has been imagined as inseparable from it. I offer here a theory of democracy that is not only before liberalism but also before Marxism, before philosophical anarchism, before libertarianism, before contemporary Confucianism or other theories based on "Asian values." My hope is to show that democracy in and of itself effectively promotes various desirable conditions of existence, and that it does so quite independently of liberalism or any other theory of moral value.

The goal is not to denigrate moral value-centered political theory. I do not hope to convince anyone that "just plain democracy" is inherently superior to the various political hybrids that have been advocated by political theorists working within liberalism (or Marxism, and so on). Rather, my aim is to demonstrate what a basic form of democracy does have to offer on its own terms. Basic democracy may be analogized to a wild species in an era of well-meaning programs of hybridization. The wild species is not intrinsically *better* than the hybrids, nor should successful hybrids be uprooted in favor of a nostalgic preference for the wild original. But for reasons analogous to a biologist's interest in the genetics and behavior of native species, we may gain from studying democracy "in the wild." By focusing primarily on hybrids, I suppose that value theorists have failed to appreciate the relationship between the conditions necessary for democracy and liberal values and have overlooked specifically democratic goods.

This is a book about what collective self-government costs and what it can provide to people willing to pay those costs: a recognizable and potentially attainable sort of human flourishing – the chance to live as an active participant in a reasonably secure and prosperous society in which citizens govern themselves and pursue other projects of value to themselves. I suggest that the easiest way to think about the costs and benefits of democracy

---

[1] That mistake may be predicated on statements such as that of Ronald Reagan in his famous "time to choose" speech of October 27, 1964, in support of Barry Goldwater's presidential candidacy: "This is the issue of this election: Whether we believe in our capacity for self-government or whether we abandon the American revolution and confess that a little intellectual elite in a far-distant capitol can plan our lives for us better than we can plan them ourselves." On anarchists and Schmittian agonists, see Chapters 3 and 8.

without liberalism is to describe a democracy that did or might pertain in a community *before* liberal value commitments have been added to the constitutional order. But, we may also think, in either a utopian or (more likely) dystopian register, of democracy *after* liberalism, where citizens confront a society in which constitutional features associated with contemporary liberalism are crumbling or have been abandoned. I address democracy after liberalism in the epilogue.

Liberalism emerged, in the seventeenth to twentieth centuries, as an answer to certain dire problems, including wars of religion, fascism, and authoritarian communism. Those problems have not disappeared. But we now face new and pressing problems arising from the very success of the liberal solutions: technocratic government, economic disruption, political polarization, alienation conjoined with nationalistic populism and a partisan politics of identity. A theory of democracy before liberalism is no panacea for these, or other, ills of modernity. But it may point to a new direction for democratic theory and, perhaps, for political action.

Democracy without liberalism is sometimes depicted by liberal political theorists as being a fundamentally, even viciously, *antiliberal* ideology, inspired by a Rousseauian fantasy of a unified popular will and powered by unconstrained majoritarianism. I hope to show that pure majoritarianism, although a readily imaginable (if unstable) form of politics, is a corruption of democracy. It is neither the original nor the normal and healthy form of the regime type. So I hope to offer a degree of reassurance to liberal democrats by showing that some of what they value is delivered by democracy in itself and that nightmarishly illiberal consequences need not necessarily follow upon a crisis of liberalism in a democratic state. But I also hope to have something to say to traditionalists who are tired of being ruled by tyrants but who reject certain tenets of contemporary liberalism – notably, state-level neutrality in respect to religion. As matters now stand, such people may doubt that democracy of any kind is really an option for them. Their doubts are well grounded only if democracy is available uniquely as a package deal of which liberalism is an integral part.

This book presents a political theory that is at once historical and normative. It is concerned with both adaptability and stability. It is decidedly nonideal. It accepts Kant's famous claim (in Proposition 6 of his 1784 "Idea for a Universal History with a Cosmopolitan Purpose") that "out of the crooked timber of humanity, nothing entirely straight can be made." But it assumes that, under the right conditions, crooked timbers can be assembled into a sturdy and adaptable framework for living together without a master. It describes a political solution to a fundamental problem of social cooperation in a diverse community rather than a morally satisfactory solution to the problem of social justice. The solution proposed here offers people who agree on a few fundamentals a way to achieve certain valued ends. But those ends do not include the moral end of "a fully just society" – no matter how justice is imagined – much less a fully just world.

The account of democracy offered here is guardedly optimistic, in the "cup half full" sense. I seek to show what democracy without liberalism could be at its best – in the form that would most fully support the possibility of human flourishing for many people in a diverse community, if not for all people, everywhere. Even that half-filled cup requires certain conditions, backed by rules, enforced by citizens. The conditions are demanding; the rules depend on good design; the citizens must be well motivated. None of that is guaranteed. No form of government is proof against corruption, and too many regimes, self-described as democracies, have brought about conditions intolerable not only to liberals but also to nonliberals seeking a decent alternative to autocracy.

The relevant question for the sort of nonideal theory I offer here is not whether things can go wrong in a democracy – they obviously can, and often have. Rather, the relevant questions are, What would it mean for collective self-government to go right? What conditions would make that possible? Can those conditions be achieved by ordinary people in the real world? The requirement that collective self-government be humanly achievable and sustainable leavens the optimism of my account of democracy before liberalism. I consider the empty half of the cup in the epilogue.

Acknowledgments

The ideas in this book have been incubating for a good many years. They took their present form when an invitation from Cambridge University's Centre for Political Thought gave me the opportunity to present the Seeley Lectures in October 2015. My deepest thanks to the Cambridge Faculty of History; to my extraordinarily kind and generous hosts John Robertson and Christopher Meckstroth; and to the many students and faculty at Cambridge who attended the lectures and seminar, posed deep questions, and made penetrating comments, for making my visit immensely rewarding and enjoyable. Clare Hall provided ideal accommodations during my stay. A research leave from Stanford University and a fellowship at Stanford's Humanities Center in the academic year 2013–2014 allowed me time off from my ordinary teaching duties to develop a preliminary draft of the lectures. A visiting Leventis Professorship at the University of Edinburgh in the autumn term of 2015 presented the opportunity to do a first round of editorial revisions in delightful surroundings and in conversation with congenial and erudite colleagues.

Before and after delivering the lectures in Cambridge, I was invited to present parts of the argument at several lectures, workshops, and seminars. I received very helpful comments and questions at the University of California at Berkeley, the Central European University, Charleston College, Dartmouth College, the University of California at Davis, the University of Edinburgh, the EHESS (Paris), Emory University, the IHR (London), McMaster University, the University of Maryland at Baltimore, the University of New Hampshire, Princeton University, St. Andrews University, Stanford University, Trinity College (Dublin), UNISA (Pretoria), the University of Washington, Wellesley College, Wesleyan University, and William and Mary College.

Two anonymous readers and many friends and colleagues have helpfully commented in detail on part or all of the manuscript, saving me from interpretive and factual mistakes, encouraging me to read more widely, and urging me to think through my arguments more carefully and to present them more clearly. I owe a profound debt of gratitude to Danielle Allen, Ryan Balot, Annabel Brett, Mirko Canevaro, David Carter, Paul Cartledge, Federica Carugati, Emilee Chapman, Sean Corner, Paul Demont, Huw Duffy, Jacob Eisler, Amos Espeland, John Ferejohn, Luc Foisneau, Catherine Frost, Charles Girard, Deborah Gordon, Ben Gray, Stephen Halliwell, Jon Hesk, Kinch Hoekstra, Bob and Nan Keohane, Melissa Lane, Tony Lang, Jacob Levy, Steve Macedo, Bernard Manin, Adrienne Mayor, Alison McQueen, Chris Meckstroth, Jan-Werner Müller, Rob Reich, Nicholas Rengger, John Robertson, Stefan Sciaraffa, Artemis Seaford, Matt Simonton, Sarah Song, Peter Stone, David Teegarden, Mathias Thaler, Barry Weingast, and Leif Wenar. Their generous help has improved this book immeasurably, in form and substance. But it remains a personal take on democratic theory, and no one should be assumed to agree with what I have written here. The usual disclaimer, to the effect that remaining flaws are the result of authorial pig-headedness, is very much in force. Special thanks are due to Michele Angel, for the original art that graces the book's cover; to my Cambridge editor, Elizabeth Friend-Smith; and to the staff of Cambridge University Press.

Above all, I thank Adrienne Mayor, my life's partner, without whom I would never have written anything worth a damn.

Section 2.2 is adapted from "The Original Meaning of Democracy: Capacity to Do Things, Not Majority Rule," *Constellations* 15, no. 1: 3–9 (2008). Section 5.4 is adapted from "Natural Capacities and Democracy as a Good-in-Itself," *Philosophical Studies* 132: 59–73 (2007). Sections 6.6–6.8 are adapted from "Democracy's Dignity," *American Political Science Review* 106, no. 4: 827–846 (2012). Sections 7.6 and 7.7 are adapted from "Democracy's Wisdom: An Aristotelian Middle Way for Collective Judgment," *American Political Science Review* 107, no. 1: 104–122 (2013). My thanks to these journals for adopting rules allowing authors to reuse their own original materials.

Note on the Text

Works by classical Greek authors are cited according the ordinary conventions of classical scholarship. Hobbes's *Leviathan* is cited by chapter and page number in the Cambridge edition (1991).

Basic Democracy

This book answers some basic questions about a basic form of democracy: What is it? Why does it arise? How is it sustained? What is it good for? For people interested in politics, these are important questions. My answers are based in part on political theorizing, in part on ancient history. Those interested in both politics and history may find democracy's deep past worth considering. But why and how democracy *before liberalism* is relevant to contemporary political theory or practice may be less obvious. Demonstrating that relevance is this book's purpose.

I offer a theory of politics grounded in understanding humans as strategically rational and adapted by nature to living social lives under certain conditions. When those social conditions are most fully met, the potential for human flourishing (in the sense of joint and several material and psychic well-being) is highest. Those social conditions are, so I will try to show, uniquely well supported by democracy. Democracy is distinguishable from familiar forms of liberalism. Political conditions necessary for democracy overlap with fundamental liberal values, so democracy and liberalism are readily conjoined. But the conjunction of democracy with liberalism is not inevitable. Disambiguating democracy as such from the overfamiliar hybrid, liberal democracy clarifies what democracy is good for and how democratic goods are produced.[1]

I.I POLITICAL THEORY

According to a recent World Values Survey, residents of each of the 34 countries surveyed ranked living in a democratic country as very important (from 7+ in Russia to 9+ in Sweden, on a scale of 10). In every country, there is a substantial gap between respondents' views of democracy's importance and their assessments of how democratically their own

---

[1] On "good for," see Kraut 2007. On "conditions for democracy," see Ober 2003.

country is governed. The gap suggests that democracy remains, in part, aspirational: a hope that is not fully realized.[2] Moreover, in the contemporary world, democracy is a near-universal aspiration, although it would be foolish to suppose that democracy means the same thing to everyone. In political theory, as in ordinary language, "democracy" is a classic example of an essentially contested political concept. It goes without saying that there are many definitions on offer.[3] No one definition is authoritative in the sense of dominating all competitors in every context. My goal in these chapters is to better understand what I call *basic democracy*. Democracy is basic insofar as it is concerned with the legitimate authority of a *demos* – that is, the organized and justified political power of a citizenry or "a people."[4]

A theory of basic democracy starts with questions of legitimacy and capacity: *Why ought* a demos hold public authority – rather than, say, a monarch, a small body of aristocrats, or a technocratic elite? And, because *ought* implies *can, How can* a demos competently exercise authority in a complex society?[5] Basic democracy is not, in the first instance, concerned with questions of personal autonomy, inherent human rights, or distributive justice. "Liberalism" is, of course, another essentially contested concept. But I take autonomy, rights, and justice, along with a commitment to neutrality at the level of state authority and religion, to be among the primary commitments of mainstream contemporary liberalism, and I take

---

[2] World Values Survey, Wave 6 (2010–2014), Question V140: "How important is it for you to live in a country that is governed democratically? On this scale where 1 means it is 'not at all important' and 10 means 'absolutely important' what position would you choose?" Question V141: "And [on the same scale] how democratically is this country being governed today?" www.worldvaluessurvey .org/ (accessed July 10, 2016). Results summarized in Achen and Bartels 2016: 4–6, Figure 1.1.

[3] Gallie 1955, who coined the phrase "essentially contested concept," employs democracy among his four "live" examples; see esp. 168–169, 184–186. Such concepts have the following properties, each of which is relevant to the discussion in this book: They are appraisive, internally complex in ways that admit of a variety of descriptions in which different aspects are graded in different orders of importance; they are open in character and used both aggressively and defensively; those who use the concept typically claim the authority of a historical exemplar; the use of the concept gives rise to genuine (productive, if not resolvable) disputes as to its meaning.

[4] The Greek word *demos* can alternatively mean "citizen assembly," "majority of a citizen assembly," "nonelite citizens," and "the many who are relatively poor." These other meanings are secondary in that they are historically subsequent to, and derive from, the core meaning as "citizenry/people." See Chapter 2.

[5] Note that, while the justification for the legitimacy of the demos's rule must be offered to each citizen, in order to limit defection and preserve stability (Section 4.4), it is not (as in liberal social contract theories) an explanation for why the compromise of an assumed pristine condition of prepolitical individual freedom is rationally choiceworthy, nor (as in liberal justice theories, e.g., Christiano 2008: 232–240) based on a claim about distributive justice. Rather the justification for democracy contests the claims of rival would-be rulers to the effect that some other system is better able to fulfill the ends for which the state exists.

them to be moral commitments.[6] As a historical regime, democracy antedates the philosophical enunciation of those liberal moral commitments. As a theory of robustly sustainable and choiceworthy (in the sense of promoting human flourishing) political order, basic democracy is antecedent to them.[7]

I offer two exemplars of basic democracy "before liberalism." First (Chapter 2) is the historical record of collective self-government by citizens in the ancient Greek world. Greek democracy provides a well-documented test case adequate to refute any claim that "no such order is humanly possible" or that "it would be unsustainable in a complex society" or "uncompetitive when matched against authoritarian regimes." Those uninterested in historical cases may wish to jump directly to the second exemplar (Chapter 3): collective self-government as a theoretical model, a form of political order arising from the choices that would be made (or so I claim) by a diverse group of ordinary people – moderately rational, self-interested, strategic, social, and communicative individuals – seeking to establish for themselves a secure and prosperous nonautocratic state in a dangerous and mutable world.

The political thought experiment that I will call "Demopolis" is a barebones constitutional framework, a set of baseline rules that enables citizens to coordinate actions to their mutual benefit.[8] I assume, without specifying them, a prior history and elements of civil society. And I assume that after the frame is set, the citizens of Demopolis will adopt further rules concerning normatively weighty matters, potentially including rights and

---

[6] Per Section 1.2, later, I take the liberal theory of John Rawls as definitive of the contemporary "mainstream." Christiano 2008 and Estlund 2008 are examples of explicitly moral theories of democracy that are in some ways critical of Rawls. It is important to keep in mind that some influential strands of contemporary liberal theory are centered on maximization of some socially valued good (e.g., preference satisfaction) rather than defending rights (Singer 1993), and others do not require state-level value neutrality (Raz 1986).

[7] Basic democracy might be regarded as a variant of what Achen and Bartels 2016: 1 refer to as the "folk theory of democracy," which holds that "democracy makes the people the rulers, and legitimacy derives from their consent." Achen and Bartels claim to have invalidated the "folk theory" by demonstrating that it is based on empirically falsifiable and unrealistically optimistic premises about the political knowledge and judgment of ordinary citizens. Achen and Bartel's deflationary characterization of the "folk theory" is primarily concerned with tracking individual and (especially) group ideological preferences (rather than common interests) and is focused almost entirely on theories and studies of American voting behavior. I leave it to readers to decide whether the theory of basic democracy developed here is invalidated by their empirical challenge.

[8] On basic agreements, which make coordination possible among many individuals with otherwise diverse preferences, see Hardin 1999. My fictive Demopolis is not to be confused with the real town of Demopolis, Alabama (population ca. 7,500 in 2010), whose nineteenth-century French founders reportedly chose the name to honor their founders' democratic ideals; https://en.wikipedia.org/wiki/Demopolis,_Alabama (accessed July 19, 2016).

distributive justice. Decision making on normatively weighty matters is likely to produce disagreement; the frame is meant to allow decisions to be made and democratic mechanisms to be designed (Vermeule 2007) without violence or the need for third-party enforcement. While a basic democracy promotes flourishing through certain ethical commitments (discussed in Chapters 4, 5, and 6), I do not suppose that these commitments will, in and of themselves, answer all the normative questions that the citizens of Demopolis will eventually need to confront. The framework is meant to make morally salient collective deliberations and decisions possible, but it is not meant to predetermine their outcome.[9]

Demopolis is an ideal type, in the Weberian sociological (rather than the moral philosophical) sense. That is, it is meant to capture real but hard-to-observe features of a basic democratic political regime by abstracting from readily observed features of real-world polities. Demopolis lacks some aspects of actual political systems in which hard (assuming a pluralistic society) choices about moral questions have been at least contingently decided. Demopolis's imagined Founders limit themselves to establishing the rules necessary to secure the stable, secure, and prosperous political foundation, leaving decisions about difficult moral questions to another day. The rules the Founders do establish are intended to enable Demopolis to be robust to exogenous shocks and to the threat of elite capture, to be capable of further development while sustaining its democratic character.

Real modern polities with good claims to call themselves democracies lack some of Demopolis's institutions. They do not closely resemble classical Athens or any other ancient direct democracy. They have features that ancient Greek polities and Demopolis lack. The goal of limning basic democracy is not to show that any regime that fails to measure up (or down) to the historical case of Athens or the thought experiment of Demopolis is unworthy of the name "democracy." But if things work out as I intend, the historical case and the results of the thought experiment will be mutually supporting (like the timbers of a tipi frame) and mutually enlightening. The goal is regulative rather than prescriptive. By conjoining theory with history, I hope to bring to light certain fundamental competencies to which democratic citizens ought to aspire, and the costs they will need to pay, if they are best to achieve the ends of sustainable security, prosperity, and

---

[9] For example, basic democracy facilitates mobilization against external and internal threats to the regime, but it may not, in and of itself, be able to offer citizens reasons adequate to justify their sacrifice in war or a way to grapple with the imagined demands of the war dead. Thanks to Catherine Frost and Ryan Balot for pressing me on these issues. Moreover, it may not solve the problem of religious pluralism that liberalism was designed to address.

nontyranny in a dangerous and mutable world. I also hope to clarify certain positive goods that accrue to citizens from the practice of democracy, goods that remain relatively opaque in mainstream liberal political theory.

I.2 WHY BEFORE LIBERALISM?

Along with the homage to Quentin Skinner's seminal *Liberty before Liberalism* (1998), my subtitle makes two points. The first is historical: Democracy, as a word, a concept, and a practice, long antedates the seventeenth to twentieth centuries, when the family of ethical, political, and economic arguments that run under the banner of liberalism rose to prominence. As we will see, basic democracy historically required certain political conditions that were later embraced as values by liberals: political liberty (of speech and association), political equality, and legal limits on legislative and executive powers. But democracy was practiced long before political thinkers construed freedom as individual autonomy. Before moral philosophers defined rights as "natural" or "human" (inherent and universal, arising from nature or the moral law) rather than "civic" (shared among citizens and preserved by their collective activities). Before distributive justice was predicated on moral assumptions about autonomy and rights. Before the fact of religious pluralism was seen as requiring value neutrality at the level of constitutional law. So there is a history of democracy as it was conceived and administered before the emergence of a coherent account of liberal morality. I have spent the better part of my career trying to sort out one part of that history – democracy in ancient Greece, and especially classical Athens. This book is not about Greek history per se, but it draws upon the classical Greek experience with democracy.

The second point made by my subtitle is conceptual: Basic democracy can be an antecedent condition for liberalism (or for other value systems) in the sense that democracy is a form of politics practiced by a community of citizens, a way of organizing relations of power and interests. Liberalism, as I am using the term here, is a theory of political morality, a way of specifying and justifying ethical social relations by reference to ethical individualism, toleration, moral right, and the requirements of distributive justice in a pluralistic society. The Kantian versions of contemporary liberal political theory that are my primary concern here (exemplified by Rawls 1971, 1996, 2001) share an ethical commitment to freedom understood as individual autonomy and a belief in the moral equality of persons. At the level of society, the dominant forms of contemporary liberal political theory typically commit rulers to seek value neutrality in the public domain and to protect and promote inherent and inalienable human rights. Each contemporary version of liberalism advocates a specific approach to distributive justice; mainstream approaches range from libertarian to egalitarian.[10]

Liberalism, understood as a moral system centered on personal autonomy, rights, distributive justice, and state-level religious neutrality, is neither, historically, prior to basic democracy, nor, conceptually, its basis. As a set of political practices, democracy can be modeled as simple games played by ideal-type rationally self-interested persons. Indeed, I seek to show that basic democracy can be modeled as a dynamic, self-reinforcing equilibrium. In contrast, the contemporary political theory of liberalism, as a set of moral commitments to ideals of right and social justice, has no equilibrium solution in a population of rationally self-interested agents who recognize their own interests and pursue those interests strategically. Nor, I suppose, is it meant to have such a solution.[11]

Contemporary liberal theory, in the Kantian tradition refounded by John Rawls's epochal *Theory of Justice* (1971), tends to take the security and prosperity typical of a modern liberal/republican/democratic order more or less for granted. It seeks to transcend mere "getting along together" (*modus vivendi*) in a society characterized by value pluralism by providing a moral justification for a just social order. That order is meant to be hypothetically acceptable to people with very different religious beliefs. Rawls's famous "veil of ignorance" thought experiment abstracts moral agents from knowledge of their own individual circumstances and thus enables them to come to an agreement on the "basic structure": the fundamental rules for a just society.[12] The difficulty of sustaining a just social order, once the "veil"

---

[10] Bell 2014 traces the history of the use of the term "liberalism" in political discourse. Critical overview of moral liberalism: Gaus 2014; in turn critically discussed by Runciman 2017. I do not assume that liberalism is necessarily metaphysical (rather than political) or a comprehensive system of value (Rawls 1996 argued that it is not). My approach here is like that of Williams 2005: Chapter 1 ("Realism and Moralism in Political Theory") in rejecting the necessity for political theory of establishing a prior ground of morality. But, as with Williams on legitimacy, ethical principles do prove to emerge from the practice of democratic politics (Sections 3.6, 5.4, and 6.1). See also Hardin 1999 on coordination theories of mutual advantage and Waldron 2013 on "*political* political theory." For a survey of contemporary versions of political realism, and the contrast with "high liberal" theory, see Galston 2010, with response of Estlund 2014.

[11] I do not claim that real people are purely rational, in the sense of being self-interested, strategic, nonaltruistic, or unmoved by ethical emotions or intuitions – i.e., Richard Thaler's (2015) "Econs." Rather, my claim is that (1) some degree of strategic rationality is manifested by most ordinary persons and that (2) it can provide the microfoundations for a *modus vivendi* among people with otherwise diverse moral psychologies who have not (yet) agreed on shared value commitments that would move them beyond that *modus vivendi*.

[12] Early-modern "classical" liberalism, predicated on natural law, on assumptions about inherent freedom and equality of persons, and on the necessity of limiting the power of government, emerged, as a *modus vivendi* for a modern state, in conjunction and in debate with republicanism (Kalyvas

is lifted and knowledge of individual circumstances is regained, is why Rawls defined his original theory of justice as an *ideal* theory. It is a theory that assumes full compliance with agreed-upon rules, rather than providing nonmoralized motivations for strategically rational agents to comply with the rules (Rawls 1971: 8, 89–91; Valentini 2012). The fact that liberal values are not, in and of themselves, self-sustaining as a social order is an issue addressed by Rawls in subsequent work (1996, 1999) and highlighted in Skinner's *Liberty before Liberalism.* Skinner proposed a "Roman" version of republicanism as his solution to the problem of ensuring compliance to a choiceworthy, if not necessarily liberal, social order. Here I propose an "Athenian" version of democracy.[13]

Ethical and political theories can be tightly intertwined (as they were in Aristotle's *Nicomachean Ethics* and *Politics*), but they are not necessarily or causally related: Some ethical theories reject politics; some theories of politics avoid taking an ethical stance. My claim is that a secure and prosperous constitutional framework can be stably established without recourse to the ethical assumptions of contemporary liberal theory, and indeed without the central assumptions of early-modern liberalism or republicanism. The political practice of democracy requires conditions that map onto core liberal and republican values of freedom and equality. It promotes certain ethical commitments, although not necessarily those of Kantian liberalism. Insofar as it is compatible with the commitments of contemporary liberal theory, democratic politics can help to provide a behavioral foundation for liberal principles in a population of more or less rational, self-interested, and strategic individuals. But liberalism is not entailed by democracy and questions of distributive justice that arise after a democratic foundation has been laid lie outside the scope of this book.

and Katznelson 2008). This classical form of liberalism was indeed intended and instantiated as a regime type, in Britain and the US. Sorting out the historical priority of democratic (or republican) and classical liberal elements in late-seventeenth- through early-nineteenth-century British and American regimes would take me far beyond my areas of expertise and is not directly germane to my argument. Thanks to Robert Keohane and Stefan Sciaraffa for pressing me on this issue.

[13] Dynamic self-reinforcing equilibria in social theory: Greif and Laitin 2004. The lack of an equilibrium solution is, in brief, what divides ideal theory (paradigmatically Plato's *Republic* and Rawls 1971) from the kind of "nonideal theory" I am engaged in here. Hardin 1999: 6–9 points out that contemporary liberalism, insofar as it focuses on distributive justice, is not an equilibrium theory. Galston 2010: 398–400 makes a similar point in emphasizing that political realism seeks conditions enabling social stability and that what he calls "high liberalism" lacks an answer to how a society of diverse individuals could be stabilized. Although not put in the language of equilibrium theory, the inability of liberalism to secure the conditions of its own existence without a political form that gives citizens reasons to defend the state is one of the central points of Skinner 1998. Note that the lack of an equilibrium solution does not imply that moral liberalism lacks a concern for or an engagement with power; see further Runciman 2017.

Putting democracy "before liberalism" may seem to put the cart before the horse, conceptually, insofar as liberalism is concerned with substantive as well as procedural justice and substantive justice is regarded as the primary concern of political philosophy. It may seem to get things the wrong way around historically, insofar as ideas about fair distribution of goods antedate the practice of democracy in complex societies.[14] Justice will certainly come into any story about democracy. For many democrats (e.g., Christiano 2008), the value of democracy lies in its role in realizing a more just social order. But democracy is, conceptually and historically, an answer to the question "who rules?" rather than to questions about who deserves what share of the goods produced by social cooperation. Both the ancient Greek inventers of democracy, and the founders of the hypothetical nonauthoritarian society in the Demopolis thought experiment, approached the problems of "why and how to create a nonautocratic government?" with some preconceptions about substantive as well as procedural justice.[15] But they did not need to agree about the requirements of substantive justice before they embarked on the project of building a viable nontyrannical political order.

If we want to understand democracy, there are good reasons to choose a "nonautocratic state" rather than a "substantively just society" as the first target we aim at.[16] In sixth-century BCE Athens, as in eighteenth-century America, the revolutionary path to democracy was opened by delegitimation of autocratic public authority, a broad-based preference for nontyranny (rather than merely a hope for a more benevolent ruler), and a clear demonstration that many citizens were capable of acting as a collective political agent. Although the experience of injustice fed the revolutions, the Athenian and American designers of nonautocratic postrevolutionary political orders focused first on institutional mechanisms to prevent the recurrence of tyranny. They left questions of how to create a fully just or otherwise virtuous social order to their successors. The very fact that those

---

[14] Ancient Near Eastern conceptions of social justice: Westbrook 1995; Early Greek ideas of justice: Lloyd-Jones 1971.

[15] On the ways in which early Greek law employed conceptions of justice as fairness in distribution of goods, see Ober 2005b.

[16] Contrast Pettit 2013, who starts with justice (which he seeks to derive from freedom as nondomination) in building his republican theory of democracy. McCormick 2011 offers a theory of "Machiavellian democracy" that is, like Pettit's republicanism, centered on nondomination but, like my account of basic democracy, is also concerned with active citizen participation in making and enforcing the law (Chapter 3) and is explicitly democratic rather than republican in its focus on the dangers of elite capture (Chapter 6). McCormick centers his theory on Machiavelli's depiction of Roman republicanism in the *Discourses on Livy*, while noting (p. 78) that Machiavelli misrepresented some of the institutions of the real Roman republic.

questions are so hard to answer is one reason for deferring them until after a political framework has been established.[17]

The history of successful democratic constitution building does not imply a normative claim that democracy in its basic sense outweighs substantive justice in the scale of human values. On the other hand, attention to the *conditions* necessary for establishing democracy draws attention to *values* of political participation and civic dignity that remain beside the point for liberal political theories primarily concerned with distributive justice. It is only when values are made visible, and after they have been disaggregated, that we can pose the question of their relative weights. So one reason for studying democracy before liberalism is to refocus attention on the intrinsic value to individuals of participation in collective self-government, a value that has often remained cryptic, when it has not been denied, within contemporary analytic political theory.[18]

Among my goals in these chapters is, first, to determine how much of what a liberal democrat values is, and how much is not, delivered by democracy *eo ipso*, before the admixture of liberalism. I do not suggest that a liberal democrat could get what she would regard as a just social order from democracy alone. As we will see (Chapter 6), there are variants of liberalism that are incompatible with democracy, at least in the form I will be discussing here. But I also show (Chapter 8) that there is reason to think that democracy can in fact provide both a stable foundation for a liberal social order and bring to attention other valuable conditions of human life.

A second goal is to provide an account of democracy that could be of value to people who are not attracted by the moral claims of liberalism but are attracted to the idea of nontyranny, that is, who hope to rule themselves under a stable, nonautocratic government. Such persons (they are, I think, numerous) may reasonably ask for an account of what democracy *offers* in terms of security and welfare, what it *requires* in terms of rules and behavioral habits, and what it *implies* in terms of values and commitments. While some liberals may regard distinguishing democratic politics from liberal morality as pernicious (the moral equivalent of handing out knives to madmen), I suppose that contemporary political theory ought to have something to say to those who are unwilling to embrace

---

[17] Contrast the postrevolutionary trajectories of reformers seeking to create a fully just or virtuous society after the French Revolution of 1789, the Russian Revolution of 1917, or the Chinese Revolution of 1949. The substantive injustice of, for example, institutionalizing slavery in the US Constitution is just one example of deferral.

[18] Notable exceptions, in which civic participation (beyond voting) is central to theory, include Pateman 1970; Fung 2004; Macedo et al. 2005; McCormick 2011.

the full "liberal democracy" package but nonetheless aspire to living without a political master. Moreover, a better understanding of the conditions required for democracy before liberalism exposes the fatuousness and falsity of claims made by contemporary illiberal populists on behalf of what they call "democracy."[19]

I concentrate on democracy both because it is something about which I suppose that I have something new to say and because there is a great deal of fine analytic scholarship on liberalism as such already available. There is less work on democracy as such, at least in the contemporary Anglo-American analytic tradition of political theory. That is in part, I suppose, because so much high-quality democratic theory concerns the hybrids "democratic liberalism" or "liberal democracy."[20] There is good reason for such theorizing, insofar as it is those democratic-liberal hybrids that appear to offer the best available solutions for pluralistic societies characterized by deep value pluralism and intensely held religious identities. Moreover, it is those hybrids that many people in the modern world (including myself) have long regarded as normatively most preferable as a framework for social order. Yet, in our haste to fully specify all we need and want from a political order, contemporary liberal democrats may have conflated matters in ways that make it harder to understand just what the relationship between liberalism and democracy actually is – and what it is not.

Many contemporary political theorists regard democracy as integral to liberal theories of justice.[21] Although I seek to show why certain applications of liberal ideas of justice are incompatible with democracy, moral liberalism can, I believe, be compatible with basic democracy. But in order to decide if and when the relevant conditions and values are compatible, or mutually supportive, or mutually exclusive, we need to pry democracy and liberalism apart. This should be possible. As Duncan Bell has shown, the idea of "liberal democracy," as we now know it, emerged only in the mid twentieth century.[22]

---

[19] "Populism" is another essentially contested concept; here I follow Müller 2016 in defining populism as an autocratic perversion of democracy as collective self-government.

[20] A small sample from a large literature: Gutman 1980; Dahl 1989; Christiano 1996; Brettschneider 2007; Estlund 2008; Stilz 2009. Contrast Rosanvallon 2006: 37 on the "duality . . . between liberalism and democracy."

[21] Rawls 1996, 2001; J. Cohen 1996; Habermas 1996. Rawls 2001: 5 seems to accept a "democracy before liberalism" postulate in claiming that his theory of justice as fairness draws its principles from the "public political culture of a democratic society" (cited in Galston 2010: 388). Ellerman 2015 offers a cogent argument to the effect that classical liberalism does in fact imply democracy in the sense that individuals must be principals in their own organizations.

[22] Bell 2014: 694–704 traces the association of democracy and liberalism back to the nineteenth century but shows that the hybrid "liberal democracy" emerged only in the mid-twentieth century:

Other contemporary liberal theorists suggest that a benevolent autocrat may create antecedent conditions for liberalism, which may or may not eventually be conjoined with democracy (Zakaria 1997, 2003; Fukuyama 2011, 2014). An autocrat might make and enforce the rules for a liberal but nondemocratic society. Such a society would, however, depend on third-party enforcement: the will of the ruler. Unless the people, as a capable collective agent, retains ultimate political authority, liberal rules are hostage to the ruler's benevolence.[23]

A leader with the power to make and enforce laws impeding coordinated resistance, in the form of effective joint action by his subjects, rules at his own pleasure. He does so despite any "parchment barriers" he allows to be placed in his way.[24] Dangers inherent in that kind of power motivate democrats to establish rules facilitating popular resistance. Democracy is, both historically and theoretically, a rejection of autocracy – even of the most benevolent kind. But what about the danger posed by "illiberal democracy"? Liberal critics have argued that democracy, before the admixture of liberalism, is viciously illiberal populism (Riker 1982). I seek to show that, while the conditions necessary for the practice of democracy are not inherently liberal, neither are they inherently illiberal. Just as it is misleading to conflate democracy with liberalism, so, too, is it a mistake to regard democracy before liberalism as antithetical to liberalism.[25]

1.3 NORMATIVE THEORY, POSITIVE THEORY, HISTORY

Answering questions about what democracy is, what it is good for, and what conditions make it possible demands an approach to political theory

---

"Arguably, the most significant conceptual move of the interwar era was the emergence of the idea of 'liberal democracy.' Barely visible before 1930, in the ensuing decade it began to supplant existing appellations for Euro-Atlantic states. During the 1940s and 1950s it became a commonplace" (p. 703). See also Müller 2011.

[23] Classical liberals (notably Locke in the *Second Treatise of Government* 1988 [1690]) have long sought ways to limit the powers of rulers, such that the ruler's authority would be subject to laws that would be enforced by a popular "right of resistance"; see further Bell 2014. But without the right institutions, the people have limited means of coordinating action against a violating ruler.

[24] Parchment barriers: *Federalist* 48. If the ruler is actually constrained by the barriers, i.e., can expect to be punished or deposed for violating the rules, then he is not an autocrat in the strong sense.

[25] Galston 2010: 391 regards it as a premise of any realist theory of politics that "individuals must agree that the core challenge of politics is to overcome anarchy without embracing tyranny." But his definition of tyranny, which is predicated on brute terrorization and domination, excludes "benevolent autocracy." Given that the Greek term *tyrannos* did not originally refer uniquely to brutal rulers, I feel justified in using nontyranny as a synonym for "nonautocracy." But I differ from standard Greek usage in including a narrow ruling coalition (which in Greek evaluative political vocabulary was a *dunasteia*) in my definition of "tyranny."

that is at once evaluative, explanatory, and historical. It requires conjoining three domains of inquiry: first, *normative political theory*. The normative theory employed here is concerned with what we require, as human beings, in order to flourish as individuals and as members of communities, and how we might go about securing it. Next is *positive political theory* that is concerned with analyzing strategic behavior to explain how problems of collective action might be solved such that the social order is at once stable and adaptive and the benefits of social cooperation are relatively abundant. Third is *historical reasoning* that is aimed at tracing changes over time in the dynamic relationship of norms to institutions and social behavior. Although this hybrid approach is not the method of most contemporary political theory, it is arguably the method employed by many of the most prominent political theorists of classical antiquity and the early-modern western tradition, for example, Thucydides, Aristotle, Machiavelli, Hobbes, Locke, Rousseau, Hume, Smith, Montesquieu, Madison, Paine, and Tocqueville. The contrasting and (occasionally) overlapping political theories of two of these, Aristotle (especially in the *Politics*) and Thomas Hobbes (especially in *Leviathan*), will figure prominently in the following chapters.[26]

Aristotle, Hobbes, and other ancient and early-modern theorists posed fundamental questions about politics in normative terms: How ought choice-making moral agents order their polity in respect to authority, decision, judgment, distribution, and in relation to other collectivities? What would it take to make those polities more just, more legitimate, or more democratic? Yet they also asked fundamental "positive theory" questions:

---

[26] The conception of "normative and positive political theory" that is, along with historical testing, the methodological basis for this book is the product of a joint project with Federica Carugati and Barry Weingast, developed in various papers in progress and in Stanford seminars on "High Stakes Politics." It is sketched in Carugati et al. 2015 and in progress. Our approach seeks to get beyond the "Manichean dualism" that Williams (2005: 12) pointedly noted was characteristic of American political theory and political science. Others seem to be engaged in a similar project, e.g., in quite different registers, Hardin 1999; Rosanvallon 2006. Two recent books by prominent specialists in American politics, Achen and Bartels (2016) and Shapiro (2016), offer contrasting "realist" theories of democratic politics, conjoining normative and positive political theory, and (mostly American) history. While both books are deeply informed by contemporary liberalism, the authors come to starkly opposed positions. Achen and Bartels call for a much greater role for depoliticized regulatory agencies, and for limiting the role of voting by ignorant citizens. Shapiro calls for a strengthened form of Schumpeterian competitive majoritarianism, decrying the sclerotic tendencies of republican limits on majority rule. Each book starts with "where we are now" (in the US, in the early twenty-first century) and neither focuses on the high-stakes historical conditions of the American founding era. Neither addresses the problems (for Achen and Bartels: unaccountable technocracy, for Shapiro: populist autocracy) raised by their preferred solutions, but each helpfully articulates the problems raised by other's position.

Why do individual agents choose as they do, and how do their choices result in a given polity being ordered as it is, in respect to authority, decision, judgment, distribution, and in relation to other collectivities? What would it take to change that order in ways that would make it more efficient – reliably delivering more and better goods to more people at a lower cost?

The ancient and early-modern writers recognized that their normative and positive theories needed an empirical grounding, and they typically sought that ground in history. They were well versed in history and very interested in historical development. But they were not adherents of a strong historicism that approaches every society as the unique and incomparable product of its own past or that sees historical processes as inexorably driving toward specifiable ends. Rather, they used history to define and to expand the bounds of possibility. They recognized that the prior existence of a given social order refutes any argument that "such a society is impossible." They believed that they could learn from historical examples of success and failure.[27]

If normative political theory and positive theory today seem to belong to different intellectual worlds, it is at least in part because the practitioners in each subfield use such different languages: on the one hand, the language of analytic or continental philosophy and, on the other hand, the language of causal inference and mathematical game theory. Each of these languages can be highly technical and impenetrable to noninitiates. But, as Bernard Williams (1993, 2005, 2006) demonstrated, political philosophy can be written in graceful prose, and Michael Chwe (2013) has shown, with reference to the novels of Jane Austen, that analyzing social interaction on the basis of game theoretic intuitions does not require algebra. When we attend to the similarities in the fundamental questions posed by ancient and early-modern political theorists, rather than to the divergent languages in which theories of politics are expressed by contemporary political philosophers and social scientists, we can see that normative and positive theory are logically conjoined. They constitute two aspects of the common enterprise of seeking to understand how choices made by agents in communities do or might lead to forms of social order that are more or less desirable.

---

[27] Herodotus, *Histories*, is a particularly clear case in point. Meckstroth 2015 is a striking recent example of normative democratic theory that is explicitly grounded in history. Green 2015 urges a rapprochement between intellectual history and normative political theory, but he is concerned primarily with historical ideas about politics rather than the history of political practices.

1.4 SKETCH OF THE ARGUMENT

Looking ahead, these chapters seek to demonstrate the validity of three sets of general claims:

I   Basic democracy is reasonably stable collective self-government by an extensive and socially diverse body of citizens. To be stable over time, a democracy requires rules, reliably backed by habitual social behaviors. Those rules must, inter alia, limit the absolutist tendencies of the collective rulers and allow for punishing violations by government agents and other powerful social actors whose actions threaten the democratic order. Basic democracy is not majoritarian tyranny. It is neither morally committed nor opposed to value neutrality, universal human rights, or egalitarian principles of distribution. Democracy in its basic form is neither the antithesis nor the fulfillment of liberalism.

II Basic democracy can be at once legitimate and effective. It is good for citizens in that it enables them to live relatively well and securely without a master (keeping in mind that noncitizens may do less well).[28] It is good for citizens because, inter alia, it
  1   provides for material conditions of human flourishing: adequate security from external and internal threats to life and property; sufficient welfare in the form of (at least) food, shelter, and health; and adequate opportunity to pursue socially valued projects[29]
  2   promotes free exercise of constitutive human capacities: sociability, reason, and interpersonal communication
  3   sustains desirable conditions of social existence, notably political liberty, political equality, and civic dignity[30]

III A theory of basic democracy highlights the importance of civic education. It foregrounds the relationship between political practices and certain values that tend to be marginalized in liberal political theory, notably the intrinsic value of participation and the independent value of civic dignity. It also answers two queries posed by liberals and by nonliberals: How can a liberal society be made both stable and adaptive? How might a nonliberal society be sustained without autocratic rulers?

---

[28] "Good for" need imply neither "necessary for" nor "sufficient for." Ancient Athens (like the US before 1865) was a slave society in which women and resident foreigners lacked participation rights, although noncitizens, including at least some slaves, were given some protection in law: Ober 2010; Sections 4.3 and 8.3.

[29] On sufficiency versus equality, see Frankfurt 1987.

[30] N.B. contemporary liberals typically value deeper and more extensive forms of liberty, equality, and dignity than are required by basic democracy. See Chapter 6.

The fundamental question I hope to answer is whether a democratic political order can, in and of itself (without the admixture of liberalism), be at once stable, limited, and an efficient provider of adequate levels of security and material welfare. Some modern theorists of democracy have argued that the three definitional conditions specified above (rule by citizens that is collective, limited, and stably effective) are either noncompossible, for reasons emerging from positive political theory, or undesirable for normative reasons. Joseph Schumpeter (1947), for example, followed by William Riker (1982, and others), argued that democracy cannot be collective self-government, on the basis of the assumption that truly collective self-government is unachievable given the supposed impossibility of collective will formation and expression. Sheldon Wolin (1996), joined by some "democratic agonists," has argued that true democracy cannot be stably effective, arguing that collective agency disappears (goes fugitive) as soon as rules are stabilized in a constitutional order.[31] Benjamin Barber (1984), following Rousseau, argued that democracy ought not be limited, claiming that, to be genuine, democracy must also be "strong."

The fundamental challenge to basic democracy long antedates modern democratic theory. In *Leviathan*, Thomas Hobbes (1991 [1651]) famously asserted that no form of limited government, that is, without a third-party enforcer, could provide the security and welfare necessary to lift a society out of the dire conditions of the "state of nature." Hobbes, in essence, denied the possibility of a self-reinforcing social order that could provide anything approaching a decent level of security and welfare. Hobbes's assertion regarding the necessity of autocracy (in the sense of a lawless ruler with unlimited authority) challenges political theorists to show how a regime that offers a normatively preferable alternative to the stark choice between "brutality" (in the state of nature) and "security and at least minimal welfare under a lawless, absolutist ruler" could also answer to the demands of positive political theory. These chapters sketch one answer to Hobbes's challenge.[32]

The answer offered here is presented in minimalist terms. I do not propose to specify all the conditions that a normative theorist (liberal, perfectionist, or otherwise) will hope for from a democratic society. Specifically, in reference to liberalism, I do not claim that democracy, in and of itself, will be committed to value neutrality in the space of public reason, will

---

[31] Democratic agonists: Chapter 8, with note 6.

[32] Hobbes's social theory is discussed in more detail in Sections 4.3, 5.1, 5.2, and 5.3. My interpretation of Hobbes, as discussed there, takes him as a theorist of absolutism, not as a proto-democrat, a position urged by Tuck 2007, 2016.

guarantee individual autonomy or universal human rights or will ensure distributive justice. Democracy, as it is defined here, will not provide all of the rights that are required by contemporary liberalism (as exemplified by Rawls or other egalitarian social theorists), even for citizens.[33] By the same token, the institutions and behaviors essential to sustain democracy need not obstruct the achievement a more extensive regime of rights. Democracy may, furthermore, provide human goods to that are not promoted by liberalism as such. Democratic goods can be analytically distinguished from liberal goods even while, as I will suggest, basic democracy proves to be broadly compatible with at least some versions of liberalism. I claim, in brief, that it is conceptually possible for a democracy to be choiceworthy before it is liberal. If that claim holds true in practice, as well as in theory, it has considerable implications for public policy.[34]

The rest of the book proceeds as follows: Chapter 2 reviews the history of political development in classical Athens, our best-documented case study of a working democracy untouched by the philosophical ideas of early-modern or contemporary liberals. We pay special attention to the original and "mature Athenian" meanings of the Greek term *demokratia*, that is, what democracy meant to the Greeks who practiced it. Chapter 3 introduces the Demopolis thought experiment: a constitutional public order brought into being by an imagined society of persons who are, by stipulation, diverse except in their shared preference for living in a country that is secure, reasonably prosperous, and not ruled by autocrats. The residents of Demopolis are willing to pay some costs to live in such a country, but they also demand that they have adequate opportunity to pursue projects of value to themselves outside the realm of politics.

Chapter 4 begins to address the question of Demopolis's legitimacy, on the assumption that it has not yet adopted a liberal superstructure. A justificatory argument, in the form of the civic education provided to potential future citizens, answers the question of what democracy is good for in material and nonmaterial terms. Chapter 5 argues that, despite their fundamentally different accounts of moral psychology, Aristotle and Hobbes agreed that humans have innate capacities for sociability, rationality, and verbal communication. Democracy offers citizens unimpeded opportunity

---

[33] Democracy assumes a common commitment to (at least) achieving collective security and minimal welfare through collective self-governance by citizens and will *not* offer equal standing to comprehensive conceptions that are antithetical to those ends (Section 8.5). Yet a basic democracy *will* allow, indeed provoke, political dissent: Ober 1998.

[34] See Ober 2012, conclusions. I do not here address the question of democracy (or democratic deficits) in international institutions that transcend the bounds of the state, as important as that question is for contemporary normative theory.

to exercise these fundamental capacities through participation in collective self-government. That opportunity is, I propose, a choiceworthy end in itself.

Chapter 6 reviews basic democracy's enabling conditions of political liberty, political equality, and especially civic dignity as worthiness to participate in politics. The rationally self-interested activity of citizens in defense of one another's civic dignity addresses the endemic social problem of how to control the behavior of arrogant individuals who seek to demonstrate their own superiority by humiliating and infantilizing others. The dignitary requirement that participatory citizens be treated as adults furthermore constrains extreme versions of libertarian and egalitarian distributive justice. Chapter 7 turns to delegation of authority to representatives and to institutional design aimed at making use of relevant expertise in democratic judgments on matters of common interest, while avoiding elite capture. If the citizens are, as a collectivity, capable of ruling themselves, representatives are thereby discouraged from seeking to rule as autocrats. To the degree that a democracy can make effective use of expertise, its citizenry are insulated from the dangers of collective ignorance.

Chapter 8 summarizes the theory of basic democracy developed in the previous chapters. Some readily imaginable variants of liberal and nonliberal societies would be unable to make use of a basic democratic foundation while remaining true to their values. Yet basic democracy could be of use to a wide range of liberals, and potentially to some religious traditionalists, who seek a political framework on which they might hope to build a society committed to a specifiable moral order. Finally, an epilogue tempers the guarded optimism of the preface by sketching a "democracy of fear" in the hope that a basic democratic framework might serve as a bastion against a descent into abysmal social conditions in a possible future "after liberalism."

CHAPTER 2

The Meaning of Democracy in Classical Athens

If it is to be realistic, rather than utopian or otherwise idealized, a political theory of democracy before liberalism rests on a demonstration of feasibility. Since reality proves possibility, a single case will serve the purpose. The new form of popular government that the Athenians established in the immediate aftermath of the popular revolution of 508 BCE was the world's first political regime to name itself "democracy." Classical Athens, from the late sixth to the late fourth century BCE, is also the best-known and most fully documented example of a long-lasting democracy in a complex society in the era before the development of liberal political thought.

I have discussed the history of democratic Athenian political culture and institutions in more detail in other work.[1] Here, after a brief survey of Athenian political development, I turn to the question of the original and mature meanings of the Greek word *demokratia*, as it was used in political discourse by partisans and critics of democracy in the ancient Greek world. The point of the exercise is to show that, in our best-documented historical case, both the conceptual understanding and the institutional form were very different from the unstable, arbitrary, and casually brutish form of populist-driven majoritarian tyranny that democracy before liberalism is often taken to be.

Ancient Athenian society obviously had many historically contingent features. The Demopolis thought experiment offered in the following chapter abstracts from history in order to show that a state adopting a system of self-government relevantly similar to Athenian democracy need not be burdened by, for example, slavery or exclusively male franchise nor limited in scale by its reliance on directly democratic modes of decision making.

---

[1] Athenian demography, political institutions, and historical development in relationship to Athenian politics and society: Ober 1989, 2008a.

2.1 ATHENIAN POLITICAL HISTORY

With a total resident population of perhaps 250,000 persons, a citizen (adult male) population in the tens of thousands (perhaps as high as 50,000+ in ca. 431 BCE; ca. 30,000 in the fourth century BCE, the age of Plato and Aristotle), and a home territory of about 2,500 km², Athens was an exceptionally large city-state. It was also exceptionally diverse, encompassing several distinct regions, many local cults, and hundreds of economic specializations. Like most city-state residents, Athenians were highly aware of class differences. Managing diversity across the citizen population was a primary aim of city-state institutions (Ober 1989). Athens's size became an asset only after a series of dramatic reforms in the aftermath of the revolution of 508 BCE strengthened civic identity and enabled coordinated political action on matters of common interest by large numbers of citizens.

Key postrevolutionary democratic reforms made participatory citizens of all resident males and (prospectively) their male descendants without regard to property or income qualifications. The new order also created a council of citizens, chosen by lot and recruited from across the polis's several regions. The council conducted much of the ordinary business of government and set the agenda for a legislative assembly, open to all citizens. In the fourth century BCE, there were 40 assembly meetings each year, and a typical meeting attracted one-fifth to one-quarter of the citizen body. The assembled citizens debated legislative proposals and voted directly on them. Each citizen's vote was given equal weight. Jurors in the People's Courts and most magistrates were likewise chosen by lottery. A few magistrates, notably military commanders, civil engineers, and (eventually) certain financial officials, were elected for one-year renewable terms. All citizen-officials were legally accountable for their performance and underwent a formal review upon completion of a year's term.

Athen's democracy was a direct form of government by citizens. The assembled citizens voted directly on policy; they did not elect representatives to make policy for them. Yet the common notion that representation is a uniquely modern concept, utterly foreign to ancient democratic thought (e.g., Rosanvallon 2006: 62), is misleading. The Athenian demos (as the whole of the citizen body) was imagined as present in the persons of those citizens who chose to attend a given assembly. So the demos was conceptually represented, *pars pro toto*, by a fragment of the citizenry. In a related sense, the decisions made by the 500 lottery-chosen councilors, by juries (typically of 201 or 501 citizens over age 30), and by boards of "lawmakers"

(Section 2.3), stood for decisions of the people as a whole and were binding upon the entire community (Ober 1996: Chapter 8). Because Athens
was very small compared to most modern nation-states, the Athenians did
not face the problems that arise when authority over rule making is delegated to elected legislative representatives (Chapter 7). But there is nothing
in the Athenian conceptualization of democracy, to which we turn below
(Section 2.2), that renders political representation inconceivable.

Athens's democracy lasted, with two brief oligarchic interludes (410 and
404 BCE), until 322 BCE. For 180 years, Athenian political culture evolved
and Athenian government proved itself to be highly adaptive. Athenians grew increasingly sophisticated in their understanding and practice of
democracy. The fundamental conditions of freedom in respect to public speech and association, equality of votes and opportunity for office,
and civic dignity as immunity from humiliation and infantilization were
robustly supported by formal rules and related behavioral norms. The
Athenians regularly adjusted the institutional mechanisms of their government. Legislation, passed in the course of the fifth century BCE, introduced pay for many forms of public service, including serving as a juror
in the People's Courts. In 451 BCE, natal citizenship was legally limited to
legitimate sons born to a female native married to a male native, effectively
recognizing Athenian women as coparticipants in the formation of the citizen body (while denying the franchise to sons born to Athenian men who
had taken foreign wives). In the late fifth and fourth centuries BCE a series
of constitutional changes, discussed below in this chapter, legally limited
the direct legislative authority of the citizen assembly, without restricting
the citizens' collective authority over all aspects of state government. We
will consider some other Athenian institutional innovations in subsequent
chapters. Yet from the beginning to the end of the democratic era, the core
meaning of democracy as citizen self-government remained stable.

Athenian political development offers initial, historically contingent
answers to the questions with which we began, concerning what basic
democracy is, why it arises, how it is sustained, and what it is good for.
When measured against contemporary norms, Athens was far from a liberal
society: Athenian democracy arose within a cultural framework in which
active participation in government, as a legislator, juror, or public official,
was strictly limited to males, and ordinarily to native males. Slavery was
very common (perhaps one-third of Athenian residents were slaves) and
taken largely for granted. Impiety, while not defined in detail in Athenian
law, was a capital offense. The institution of ostracism allowed for the occasional (albeit temporary) expulsion from the state territory, without a trial

or criminal charges, of an individual regarded as dangerous or otherwise objectionable by a plurality of his fellow citizens. And yet the classical Athenian definition of democracy, so I will argue, fits the preliminary definition of basic democracy offered in the first chapter. The Demopolis thought experiment, sketched in the next chapter, seeks to generalize the features of basic democracy, abstracting it from the specifics of ancient Greek history, culture, and political practice.

As noted in Chapter 1, no definition of democracy can claim final authority. But it is worth noting that the original meaning of *democracy*, and the meaning that was embraced by Greek democrats across classical antiquity, was not "majority tyranny." Rather, it was "collective self-government by citizens." Moreover, in practice, the collective authority of the citizens to do just as they wished, whenever they gathered as a body, was limited in practice from the beginning, by what amounted to constitutional rules. It was certainly possible for Athenian populists to claim that "it is monstrous if the *demos* cannot do as it pleases." Populist demagogues occasionally persuaded the assembled demos to act rashly, against its established norms, against it interests, and in ways the Athenian citizens subsequently came to regret.[2] But those instances were exceptions to the standard practice of rule- and norm-bounded decision making. Were such irrational public acts typical rather than exceptional, Athens would quickly have failed in the competitive world of Greek city-states. Moreover, the historical arc of Athenian government reform bent in the direction of clearer and more formal rules, aimed at imposing sanctions on populist opportunism by would-be leaders. Athenian democracy proved robust to extreme shocks, including physical destruction of the city by foreign invaders, a plague that killed at least one-quarter of the population in a few years, and devastating loss in a protracted war. It also proved capable of providing, most of the time and for much of Athens's population, relatively high levels of security and welfare.[3]

Since Athenian political history shows that democracy of the basic form existed more or less stably and effectively over a long period of time in a complex society, the argument that basic democracy cannot have existed is ipso facto refuted. Basic democracy is thus proved to be compatible with the demands of human nature and behavior as it is manifest in relatively

---

[2] Monstrous: Xenophon *Hellenica* 1.7.12: assembly condemns the Arginousai generals en masse. Regret: ibid., 1.7.35.

[3] Ober 2008a: Chapter 2 measures Athens's capacity as a state relative to other Greek city-states. Ober 2017 estimates welfare and income inequality across the Athenian population in the late fourth century BCE.

large societies. Of course ancient Athens, with a total population in the hundreds of thousands, was tiny compared to major modern nation-states. Moreover, although the resident population of Athens was exceptionally diverse by the standards of Greek antiquity, and diversity was readily identified as a feature of democracy (Plato, *Republic*, Book 8), Athens was certainly not pluralistic in the sense of including sizable minorities with primary identities and political preferences defined by inflexible and demanding monotheistic religious traditions. Questions about *how far* a basic democracy might be scaled up, and whether it could answer to the requirements of a large and pluralistic contemporary nation-state, are addressed in subsequent chapters.

2.2 ORIGINAL GREEK DEFINITION

As is well known, the ancient Greek word *demokratia* conjoins the words *demos* (people) and *kratos* (power).[4] But what sort of power, and who are the people? The compound term was almost certainly coined in Athens, within a generation of the revolution of 508 BCE. By the mid fifth century BCE, hostile critics were claiming that the true meaning of the word was "the unconstrained domination of the many poor over the wealthy few" – i.e., the tyranny of a self-interested majority faction. That critical rebranding informed Thomas Hobbes's account, in *Leviathan*, concerning the kind of large assembly that might serve as an appropriately lawless sovereign (albeit only as a third-best option, after a single monarch and a small ruling council); we will return to Hobbes on democracy in Chapter 4. *Mutatis mutandis*, the ancient critics' definition fits Carl Schmitt's (2007) conception of politics as a system of power defined by existential contests engaged by friends against enemies. Schmitt's emphasis on contestation is, in turn, the basis of a range of political theories developed by contemporary democratic agonists. Yet majoritarian tyranny is decidedly not the sort of government envisioned by the ancient Greek originators of term.[5]

There is no good reason to take the hostile testimony of democracy's ancient Greek critics, or those subsequently influenced by them (at whatever remove), as evidence for what the term originally meant to democracy's Greek inventors in the late sixth and fifth centuries BCE. Nor, a

---

[4] This section is adapted and updated from Ober 2008b, in which the philological argument for the original meaning of democracy was first presented.

[5] Possible dates for coinage of the term *demokratia*: Hansen 1986. Critics of democracy: Ober 1998. Democratic agonists: Chapter 8, note 5. Canevaro (forthcoming) demonstrates that, at least in cases for which the numbers of votes were recorded, decisions of democratic Greek legislative assemblies tended to be consensual, with few or no dissenting votes.

Table 2.1 *Greek (and neo-Greek) terminology for regime types*

1. Empowered body	2. *-kratos* root	3. *-arche* root	4. Other regime-name terms	5. Related political terms: persons, abstractions
One	*autocracy*	**monarchia**	tyrannia	**tyrannos**
			basileia	**basileus** (king)
Few Many	**aristokratia**	**oligarchia**	dynasteia	**hoi oligoi** (few)
	demokratia	*polyarchy*	isonomia (law)	**hoi polloi** (many)
	isokratia		isegoria (speech)	**to plethos** (majority)
	ochlokratia (mob)		*isopsephia* (vote)	**ho ochlos** (mob)
				isopsephos (voter)
Other	timokratia (honor)	**anarchia**	isomoiria (shares)	**dunamis** (power)
(exempli	gunaikokratia		**eunomia** (law)	**ischus** (strength)
gratia)	(women)		politeia (mix of	**bia** (force)
	technocracy		democracy and	**kurios** (master)
			oligarchy: as used	**exousia** (authority,
			by Aristotle)	license)

Notes: Earlier (fifth-century BCE attested) forms in bold, "standard" terms used in the later fifth and fourth-century in bold underline, exotic ancient inventions in plain type, post-classical/modern inventions in italics.

fortiori, is there reason to apply that hostile definition to the mature practice of democracy as it developed in Athens and other Greek city-states in the fourth through the second centuries BCE.[6] A philological comparison with other compound Greek terms for regime types (*monarchia, oligarchia, aristokratia, timokratia*, etc.) suggests that the *demos* of *demokratia* was more expansive than its critics alleged. Linking *kratos* to *demos* was an optimistic assertion of the demos's collective strength, rather than a cynical claim regarding the domination or subordination of others. As a matter of historical fact, collective strength enabled Athenians to dominate others, especially during the mid-fifth-century imperial era. But that fact ought not to be confused with the term's original or mature meaning.

The ancient Greek vocabulary for political regimes was focused on the question "who rules?" The choice was from among a set of three options: an individual, a small and exclusive coalition, and an extensive and inclusive body of citizens. Table 2.1 offers a schematic map of the terminological terrain. Three key terms for the authority of an individual, elite coalition, and

[6] On democracy in the Hellenistic third and second centuries BCE, see Grieb 2008; Hamon 2010; Ma 2013; Teegarden 2014.

extensive citizenry are *monarchia, oligarchia,* and *demokratia.* Even in this small sample, two things stand out: First, unlike *monarchia* (from the adjective *monos,* "solitary") and *oligarchia* (from *hoi oligoi,* "the few"), *demokratia* (from *demos,* "the citizenry/people") is not specifically concerned with "number." The term *demos* refers to a collectivity of unspecified size (see below). Unlike *monarchia* and *oligarchia, demokratia* does not, therefore, answer the question "how many are empowered as rulers?" Second, Greek names of regimes divide into terms with an *-arche* suffix and terms with a *-kratos* suffix.[7] Table 2.1 lists the primary classical Greek terms for regime types along some postclassical and modern Greek-derived terms.

Given the Greek penchant for creative neologism, not least in the realm of politics, it is notable that some regime names are missing from the list. The standard Greek term for "the many" is *hoi polloi,* yet there is no ancient Greek regime was named *pollokratia* or *pollarchia.* Nor is *monokratia, oligokratia,* or *anakratia* ever attested.[8] I focus in the first instance on the six bold-faced terms in columns 2 and 3 of Table 2.1: *demokratia, isokratia, and aristokratia* among the *-kratos* roots and *monarchia, oligarchia,* and *anarchia* among the *-arche* roots.[9]

Each of the three primary *-arche* root terms (Table 2.1, column 3) is concerned with "monopoly of office." A Greek magistracy was an *arche.* The public offices as constitutional entities were (plural) *archai.* An *archon* was a senior magistrate: the holder of a particular office with specified duties.[10] Each of the three *-arche*-root regime names thus answers the question "how

---

[7] The primary Greek terms are as follows (with sample citations in classical authors): *Anarchia:* Herodotus 9.23; Aeschlus *Suppliants* 906. *Aristokratia:* Thucydides 3.82. *Demokratia* (and verb forms): Herodotus 6.43, Thucydides 2.37. *Gynaikokratia:* Aristotle, *Politics* 1313b. *Dunasteia* (as the worst form of *oligarchia*): Aristotle *Politics* 1292b10, 1293a31. *Isegoria:* Herodotus 5.78, Demosthenes 21.124. *Isokratia:* Herodotus 5.92.a. *Isomoiria:* Solon *apud* Aristotle *Constitution of Athens* 12.3. *Isonomia:* Herodotus 3.80, 3.142 (opposed to *dunasteia:* Thucydides 4.78). *Isopsephia:* Dionysios of Halicarnassus 7.64. *Isopsephos:* Thucydides 1.141. *Monarchia:* Alcaeus Fragment 12; Herodotus 3.82. *Oligarchia* (and active and passive verb forms): Herodotus 3.82.2, 5.92.b; Thucydides 6.38, 8.9; as personification (on tombstone of Critias): *scholion* to Aeschines 1.39. *Ochlokratia* as pejorative form of rule by the many: Polybius 6.4.6, 6.57.9. *Timokratia:* Plato *Republic* 545b; Aristotle *Nicomachean Ethics* 1160a. Fuller lists of citations available in Liddell et al. 1968; *Thesaurus Linguae Graecae:* www .tlg.uci.edu/.

[8] *Demarchia* refers not to a regime type but to a relatively minor local office (*ho demarchos,* chief office-holder in a town, "the mayor"). In this case the prefix refers to the jurisdiction in which authority is exercised, rather than the number of rulers. Plato, at one point in the *Republic* (8.545b), suggests *timarchia* as a synonym for the honor-centered regime he ordinarily calls *timokratia.*

[9] Each of these is attested in the fifth century, although *oligarchia* and *aristokratia* are probably somewhat later than *demokratia, isokratia,* and *monarchia.*

[10] The word *arche,* in Greek, has several related meanings: beginning (or origin), empire (or hegemonic control of one state by another), as well as office or magistracy. In classical Athens, nine archons were chosen annually – along with several hundred other magistrates: Hansen 1999. On the role of offices in classical, and especially Aristotelian, political thought, see Lane 2016.

many rulers (*quasi* actual or potential officeholders), among some larger set of possible rulers, are there in the state?" The answers are, *anarchia* (none); *monarchia* (one); *oligarchia* (few).

By contrast, the *-kratos* terms (Table 2.1, column 2) do not refer to offices or officeholders as such. Unlike *arche*, the Greek word *kratos* is not used of "office." In regime names, *kratos* must refer to political authority, but if not authority gained by monopoly control of office, then ruling in what manner? *Kratos* has a root meaning of "power" – but Greek linguistic usage of the noun *kratos* and its verbal forms ranges widely across the power spectrum, from "strength/power to" through "constraint" to "domination/power over." We can narrow the range of possible meanings for *-kratos* as a regime-name suffix. Unlike the *-arche*-root group of regime names, which, as we have seen, is composed of "number terms," none of the prefixes in the *-kratos* group refers specifically to number. Thus, on the face of it, *-kratos* terms seem not to be about distinguishing the size of the group that holds offices, dominates, or rules over others as a subset of a larger body of possible rulers. Does it nonetheless serve to distinguish those who rule by employing power to dominate from those who are thereby dominated?[11]

It is possible, on the analogy of *oligarchia* in which *hoi oligoi* (the few) monopolize public offices, to imagine that *aristokratia* pertains when *hoi aristoi* (the excellent) dominate the rest by some other means. The term might, therefore, be construed as asserting that "those who dominate are excellent – and the dominated are not." But, in light of the positive connotations of the Greek term, it seems more likely that *aristokratia* asserts, first, that excellence is the defining principle of the regime and, next, the strength or capacity of the excellent to organize public affairs accordingly. In Aristotle's taxonomy of regimes, *aristokratia* is the name of the regime in which excellent few rule justly, in the common interest of all, as opposed to *oligarchia* in which the few rule in their own factional advantage. Public offices are, on this reading, just one mechanism that the capable rulers may employ in organizing public affairs according to the regime's core principle of excellence.[12]

Among the other compounds in the *-kratos* group, only *gunaikokratia*, "feminine rule" or rule by women (*gunaikos* = genitive of *gune*, "woman"),

---

[11] On the wide range of meanings for *kratos*, see Liddel et al. 1968, s.v. Williams 1993: 105 points to *kratos* as "physical constraint" and to its association with *bia* (force) in Aeschylus's *Prometheus Bound*. Domination is what Geuss 2008 characterizes as the relation "who whom."

[12] Positive connotations: Liddel et al. 1968, s.v. Aristotle on *aristokratia*: *Politics* 1279a34–37. The difference in meaning between the ancient Greek term and medieval and modern usages of "aristocracy" are highlighted by Fisher and van Wees 2015.

could be construed as referring to monopoly officeholders. *Timokratia* refers to an abstraction: *time* (honor). In Plato's *Republic*, *timokratia* (the second-best regime, after the rule of philosopher-kings) pertains when honor (construed especially as courage: Balot 2014) is the defining principle of the regime and the honorable organize public affairs accordingly. *Isokratia* likewise refers to an abstraction, "equality." By analogy to *aristokratia* and *timokratia*, *isokratia* pertains when the general principle of the regime is equality and when public affairs are arranged accordingly by equals. In this case, it is especially difficult to see *kratos* as referring to domination, insofar as domination is inherently a relationship of inequality.

Because *isokratia* was employed as a synonym for *demokratia*, it is especially important for our comparative purposes. *Isokratia* shares its prefix-root (*iso-*, "equal") with two other terms used by the fifth-century BCE historian Herodotus as synonyms for democracy: *isonomia* and *isegoria*. Judging from *isonomia* (equal-law) and *isegoria* (equal-public address), it appears that in political discourse, *iso*-prefix-roots refer to equality in respect to access, in a sense of "right/capacity to make use of." *Isonomia* is equality in respect to access to law, legal processes, and legal protection. *Isegoria* is equal access to deliberative forums: equal right to speak out on public matters and to attend to the speech of others. Equal access in each case is a valued means for using other valued instruments (law, public speech). As in the case of *aristokratia*, the positive connotation of these evaluative political terms suggests that equal access to the specific instrument in each case conduces to a common good.[13] *Isokratia* is, by analogy, equal access to the instrument of *kratos* – to public power that conduces to a common good through enabling things to be done in the public realm.

So *kratos*, when it is used as a regime-type suffix, appears to be power in the sense, not of domination or monopoly of office, but, more positively, of strength, capability, or "capacity to do things." This is well within the range of how the word *kratos* and its verb forms were used in archaic and classical Greek. Under *isokratia*, each person who belongs to the category "those who are equal" (say, the citizens) enjoys access to public power in this "capacity" sense, and likewise, *mutatis mutandis*, for *gunaikokratia*,

---

[13] *Isomoiria*: "equal shares" is an *iso*-root term that seems to inhabit a somewhat different semantic field. Solon, who was later regarded by the Athenians as the father of democracy (Mossé 1979), speaks of the lower sort demanding *isomoiria* in the rich land of Attica with the worthy (*kakoisin esthlous is[omoirian] echein*: [Aristotle] *Constitution of Athens* 12.3): This may refer to a proposed redistribution of land (see Rhodes 1981 *ad loc.*), although other interpretations are possible. Thucydides (7.75.6) refers to the retreating Athenian soldiers in Sicily in 413 BCE as "having a certain *isomoiria* of evils," while noting that sharing of the burden of misfortune with many (*polloi*) served to alleviate its weight.

timokratia, and *aristokratia*.[14] In each case, access to public power would presumably include, but need not be limited to, access to public offices. In sum, rather than imagining the -*kratos* group as sharing the -*arche* group's primary concern for the monopoly control of public offices by a strictly delimited number of persons, I would suggest that each of the -*kratos*-root terms originally referred, positively, to the aspiration for, or fact of, the exercise of political power-as-capacity by the deserving: whether it was the female, the honorable, the excellent, the equal – or, with *demokratia*, the whole of the citizenry.[15]

Demokratia cannot mean "the *demos* rules/dominates by a monopoly on officeholding" in that the singular *demos* (unlike the plural *hoi oligoi*) must refer to a collectivity, a "public" – and that public cannot collectively be "officeholders" in any ordinary sense.[16] In classical Greek, *demos* had multiple meanings, including the primary meaning of "citizenry" and the secondary meanings of "the citizen assembly" and "the lower classes."[17] In the postrevolutionary political context in which the *demokratia* compound was coined, when all native, adult, male residents of Athenian territory were enfranchised, *demos* must refer to "the whole of an extensive and diverse citizen body" (in conformity with earlier Greek usage of the term) rather than "the many who are poor" (i.e., "not leisured"), as it later came to mean to democracy's critics. When it refers to "the citizen assembly," *demos* points to the whole of the citizenry, insofar as access to the assembly was open to all citizens. The *demos* that authorized legislation in a given meeting of the assembly stood for the whole of the citizenry.[18] In classical Athens, then, *demos* originally meant "the whole of the citizenry" (free native male population of a defined territory) – not a sociologically delimited fragment of the citizenry. *Demos* of *demokratia* was originally an inclusive term, referring to all potential rulers (in the relevant category of free, native, adult

---

[14] Albeit, I cannot positively eliminate the counterposition that, in each case, what is being asserted (in ordinary Greek political language, if not in the philosophical vocabulary of Plato or Aristotle) is the defining characteristic (excellent, female, honorable, equal to one another) of the group that rules by domination over others. But this seems less likely, in light of the positive connotations of the relevant terms (with the possible exception of *gunaikokratia*) and the general Greek disapproval of brute domination of rulers over potential rulers (free, native males as opposed, e.g., to slaves).

[15] This suggests why there is no *monokratia* or *oligokratia*: "the one" and "the few," when in authority, were regarded as *inherently* strong and capable, through control of wealth, special education, and high birth. So it was not in question whether the one or the few possessed a capacity to do things – the question was whether they controlled the apparatus of government.

[16] Aristotle worries about this issue in Book 3 of the *Politics*. See discussion of Lane 2013.

[17] Liddel et al. 1968, s.v. Donlan 1970.

[18] Athenian revolution of 508 BCE: Ober 2007a; the general enfranchisement of resident males after the revolution: Badian 2000. Demos in assembly as synecdoche for the entire citizenry in Athenian public discourse: Ober 1996: 117–122.

males) as opposed to just some. If we employ Aristotle's analytic vocabulary of parts and wholes, we may say that the *demos* was a comprehensive whole rather than a subsidiary part. Thucydides has the democratic politician, Athenagoras, make that exact point in a speech to the citizen assembly of Syracuse: "the *demos* encompasses the whole; oligarchy only a part."[19]

If we extrapolate from *isokratia* and other *-kratos* compounds, the term *demokratia* makes both philological and historical sense: *Demokratia*, which emerged as a regime type with the historical self-assertion of a *demos* after a popular revolution (Ober 2007a), asserts a *demos*'s collective capacity to do things, to rule in the positive sense of capably organizing public affairs. If this is right, *demokratia* does not refer in the first instance to the *demos*'s monopolistic control of preexisting constitutional authority. *Demokratia* is not just "the power of the *demos*" in the sense of "the dominion or monopolistic power of the *demos* relative to other potential power-holders in the state." Rather, it means, more capaciously, "the empowered *demos*" – it is the regime in which the *demos* gains a collective capacity to effect change in the public realm. And so it is not only a matter of the people's collective *control* of a public realm (Pettit 2013). Rather, it is their collective *capability* to act effectively within that realm and, indeed, to reconstitute the public realm through their joint action.

The institutions of Athenian *demokratia* were never centered on the use of a majority-voting rule to elect officeholders. Voting for generals (for example) and directly on policy was certainly important – the individual Athenian citizen could be described not only as *isonomos* and *isegoros* but also as *isopsephos*: an equal in respect to his vote. But in contrast to *isonomia* and *isegoria*, *isopsephia* is another "missing" classical Greek regime name: It is unattested until the first century BCE and was never periphrasis for *demokratia*. *Psephokratia* (vote-power) is unknown in ancient Greek. Ancient critics of popular rule sought to rebrand *demokratia* as the equivalent of a tyrannical "*polloi-archia*" – as the monopolistic domination of government apparatus through the voting power of the many who were poor. This is the strategy, for example, of the so-called Old Oligarch, an anonymous fifth-century pamphleteer (Ober 1998: Chapter 1). But we ought not to confuse this rebranding with the positive meaning of term, as it was used by Greek democrats across the long history of Greek democracy.[20]

---

[19] Thucydides 6.39.1: "It will be said, perhaps, that democracy is neither wise (*xuneton*) nor equitable (*ison*), but that the holders of property are also the best fitted to rule (*archein*). I say, on the contrary, first, that the *demos* encompasses the whole (*xumpas*), oligarchy only a part (*meros*)."

[20] Plato, in the *Statesman*, retains most of the fifth-century regime terminology but "doubles" the name *demokratia* in order to refer to the power of the demos both in the positive sense of "law-abiding,

Demokratia therefore originally meant "the People's capacity to do things" – to make history through joint action at scale.[21] As used by its inventors, the term *democracy* was descriptive, asserting that the people *do have* the capacity to effect change. As we will see (Chapter 5), joint action at scale required the exercise, by citizens, of inherent human capacities for reason and communication in the formation of shared plans for the pursuit of common purposes.[22] But its inventors also deployed "democracy" normatively, contending that the people *ought to be* capable of making and enforcing rules. The original Greek definition thus captures the core of what a nontyrannical form of democracy is, in principle and practice: legitimate collective self-governance by citizens.

2.3 MATURE GREEK DEFINITION

The Greek term *kratos* can have, as we have seen, the sense of both strength and constraint; those meanings are conjoined in acts of rule making and enforcement. The *kratos* of the Athenian demos was manifest in rules, enacted by the citizens and binding on all members of the Athenian community, and in the enforcement of those rules. In classical Athens, citizens were expected to participate from time to time in the civic activities that sustained the nontyrannical regime; not to do so was to risk the censure of fellow citizens, to be called out, as Thucydides's Pericles puts it in the famous Funeral Oration (Thucydides 2.40.2), as "useless." Athenian law and participatory behavioral norms sustained democratic conditions of political freedom, political equality, and civic dignity. Athenian democrats and their ancient critics alike regarded those conditions as essential for democracy's continued existence.[23] But the conditions of freedom, equality, and dignity in turn required restraint in the demos's exercise of *kratos*. In Greek political history, the full recognition that the demos must, and can, impose legal limits on the exercise of its own capacity to do things, by

limited rule" and the negative sense of "lawless domination." In Polybius's *History* (6.4.5), written in the second century BCE, *demokratia* becomes a generic term for "legitimate, law-respecting, republican government" – and is opposed, as such, to *ochlokratia*, a neologism for "lawless mob rule."

[21] This interpretation is consistent with the conjunction of *demos* and *kratos* in Aeschylus's *Suppliants* of ca. 463 BCE, a play that is often taken to offer the earliest periphrases of the word *demokratia*: "the ruling hand of the people" (*demou kratousa cheir*: 604); "the people, the power that rules the polis" (*to damion, to ptolin kratunei*: 699).

[22] On the philosophical underpinnings of a methodologically individualistic theory of joint action, I follow Bratman 2014; Bratman's theory of joint action is applied to democracy at scale by Ober 2008a; Stilz 2009; Pettit 2013. See, further, Section 6.2.

[23] Participation norm, which leaves ample space for pursuit of individual projects: Thucydides 2.40.2; political freedom: Hansen 1996; political equality: Raaflaub 1996: civic dignity: Ober 2012.

regulating legislative procedure, developed well after the democratic founding era. But by the end of the fifth century BCE, the need for limits had
been recognized and formalized in Athenian law.

The recognition that the authority of the ruling demos can and should
be limited by law is often thought to distinguish liberal democracy from
democracy before liberalism (Starr 2007). Limitations on legislative authority in democratic government are associated with a liberal ideal of individual liberty, understood as a natural condition or an inherent human right.
Yet the theory and practice of legal limitation of legislative authority was
well developed in Greek antiquity, long before the emergence of doctrines
of natural law or rights theory. In classical Athens, it was the imperatives
of security and prosperity that impressed upon the citizens the necessity
of limiting the power of the assembled demos to act as an unconstrained
legislative body. The necessity was reconfigured as a virtue by the realization that the essential democratic conditions of political liberty and equality were potentially compromised by the unconstrained exercise of public
authority by a democratic majority.

Democracy, as a regime type, persisted in the Greek world for some 400
years; the theory and practice of democracy evolved considerably over that
time. By the era of the historian Polybius, in the second century BCE, the
term *demokratia* was synonymous with "legitimate nonautocratic government," and the notion of "mixed government" – in which presumptively
monarchical, aristocratic, and popular elements would serve to counteract
tendencies to autocracy inherent within each element – was commonplace.
But in practice, legislative limitation came much earlier.[24]

Certain self-imposed constraints on the authority of the demos to do
what it wished to individual citizens appear to be coterminous with democracy's founding. The practice of ostracism, for example, by which an individual could be expelled from the community by plurality vote was limited by procedural rules. The rules required a prior majority vote in favor
of ostracism, permitted such a vote only once each year, and limited the
period of expulsion to ten years.[25] For our purposes, however, the key development was an innovative set of legal changes enacted in the late fifth and
early fourth centuries BCE. Those changes were motivated by the Athenians' recognition that the stability of the state required systematic constraints on the power of the people to do things, just when and as they
pleased. The constraints came in two forms: first, formally distinguishing

[24] Greek democracy outside Athens: Robinson 1997, 2011. Polybius on democracy: esp. 6.4.5; on mixed
government: 6.11.11.
[25] Ostracism: Forsdyke 2005; Ober 2015b: 174–175.

day-to-day policy, made by simple majority vote in a legislative citizen assembly (usually by show of hands), from fundamental constitutional law, made by a more cumbersome, multistage quasi-judicial process; second, formally subordinating the "decrees" passed in the ordinary meetings of the assembly to codified constitutional "laws" made through the more cumbersome quasi-judicial process.[26]

In the late fifth century BCE, in the aftermath of the Peloponnesian War, the Athenians instituted, by democratic means, a new constitutional rule whereby they required the immediate expression of the will of the assembled citizenry, in the form of "a decree of the Assembly" to be consistent with existing fundamental law. They had recently codified and archived the laws. Now they distinguished the procedure for making and amending fundamental law from the direct-vote method of passing decrees. Constitutional law could be revised, if and when a majority of the assembled citizens voted to initiate a constitutionally mandated process that allowed specific laws to be challenged and, potentially, changed. According to the usual reconstruction of the process, lawmakers responsible for considering and authorizing changes were randomly selected (by lot) from among citizens over age 30 (Hansen 1999: 167–168; cf. Canevaro 2015). The process resembled a jury trial, in which the assembled lawmakers heard detailed arguments for and against adding a new law and simultaneously repealed those existing laws that contradicted provisions of the new law. Amending the constitution was not nearly so difficult as it is, for example, in the contemporary US. But, when compared with ordinary Athenian legislative procedure, the new process for changing Athenian constitutional law was relatively protracted, public, and deliberative.

The constitutional innovation came in the aftermath of two oligarchic coups d'état and a devastating military defeat. After the democratic restoration of 403 BCE, the Athenians saw that a return to prosperity required political stability. Stability in turn required a credible commitment on the part of the ordinary-citizen majority to a legal order that would protect the persons and property of the wealthy. Elite citizens must, for their part, credibly commit to preserving the entitlements (e.g., pay for public service) that enabled the relatively poor to participate in politics. The civil war era

---

[26] Athenian constitutional reforms of the later fifth century BCE and following: Hansen 1999; their context: Shear 2011; Carawan 2013. Motivation for changes: Carugati 2015, with literature survey. Canevaro 2013, 2015, forthcoming, argues for a somewhat different procedure and suggests (per litt.) that the nomothetai were ordinary assemblymen. For my present purposes, the important thing is that under the new rules, the procedures for making constitutional laws were distinct from and more cumbersome than those for making ordinary legislative decrees.

was ended with a reconciliation agreement that took, as Edwin Carawan (2013) has shown, the form of a contract between the elite-citizen "men of the city" and the ordinary-citizen "men of Piraeus." The new constitutional order was predicated on acknowledging that the social diversity of the demos gave rise to opposing policy preferences. Yet it also recognized what Federica Carugati (2015) has called "the *patrios politeia* consensus" across that diverse population – a widespread agreement that Athenians were "ancestrally" committed to living according to their own laws. There was general agreement that behavior that endangered the ability of Athenians to negotiate diverse preferences and to live together peacefully was against the law. There was also a widely shared sense that toleration of lawlessness led to poverty and insecurity. That general consensus was enough to bootstrap recommitment to a formal system of fundamental constitutional law.

The change in the way in which constitutional law was made in Athens was, therefore, predicated on an equilibrium solution, achieved in high-stakes social conditions by people who recognized that they had more to gain by cooperating than by fighting. The result was what we may call the mature (philo-democratic) Greek definition of democracy: collective self-governance by a socially diverse body of citizens, limited by constitutional laws that were also established by citizens.

That ancient definition is consistent with two of the most famous and resonant phrases in early American political history. One is Abraham Lincoln's succinct evocation, in his Gettysburg Address, of "government of the people, by the people, for the people." Basic democracy is *for* the people, in the sense of aiming at the fulfillment of fundamental interests that are commonly held by the citizen body as a whole, rather than merely satisfying the preferences of a majority faction. It is *by* the people insofar as the citizens make, execute, and enforce public policy. And it is *of* the people in that democracy is a common possession. The citizens *own* the government, it is *their* government, because they were and are its author. That collective authorship and ownership had been asserted in the previous century in the Preamble of the US Constitution: "We the People . . . do ordain and establish this Constitution for the United States of America."[27]

The assumed and aspirational political context in 1787 and 1863 was, of course, a representative government rather than a direct democracy on the Athenian model. As noted above, ancient Greek democracies came about and were sustained in distinctive and presumably unrepeatable

---

[27] On the importance of the Preamble to a democratic reading of the Constitution, see Amar 2005.

historical circumstances. They manifested distinctive social and cultural features. Some of those features, which included slavery and denial of participation rights to women, are foreign and abhorrent to any contemporary regime that today would be considered a democracy. But, as we turn to the Demopolis thought experiment in the next chapter, we need not be burdened with ancient Greek sociocultural baggage or, for that matter, with the attitudes characteristic of political leaders in the America of 1787 or 1863. If Demopolis is imagined as a state in the twenty-first century CE, its citizens will not require a moral commitment to principles of liberalism to do without slavery and to open participation rights to women.

All ancient Greek democratic governments were, as Paul Cartledge (2016) has emphasized, procedurally different from all modern democracies in relying on the regular and direct legislative activity of citizens. I suggested in Section 2.1 that the procedural distinction does not point to an unbridgeable conceptual chasm. In Chapter 7 we will turn to the question of how the basic democracy framework might support a government in which the people have delegated to representatives the primary responsibility for most (although not necessarily all) rule making and enforcement. For now, I assume that until it is shown that a representative government of a large state *cannot* be a basic democracy, that is, a system of self-government in which citizens are capable and (directly or through representatives) collective rulers, it remains possible that democracy before liberalism could be relevant for a modern state.[28] Thus, as we turn to the thought experiment of Demopolis in the next chapter, I consider it possible that the government that will emerge from the experiment could be provisionally delegated to representatives. By abstracting from the specific historical circumstances in which ancient citizen self-government arose, the thought experiment allows us to posit a system of basic democracy in different contexts – including modernity.

---

[28] Representative democracy: Pitkin 1967; Manin 1997; Urbinati 2006. Achen and Bartels 2016 and Caplan 2007 are prominent examples of the argument that the people are incapable of effective collective self-government, under the conditions of modernity. Like other liberal critics of democracy, they seem, however, eager to retain the term "democracy" for their preferred form of government, a strategy reminiscent of Polybius, above. Of course, democracy, as a form of organizational governance, is not limited to states; see, for example, Manville and Ober 2003.

CHAPTER 3

Founding Demopolis

The thought experiment that follows is indebted to a grand tradition in political philosophy that includes Plato's Callipolis and Rawls's original position. But, unlike these two great exemplars, my "Demopolis" experiment leaves the conditions of social justice unspecified. Rather than being the basis of a theory of justice, Demopolis addresses a question about social order. It posits that democracy, in its basic form, is an answer to one variant of the fundamental question of how a human community can reliably realize the benefits arising from social cooperation. How to gain the benefits of security and prosperity without being ruled by a master – without submitting to the authority of an autocratic monarch or oligarchic ruling coalition – is the variant of the cooperation question to which basic democracy is the answer. [1]

In any historical democracy, that answer comes with a variety of historically contingent features; for Athens, along with slavery and restriction of the franchise to men, those features included its small scale. In addition to abstracting from circumstances specific to any given historical era, Demopolis is intended to answer whether basic democracy is a plausible regime at a scale larger than the city-state.

The difficulty of the question of how cooperation can be achieved without a master varies with scale. The answer is relatively easy when the size of the group remains at the level of a face-to-face society in which each of the group's individual members knows one another. Think of the faculty of a university department, the partners of a firm, or the members of a hobby club. As we will see (Section 5.1), modern humans came into being and long existed in small, face-to-face foraging groups, and the earliest social-political systems are plausibly described as democratic. Democracy of some sort appears, therefore, to be the natural default of humans as a

---

[1] Cf. Williams 2005: 3 on the "first" political question as "securing of order, protection, trust, and the conditions of cooperation."

species. But when social scale increased, the natural democratic default was no longer available as an easy answer to the cooperation question. When a group becomes so large that mutual monitoring and informal norm-enforcement are no longer practicable, free riding and commons tragedies reduce the benefits arising from cooperation, threatening the group's survival and demanding a new answer to the fundamental question of political order. With the advent of agriculture some 12,000 years ago, followed by related technologies of food processing and storage, societies gained the potential to become much larger. As human communities grew in size and complexity, they also became more autocratic, a trend that persisted, with notable exceptions, throughout most of recorded history.[2]

For reasons specified a half-century ago by the political scientist Mancur Olson (1965), autocracy readily solves the problem of cooperation at scale, through the imposition of clear hierarchies of status and authority. Those at the top of the hierarchy have a strong incentive, in the form of rents extracted from those below them, to punish free riding and other forms of social deviance. If rents are distributed so that those with high violence potential use that potential to sustain the autocrat and punish deviation, then the incentive to deviate is reduced.[3]

Fear of punishment gets autocracy part of the way to a cooperative equilibrium, but autocracy, like any form of government, requires legitimacy – which I define in a preliminary way as the condition in which obedience to authority is normal and predictable, because most people, most of the time, accept authority as mandatory and right. They obey because the ruler (or, more immediately, the background culture that sustains the ruler) has offered them an acceptable set of reasons for why they should obey.[4] Historically, the legitimacy of autocracies long rested on claims that the rulers had a special and unique relationship to a divine order, backed up by ideologies asserting the naturalness of social and political hierarchy.[5] When subjects

---

[2] For the big picture of human development, from deep prehistory onward, see Morris 2010; Harari 2015. On the turn from foraging democracies to complex society autocracy, see survey in Turchin 2015, with literature cited.

[3] See North et al. 2009; Cox et al. 2012, discussed in more detail in Section 4.2.

[4] This is a practical, rather than a moralized (e.g., Christiano 2008: 232–240), conception of legitimacy. On the distinction, see Williams 2005: 5. It is the answer to the question, why does government not require constant use of overt violence in extracting rents from subjects, rather than the answer to the question of why a subject *ought*, as a moral duty, to obey governmental authority. See, further, Chapter 4.

[5] God-like Kings: Morris 2010. Contemporary attempts to legitimate autocracy have relied on ideology, cult of personality, or impersonation of the forms of democracy. The reasons offered by autocrats tend to become less compelling when practical alternatives are well publicized, which is at least one reason democracy made headway in classical Greek antiquity and in modernity.

regard autocracy as legitimate for these (by a democrat's lights, spurious) reasons, the autocrat's orders will be passed down through a chain of command and obeyed (more or less accurately and voluntarily) at each level – thereby promoting social cooperation at scale.

Its historical prevalence suggests that autocracy often works well, insofar as it has established social order at scale for many people in many times and places. It is only when legitimacy collapses, when subjects no longer find the reasons for obedience offered by autocrats compelling, when people reject autocracy along with its supporting hierarchy, that they will be motivated to seek answers to the difficult question of how to secure the benefits of cooperation at scale without a master. The question was answered, in the ancient world, by the democracies established by Athenians and by the citizens of a number of other Greek city-states. Athens was much too large to avail itself of the "natural" small-group solution. But it was, as noted in Chapter 2, very small compared to many modern nation-states. Moreover, as noted above, ancient city-states developed democracy under certain conditions, cultural as well as social and economic, that were specific to a certain time and place. At least some of those conditions are unlikely to be repeated. The Demopolis thought experiment is intended to show how people might solve the puzzle of masterless cooperation without the special conditions of culture and scale that pertained in ancient Greece.

3.1 FOUNDERS AND THE ENDS OF THE STATE

We begin with an ordinary human population that is both numerous (above face-to-face size) and socially and economically diverse. The population is likewise diverse in its values, although not so deeply divided in fundamental beliefs as to be in the midst of, or on the brink of, religious or ethnic warfare. These people share some (nonspecified) prior history and elements of civil society. They can easily communicate with one another (they share a language or can readily translate).

We sort that population according to individuals' preferences for government by autocrats. Suppose the result, when charted, is a normal (i.e., bell-shaped) distribution; this is illustrated in Figure 3.1. On the left tail of the distribution are those fiercely opposed to being ruled by a master; on the right tail are those with a strong preference for autocracy. Most of the population lies between these extremes.[6]

---

[6] We might, of course, imagine a different distribution, with many more supporting either autocracy or nonautocracy, and with more or fewer people on longer or shorter tails; the normal distribution is a simplification device, implying nothing about actual preference distributions in actual populations.

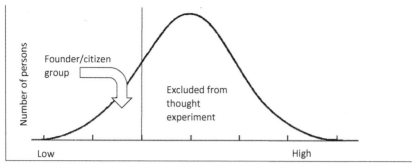

Figure 3.1 Distribution of people in Demopolis thought experiment.

Now imagine dividing the population with a vertical line somewhere to the left of the center of the distribution. Those to the right of the line have a fairly high tolerance or even an active preference for autocracy. People situated to the left of the line range from those who actively detest autocracy to those with a fairly low tolerance for it. These "left of the line" people are those with whom our thought experiment is concerned.

By stipulation, the "left of the line" group matches the original population in all other forms of social, economic, and value diversity. Now suppose that this "antiautocracy, but otherwise diverse" group of people inhabits a defined territory and that they seek to answer the question about achieving social cooperation without a master. Despite their other differences, the members of the group are in general agreement concerning their unwillingness to live under a master.[7] This general agreement may be thought of as the first step in a three-stage constitutional process. The second step is the establishment of basic rules discussed below (Sections 3.3, 3.4, and 3.5). The third step will be the elaboration of other rules that will answer, inter alia, difficult questions about distributive justice. The first two stages do not predetermine the substantive rules that will be established in the third stage: The core idea of basic democracy is that it could provide a secure foundation for a variety of quite different democratic regimes (Chapter 8). Meanwhile, in the situation enabling the first step of general

---

[7] Historically, this situation may be rare, but it is hardly unknown, e.g., Athens in 508 BCE, America in 1776. Acemoglu and Robinson 2016 argue that democracy (in a somewhat broader sense than used here) may be coterminous with state formation and that democratic transitions are better explained by reference to strong pressure from those demanding a part in governance than as a matter of elite choice. Note that general agreement need not presume unanimity, in the sense of all agreeing on the same thing for the same reasons.

agreement on nontyranny, we assume that those in the original (bell curve) population who fall to the right of the line, i.e., those who have a moderate to high preference/tolerance for autocracy, now inhabit another territory.[8]

The thought experiment is not predicated on a liberal premise of value neutrality in that it excludes a large part of the original population, based on their political attitudes. While other sorts of value pluralism remain, the problem of diverse preferences over autocracy is solved by division and separation rather than by, for example, an overlapping consensus achieved via deliberative reason giving (Rawls 1996) or any other liberal procedure. The experiment assumes that a particular group of people controls a particular part of the earth, but it is not concerned with their moral right to control that territory (Stilz 2011, 2013). The experiment starts within history, assuming that things have happened in the past (good, bad, just, unjust) that resulted in a specific group of people possessing a certain country at a particular moment in time. Now they need to decide how to govern themselves so that, inter alia, they can defend their territory if confronted by hostile rival claimants.

This setup assumes that the original population has split, perhaps dividing a territory they once shared (think of the US and Canada after 1776). It is meant to recognize the fact that, while a good many people *have*, throughout history, sought to live without a master, a great many other people, in all periods of human history, have tolerated or even preferred autocracy.[9] While democracy may be regarded as *natural*, and while I will argue that certain human goods are uniquely well supported by democracy (Chapter 5), democracy has never (in historical times) been globally preferred to autocracy. I believe that rational people would choose democracy under a specifiable set of ideal conditions. But democracy before liberalism is not ideal theory.

We start, then, with an extensive and diverse group of people – who share a preference for nonautocracy – seeking to establish rules for themselves, as residents of a masterless state.[10] That state will exist in a world of rival

---

[8] This three-stage process may be seen as an elaboration on Hardin's (1999) two-stage constitutional process, in which the first stage is broad enough agreement on general issues to enable coordination and the next stage is making more conflict-ridden decisions on specific issues.

[9] Scheidel 2017 presents data on frequent, unsuccessful peasant revolts in medieval Europe, which at least suggests that true contentment with the rule of a particular master may not be a general historical norm.

[10] The setup assumes simultaneity in the establishment of a state and a basic democratic constitutional order. This would be implausible if we follow theorists of state formation (notably Huntington 1968) who claim that state formation (with an autocratic government) must precede democratization. But the "first state with established capacity then inclusive democracy" sequence has been effectively challenged, both empirically and theoretically. See Acemoglu and Robinson 2016: 4–5,

states ruled in various ways; one of them is occupied by those to the right of the line in the original distribution, above. The world of states is potentially dangerous: Rivalry may mean attempts at conquest. It is also mutable: States will change their government; populations will grow or shrink; technology, climate, etc., will change. I do not specify the no-autocracy group's size, but, as noted above, it is greater than face-to-face. The group is diverse in terms of economic standing (wealth and income), life experiences, and knowledge. But, as noted, those in the group are able to communicate with one another at a sophisticated level.

The group's members have no special psychology. There is no veil of ignorance, no "hive mind," no strong antecedent national (as opposed to civic) identity. They are sociable (in a basic sense), reason using (but also ordinarily emotional with ordinary cognitive limits), fairly (but not narrowly) self-interested, strategic, communicative human beings. They are not exceptionally altruistic or completely selfish. Each wants to flourish, at least in the simple sense of "doing well" in material conditions of life, as an individual and as a member of social subgroups (e.g., families). Each recognizes that an extensive system of social cooperation is necessary for flourishing.[11] They share some background knowledge of political and social history and of social and natural sciences. The group includes within its membership a range of interests and skills. Some are expert in various domains relevant to governance. The group's members are provisionally willing to take expert knowledge into consideration in decision-making contexts. They will not, however, defer to experts unless they are confident that deference does not risk capture of the rule-making process by experts, in ways that might produce autocracy.

The persons in the group are "Founders" in that they share an intention to establish the fundamental rules, a basic constitution, for an independent state in a bounded territory.[12] Let us call that state Demopolis. The state established by the Founders must have the capacity to achieve three ends, on which the Founders agree ex ante. Each of the three ends listed below must be robustly sustained. No one end can be traded off against another.

with literature cited; Rosanvallon 2006: 34, "the political means the process whereby a human collectivity is . . . constituted by an always contentious process whereby the explicit or implicit rules of what they can share and accomplish in common . . . are elaborated."

[11] They are, in short "Humans," not "Econs," in the terminology employed by Richard Thaler (2015) and borrowed by Daniel Kahneman (2011), among others.

[12] In the twenty-first century, politics is certainly not limited to the activities of states within bounded territories; see Runciman 2017. But as Stilz (2009, 2011) and other contemporary theorists demonstrate, the territorial state remains a highly significant object of theoretical attention and practical importance. I leave it to future work to determine whether democracy before liberalism is relevant in the kinds of nonbounded communities imagined by Runciman and other theorists of globalism.

1   *Security.* The state is capable of responding to exogenous shocks (e.g., hostile neighbors, environmental changes). It is reasonably robust to both external threats and civil conflict or subversion. It has, therefore, the potential to persist over time. Residents are reasonably secure against arbitrary threats to their persons and property.

2   *Prosperity.* The state is overall prosperous rather than impoverished. Residents have ample opportunity to gain wealth and income at levels that will allow them to pursue life plans beyond subsistence. Collectively, prosperity allows the state to compete successfully with rival states, autocratic and otherwise, without impoverishing its own residents.[13]

3   *Nontyranny.* No individual or faction monopolizes political authority; there is no fixed hierarchy of political power.

Nontyranny (masterlessness, nonautocracy) is the key stipulation. I take security and prosperity to be generic ends sought by the residents of real states throughout history. In brief, the Founders want what other people have historically wanted, but they are distinctive in their unwillingness to accept either a boss or the hierarchy that comes with a boss. They lack faith in the benevolence of dictators, the wisdom of ruling elites, the ideologies of divine kingship and aristocratic natural right. On the other hand, they hold different opinions about exactly what is wrong with autocracy: a tendency to cruelty, violence, or domination; an affront to freedom, equality, or dignity; a predatory threat to economic interests or personal privacy; the risible, contemptible, or aesthetically revolting features of its public products – parades, rallies, speeches, architecture.

   Just as they vary in their reasons for rejecting autocracy, the Founders of Demopolis embrace a range of ethical commitments. Their beliefs represent, in Rawls's terms, different comprehensive conceptions of the good. Some are theists, ethical liberals, libertarians, republicans, egalitarians, etc. They do not agree, ex ante, on specific conceptions of justice or even on the intrinsic value of individual liberty or equality. But their disagreement is not, as noted above, at the fever pitch of current or imminent religious or ethnic war. After the rules are set, some conceptions of the good may be supported through the tax structure or actively promoted through state education. Other conceptions will not be supported or promoted but will

---

[13] In reference to Plato's *Republic* (2.372d), we might say that the state, when complete, will not be limited to subsistence conditions because the citizens share Glaucon's preference orderings concerning basic conditions of life. Glaucon rejects Socrates's simple and healthy "First Polis" as a city fit only for pigs, because he wants to live further above subsistence.

be available as options. Comprehensive conceptions that aim at autocracy will be disadvantaged. Thus, the basic constitution is not committed to value neutrality, although it will not, in and of itself, determine which values, other than those arising directly from the three ends, will be privileged.[14] Whether choices made after the foundation will favor or preclude liberalism remains to be seen (Chapter 8).

The Founders do not assume that they are setting up a regime that is best for all people, everywhere. Rather, they seek a government that suits themselves, in recognition that their preference for nontyranny is their own. They are, in terms of their rejection of autocracy, localists of the Bernard Williams type rather than cosmopolitans or universalists. They seek the best nonautocratic solution for, in Williams's phrase, "now and around here."[15]

In addition to the three fundamental ends, each of the Founders will have other social goals on which there is substantive disagreement. The constitution established by the Founders must allow for subsequent legislation that will instantiate, however imperfectly, some standard of justice. But distributive justice is not the immediate goal of the group in establishing the basic rules. Although, as we will see (Sections 3.4 and 6.8), the question of distribution will enter the picture as we specify the conditions necessary to achieve and sustain the three ends, distributive justice is not the goal sought, in the first instance, by the Founders. They recognize that before seeking to establish all the social conditions (whatever these may be) demanded by justice (however defined), they must first live in a secure, prosperous, nonautocratic state with a workable procedural system for rule making. Before seeking to legislate fairness or desert in respect to distribution of wealth or income, they must, as a society, securely possess the relevant goods that might be distributed and must have a robust institutional process for making and enforcing decisions about distribution and much else.

Each of the Founders is willing (if not eager, below) to pay some costs (time, disclosed knowledge, taxes) in support of the conditions necessary for cooperation without a master. The Founders do not, however, intend to devote their lives to governing. Nor are they ready to pay costs that are so high as to preclude pursuit of all other projects. In some social systems

---

[14] Nonneutrality allows for a regime that differentially advantages certain comprehensive conceptions: So, for example, those who are exemplary citizens (because they value political participation) may be rewarded for service from which they gain utility. On civic education, see Sections 4.4 and 5.5.

[15] Williams 2005: 8ff. Because of this recognition, members of the group may feel no ethical obligation to promote democracy beyond their own borders.

that could emerge from the original foundation, such projects might be autonomously chosen on the basis of freely formed individual preferences (i.e., ethical individualism). In other systems, some projects falling outside the domain of collective self-governance may be mandated by a traditional culture or religious belief. I will call these other projects "socially valued," to distinguish them from civic responsibilities.

Citizens vary in what they expect to pay in participation costs, but few of them want nontyranny at *any* cost. Most want nontyranny at a *reasonable* cost, i.e., at a level that assures adequate opportunity to pursue their other projects.[16] Few of the Founders expect to make governance their own primary life project. Some Founders may want to be free in Isaiah Berlin's (1969) "noninterference" sense of having the choice of choosing or not choosing among a range of possible ends deemed as good by themselves. Others, for example, those whose primary life project is religious devotion (and who see tyranny as a threat to their faith), may be uninterested in free choice among diverse goods. But, like those who do want freedom to choose, they will not support nontyranny if the costs are so high as to preclude pursuit of their primary project.[17]

We may represent "what a Founder wants" in economic terms as a "utility function." The utility function of the "median Founder" is schematically illustrated in Figure 3.2. Each of the Founders requires a society that will provide to each citizen at least the basic necessities of existence (white box); the public conditions ensuring state-level security, prosperity, and nontyranny (gray box); and the space to pursue socially valued projects (black box). The median Founder hopes to spend relatively little effort on securing the bare essentials of life, somewhat more time on public goods provision, and most time pursuing projects of value to herself.

Utilities of the Founders differ, both in the relative size of each of the boxes (some may, for example value civic duty more than other projects) and in the contents of the black box of socially valued projects. But each of the Founders has, and assumes that the others have, a similarly *structured* utility function. The structure presumes (as in the case of the three ends) that the contents of the three boxes cannot be traded off against each other.

---

[16] Those willing to pay high costs might seem to be exploited by those willing to pay only minimal costs. But the former may also value participation intrinsically or instrumentally. Socially valued projects may or may not be autonomously chosen: A given individual's project might be the conversion of his or her fellows, with the goal of creating a unified community of shared religious belief and practice, such that each individual would choose the same "black-box" projects.

[17] For critical discussion of Berlin's conception of freedom as noninterference, see Pettit 2013. On the question of whether the choices made by our imagined Founders might provide a foundation for a nonliberal value system, see Chapter 8.

Figure 3.2 Utility function of the median Founder-citizen.

Thus, no increase in public political goods can make up for the complete elimination of other socially valued goods. Moreover, the three boxes have an ordinal rank: white, gray, black. Each Founder ranks his own survival highest, then the public conditions of social cooperation, and then socially valued projects. This is not because the Founders gain most utility from the activities in the white and gray boxes but because they recognize that without bare existence, there is no chance for public goods arising from social cooperation, and in the absence of the public goods of security and prosperity, there will be insufficient opportunity for pursuit of other valued ends. The inclusion of nontyranny in the gray box is contingent, as we have seen, on its cost being reasonable. As we will see (Section 5.5), the costs of nontyranny will be more readily covered if democracy is seen as a source of highly valued gray-box goods uniquely available to those who participate in politics.

The ordinal ranking will be stable if public good provision is a reliable means to the end of socially valued (black-box) projects. This does not mean that all possible projects will always be protected from interference arising from the requirements of securing public goods. The ordinal ranking white/grey/black means that black-box projects may sometimes be compromised by white-box or gray-box requirements. But state interference in socially valued projects will need to be justified by reference to the

three ends for which the state exists, insofar as excessive or arbitrary interference will lead to disaffection and instability that will ultimately compromise security and nontyranny and to limits on capital investment in ways
that will ultimately compromise welfare.

3.2 AUTHORITY AND CITIZENSHIP

The Founders recognize that anarchy is not a practical option (no matter
how theoretically attractive) in light of the dangerous, mutable environment in which their society exists. On the other hand, in choosing nontyranny as a primary end for their state, they have rejected the option of
turning over jurisdiction – i.e., the authority for rule making, enforcement,
and adjudication of disputes – to any individual or group unconditionally.
To do so would be to accept a master. Rules and rule-structured behaviors may produce conditions allowing jurisdiction to be delegated to representatives (Sections 7.1–7.4). But in our thought experiment, that time
has not yet come. The Founders must make and ratify rules by and for
themselves.[18] The rules they make must enable the Founders collectively
to enforce those rules. And, given their commitment to sustainable security, they must make rules such that their descendants likewise will have
the capacity to be rule makers and rule enforcers, even if day-to-day public
authority has been delegated to representatives. Any future delegation of
jurisdiction must, at any point, be revocable, so that delegation remains a
collective choice rather than a practical necessity.

Because they refuse to be subjects of a sovereign, the Founders must act
conjointly, as a collective agent.[19] The choice of regime type is, at the most
basic level, binary. Either the people rule capably as a collectivity, or they
have a master. Because there has been a prior agreement to reject autocracy
(the first step alluded to above), even before basic rules are decided upon
and established (the second step), we may call the Founders, individually,
"citizens" and, collectively, "the demos." The citizens and the demos come

---

[18] The question of who writes the constitutional rules is not addressed here. It could be an individual
(e.g., Solon) or a small group (e.g., American Founders); the important thing is that the basic rules
must be seen to be established by the Founders collectively, in the sense that they take for themselves
collective ownership, authorship, and responsibility for them. The ratification of the basic rules must
be a collective action of the citizenry.

[19] I do not attempt to solve the philosophical problem, pointedly raised by Hobbes in the opening
passage of *Leviathan*, of whether or how the rationality or employment of reasons of a collective
agent is to be conceived of as a fictive person; on which see the helpful discussion of Stone 2015 and
Section 4.3. It is enough for my purposes that the people in question can, together, arrive at binding
decisions that enable them to achieve and sustain the three primary ends discussed above.

into existence with the general agreement upon the three ends of security, prosperity, and nontyranny – and before any decisions on the rules that will enable the achievement of those ends.[20] But who among the residents of Demopolis are the citizens?[21]

The question of who will be empowered citizens, and thereby constitute the demos, is determined, in the first instance, by the cultural norms that pertain "now and around here." In light of both contemporary and historical practices governing citizenship, it is implausible that young children will be treated as fully empowered citizens, as opposed to citizens-in-training. Likewise, it is implausible to imagine that short-term visitors, lacking any meaningful commitment to or stake in the state, will be citizens. Different cultures have devised different answers to the question of whether working men, women, long-term nonnative residents, or persons convicted of crimes will be citizens with political participation rights. There is, however, a basic inclusion norm for citizenship in a basic democracy, predicated on the requirement of security. That is, if persons who can be "culturally imagined, now and around here," as citizens are excluded from the citizen body without some compelling reason being offered for why they ought to be excluded, their dissatisfaction with their unwarranted exclusion will be an endemic source of civil strife. This is among the considerations that led Aristotle, for example, to define the category of "citizen" with special reference to the citizen in a democratic state rather than in an oligarchy.[22]

---

[20] I do not seek to specify how agreement on the three ends was achieved or determined, other than to claim that the first two ends (security, prosperity) are common to most forms of social order and to note that the third (nontyranny) is the premise that motivates the thought experiment. The problem of the original agreement that makes possible a rule-making process is inherent in democratic theory, as noted by Meckstroth 2015: 18–23, who discusses it under the rubric of "the paradox of authorization." Note that this prior agreement limits the domain of available choices and thus, by weakening the "universal domain" assumption of the judgment aggregation impossibility result, renders collective judgments potentially stable: List and Pettit 2011, with discussion in Ober 2013a.

[21] The question of "who is an empowered citizen?" is sometimes referred to in democratic theory as the "boundary problem": Whelan 1983. Because, by stipulation, the Founders of Demopolis are Williamsian localists, I limit the initial citizen-eligible pool to residents of the territory, although some political theorists regard that sort of limit as arbitrary and morally indefensible. For discussion of the question of why the boundary should ever be narrower than "all those whose interests are affected," see Goodin 2007.

[22] Aristotle *Politics* 3.1275b5. The "preconstitutional" emergence of a demos is historically attested in, for example, the Athenian and American Revolutions. What can be culturally imagined in respect to citizenship can change and has changed dramatically over time, which is one reason that a democracy's fundamental rules must remain open to revision. The "culturally imagined" requirement for inclusivity in a democracy shows why ancient Sparta, for example, was not a democracy, even though was is a citizen-centered social order: The Spartans accepted a state of permanent internal war as the cost of excluding the "culturally (in the wider Greek context) imagined as citizens" helots from civic participation.

In consideration of the security issue, citizenship in Demopolis is extended to all those who are, there and then, culturally imagined as potential citizens. The question "who *ought* to be a citizen?" is unlikely to be answered identically by each of the current residents of Demopolis. The answer the current residents settle upon is likely to change over time, as circumstances change and as the original answer is contested, whether by outsiders or by insiders who come see the world differently from their predecessors. But we may assume that at a given moment in time, there will be a culturally dominant answer to the question of who is a citizen. Those who disagree with the answer can work to change it. If they regard the answer as simply intolerable, they can opt out of the society (Section 3.6).[23]

By asserting that there is, at any given moment, a dominant cultural imagination of citizenship, I beg the question of how that imagination came about. If the Founders (and their successors) fail to acknowledge that the original answer to the citizenship question was a contextually contingent product of a particular time, they put their state at risk of ossification and thereby reduce its capacity to respond to the challenges of a mutable environment. The evolving sources of cultural imagination of citizenship will involve changing considerations of desert, insofar as citizenship is taken to be a good that is available to some, but not all, long-term residents. In regard to the fundamental question of civic belonging, ethical judgment comes into play as the democratic order is being established and remains in play forever after.

For these reasons, the answer to the question "who is a citizen" can never be regarded as settled in a way that would bind the hands of a future generation that sees reason to expand the ambit of "we the people." Notably, however, citizenship tends to be a ratchet that allows movement in only one direction: A decision by a majority to disenfranchise a category of persons currently enjoying citizenship would be to accept that a part of the citizen body can act, in the most basic way, as a tyrant, and thus would violate the third end for which the state exists. Of course, that choice might be made and has been made by democratic states (notoriously, in the case of the American government's internment of Japanese-Americans in World War II). Such "exceptions" can be temporary; democracies may subsequently

---

[23] "Culturally imagined" is less inclusive than "imaginable." For example, Aristophanes's comedy *Assemblywomen* imagines a comic Athens in which women have replaced men as politically empowered citizens (see Ober 1998: Chapter 2). But there is no reason to suppose that, outside the realm of comedy, Athenians ever imagined women as citizens in the sense of those who exercised full political participation rights (as opposed to citizens in the sense of full members of the community: see Patterson 2005).

recognize them as mistakes. But stripping any minority within the citizen body of its standing, redefining civic friends and insiders as civic enemies and outsiders, puts every citizen (given than everyone can be part of some minority) at risk. Every time a civic majority disenfranchises citizens, it becomes, in that moment, a collective tyrant, and thus, to the extent to which the decision denies a primary end on which public order is predicated, it opens the way to the collapse of social order.[24]

If we suppose that the date of Demopolis's founding is the early twenty-first century CE (rather than, as in the Athenian case, the late sixth century BCE), adult women and at least some long-term nonnative residents will be included in the body of the citizens. Demopolis exists within a competitive world of states in which information flows readily across state borders. If we assume that the temporal context of our thought experiment is modernity, the background, global cultural imagination of "who can be a citizen" will have been influenced, directly or indirectly, by principles of liberalism. We do not need to suppose that the Founders of a modern Demopolis are morally committed to liberalism in order to presume that they will enfranchise women and some nonnative residents for prudential reasons.[25]

"All persons culturally imagined as citizens are to be empowered citizens," as a general political principle, provides a floor, not a ceiling. As we will see (Section 5.5), ethical considerations, arising from assumptions about human nature, will require a democracy to justify the exclusion of long-term adult residents from participatory citizenship if and when those considerations are deployed as arguments for the regime's legitimacy. On the other hand, the political principle does not preclude the possibility of democratically establishing rules that will result in individuals being stripped, temporarily or permanently, of civic standing if and when their behavior violates civic norms. So, for example, the question of whether voting rights can legitimately be denied to convicted felons in American jurisdictions is not answered, ipso facto, by the fact that criminals can readily

---

[24] On the role of contestation in the constitution and subsequent reconstitution of a democratic citizen body, see Frank 2010; Beaumont 2014; with discussion of Müller 2016. The exception and civic enemies: Schmitt 2007. Civic friendship: Allen 2004. Danger of reversing the ratchet: Hardin 1999: 310. Liberal argument against disenfranchisement: Christiano 2008: 264–270. The question of authority to disenfranchise an individual widely regarded as profoundly dangerous, or those convicted of serious crimes is a separate question. I take up the question of ostracism, which provides a particularly clear case of depriving a citizen of civic rights, below, in Section 8.3.

[25] In 2015 women in Saudi Arabia were first allowed to vote and to stand as candidates for the nominally governing council (2,100 seats, of which 1,050 were appointed by the King). So, even in a highly religious society, in which women are not allowed to drive, the dominant cultural imagination of citizenship is now such that it is no longer feasible to deny women basic political participation rights – albeit those rights have as yet little practical value, given social restrictions on women and background limits on political freedom.

be imagined as having a right to vote. If, however, the effect of denying voting rights to felons were to delegitimize the democratic order, then curtailing felons' voting rights would be disallowed by the same prudential considerations that underpin the extension of citizenship to all those who are culturally imagined as citizens.

The Founder-citizens accept the need for authority, as organized political power, and for legitimacy, as general, willing obedience to authority. They intend to establish rules necessary to achieve the three ends of security, prosperity, and nontyranny, and they know that the rules must be enforced; they accept the requirement of coercion. By the same token, the Founders do not mean to establish all the rules the state will ever need. They assume that there will be ongoing rule making to fill in other important aspects of politics, including distributive and corrective justice (i.e., "stage 3," above). They assume that there will be exogenous change and shocks that demand legislative response. Indeed, the initial, foundational rules must foster the state's capacity for devising innovative solutions to future problems.[26]

3.3 PARTICIPATION

Like security and overall prosperity, nontyranny is, for the citizens, a public good. It is *nonrival* in that the condition of nontyranny held by one citizen does not subtract from the nontyranny enjoyed by another citizen. It is *nonexcludable* in that every citizen (the original "left of the line" group inhabiting the territory) enjoys the same masterless status.[27] As a public good, nontyranny is subject to the familiar problem of free riding and commons tragedy that potentially beset collectively held possessions. The public goods of security, prosperity, and nontyranny can be simultaneously preserved only if the citizens collectively act to make and enforce rules. Doing so entails costs – time and effort spent on the gray box of public goods could otherwise be spent on the black box of socially valued goods. *Ex hypothesi*, all citizens want to preserve nontyranny. But in the "game" of establishing and sustaining the rules, each citizen, insofar as she is assumed to be rationally self-interested, will choose to defect (i.e., not pay

---

[26] Meckstroth 2015 is distinctive in being a liberal (assuming the inherent value of equal freedom in its first principle: 11) democratic theory that is specifically about the conditions required for dynamic change within a constitutional order.

[27] The public good could devolve to a club good if we assume subsequent immigration of many people denied the opportunity of applying for citizenship (e.g., as long-term "guest workers); again the security issue will push against this exclusion. Note, however, that eligibility for citizenship will not automatically lead to admission to citizenship; see Section 4.4 on civic education and affirmative assent.

the costs) if she can fully enjoy the public good without paying the costs of contributing to it. The state will not long remain secure, prosperous, and masterless if it is beset by cascades of free riding and marginal cheating.[28]

The first rule established by the Founders is, therefore, "all participate" in the business of maintaining public goods. That means, at least, that all citizens have a duty to share, in one way or another, in making, adjudicating, and enforcing the rules. They have a corresponding duty to join in sanctioning those who shirk their participation duty.

Exactly what the duty to participate entails will depend on subsequent choices concerning details of rules governing legislative, executive, and judicial procedure. It will include, at a minimum, devoting some time to deliberating on public issues, voting on important matters of common interest (whether elections or referenda), and serving as a juror. It may also entail taking personal responsibility for rule enforcement (Section 6.6). At least for the more affluent, it will require paying taxes. Some tax revenue will be dedicated to security. Other revenues will be redistributed in the form of support for basic welfare and education.

The "all participate" rule requires that each citizen have access to at least a basic education, in order to access information and make choices responsibly as a voter, juror, and, potentially, as a state official (e.g., member of a deliberative council; Section 7.7). Moreover, in order to be full participants in the work of collective self-governance, citizens will require certain welfare guarantees: Costs of participation cannot be paid by anyone who lacks the capacity to pay those costs without putting her white box of bare existence at risk. Thus, a responsibility for helping to sustain at least minimal levels of health care, food, and housing for every citizen will be part of the participation duties of each citizen. Distribution comes into the basic democracy story as a condition of securing the three ends for which the state exists rather than as a condition of social justice. The redistributive requirement arising from the participation rule provides a floor, not a ceiling. It is antecedent to any choices the citizens subsequently make concerning the level of distribution demanded by whatever conception of justice they eventually agree upon.

Per the first two ends, the citizens aim at a secure and prosperous society. Each citizen expects that the state will promote opportunities for individual prosperity (in the sense of space to pursue socially valued projects) as well as the prosperity of the society as a whole. Whatever choices about

---

[28] Public goods and how commons tragedy can be overcome: Ostrom 1990, Poteete et al. 2011. Tuck 2008 suggests that free riding is a uniquely modern issue, but see Ober 2009; Teegarden 2014.

distributive justice are eventually made, the tax rate and the redistributive function of taxes must be structured such that neither a wealthy few (presumed to be heaviest payers of taxes) nor a middle-to-lower income many (presumed to benefit in various ways from public revenues) have reason to defect from the masterless status quo because their expectations in regard to opportunities for personal prosperity are systematically frustrated. Getting either the tax rate or benefits distribution wrong risks lowering the "revolutionary threshold" (Kuran 1991, 1995) of the relevant section of the population, thereby increasing the risk of an autocratic counterrevolution and degrading the state's security. We will revisit the bounds within redistribution is possible in a basic democracy in Section 6.8.

3.4 LEGISLATION

The second primary rule will specify the basic procedure for making future (stage 3) rules. Some rules may be made consensually, based on the agreement concerning the priority of the three ends of security, prosperity, and nontyranny. But the rule-making procedure must be able to accommodate disagreement, which on some issues will be deep enough that true consensus cannot be achieved. Disagreement, and thus political debate and contestation, will arise, first because of the fact of value pluralism among the citizens, and next because the projects variously pursued by citizens will lead to competition when resources to support those projects are scarce. The first rule (above) requires that all participate in politics; when it comes to nonconsensual decisions, participation will mean (at least) voting under some kind of majoritarian decision rule.

Nontyranny means that no defined "part" of the demos can legitimately rule, as a collective autocrat, over the whole of the demos and thus pushes in the direction of equal votes. If, in the extreme case of inequality, one individual's vote outweighs the votes of all others, that individual is, by definition, a tyrant. Likewise, if a few people's votes outweigh those of many, those few are, by definition, a collective tyrant. Furthermore, the participation requirement would be prima facie unfair and thereby productive of instability, if citizens who are required to pay similar participation costs were assigned votes of different weights – as, for example, in J. S. Mill's (1861: Chapter 8) proposal to give plural votes to citizens with "mental superiority" (as proved by their elite educations).[29] Participation plus

---

[29] Mill's concern for ensuring fair and efficient inequality of political influence on matters of common interest, is important. But, as I argue in Section 7.5, inequality of influence ought to be based on

nontyranny implies, therefore, that, as in classical Athens, each citizen must have an equal vote and an equal opportunity to take on whatever other political roles (e.g., as a lotteried council member; Section 7.6) are created in the course of establishing the rules. Although the citizens of Demopolis will be inherently unequal in some salient ways (some will be better informed, more eloquent, etc.), their votes will be equally weighted. The question of how a majority of voters might be prevented from acting as a collective tyrant over a minority of equal voters is addressed in Section 3.5.

Legislation must aim not only at nontyrannical process but also at efficiency. Assuming the requirement of security in a dangerous and mutable environment, policy decisions made by the citizens must be better than "coin-flip" random choices.[30] As noted above, citizens will require education and welfare in order to make responsible choices. They will also require freedom of inquiry, speech, and association if they are to be in a position to devise and to effect the best possible policies. In order to do so, they must be free to pursue the discovery of information relevant to their choices. Those who have knowledge that is of potential value for a given decision must not only have reason to disclose that knowledge but must be free to seek to inform (and thereby influence) their fellow citizens. Because there can be no ex ante assumption about whose information or knowledge is potentially relevant, all must be equally free in these salient political ways. Furthermore, were some or all of the citizens not free in respect to inquiry, speech, and association, they would in effect have a master – that is, deprived of conditions essential to ruling themselves, they would be ruled by whoever set and enforced the condition of nonfreedom. Thus, although, unlike contemporary republican theories of political order (Skinner 1998; Pettit 2014), political freedom need not be understood as basic democracy's principle of justice, it is a necessary condition of the masterless state.

The citizens must, per above, enjoy functional political equality and freedom. In order for equality and freedom to function in practice, citizens must treat one another with dignity, as persons worthy of civic participation. They must likewise be treated with dignity by whatever public

---

expertise in the matter at issue and can be accommodated without the expedient of unequal votes. For the internal contradictions inherent in Mill's plural voting proposal, in light of his concern for civic education and effective government, see Thompson 1976. My thanks to Prithvi Datta for this reference.

[30] On coin-flip choices as an alternative (if undesirable) form of political decision making, see Estlund 2008.

officials they eventually decide to bring into existence. A citizen who is subject to indignity, in the form of public humiliation or infantilization, is functionally neither equal nor free. Furthermore, as we will see (Section 6.8), civic dignity will prove valuable in moderating the demands of egalitarians and libertarians, once the issue of substantive justice in respect to distribution is put on the table. Meanwhile, as in the case of education and welfare, the democratic commitment to freedom, equality, and dignity remains firmly grounded in politics. Citizens with liberal values will value freedom, equality, and dignity as ends in themselves. But even those citizens who do *not* regard these as inherently valuable ends have reason to acknowledge their instrumental value as conditions essential for the preservation of nontyranny. The conditions of freedom, equality, and dignity may be expanded and elaborated by subsequent (stage 3) public choices informed by a moralized conception of justice. But meanwhile, the minimal conditions, those necessary to enacting effective legislation by democratic means, cannot be reduced without sacrificing one of the three ends for which the state exists.

3.5 ENTRENCHMENT

The third and final foundational rule entrenches the general agreement on the three ends of the state and the citizen body (stage 1) as well as the rules concerning participation and legislation. The third basic rule limits the citizens' collective ability to make subsequent rules (in stage 3) that would threaten the three ends of prosperity, security, and nontyranny or that would threaten the conditions that make those ends achievable, including political equality, political freedom, and civic dignity. Limitation on the scope of government in defense of basic liberties is, of course, a familiar feature of liberalism. In our thought experiment the limitation does not arise from assumptions about the intrinsic value of autonomy or from natural or human rights. It arises instead from the imperative of achieving the ends of security, prosperity, and nontyranny in an otherwise diverse population. The freedom, equality, and dignity required by the first two rules will be, in substance, civic and political and, as such, less deep and less extensive than will be required by liberalism (Christiano 2008: 138–154); once again, basic democracy provides a floor, not a ceiling. On the other hand, the commitment to nontyranny imposes some limits on legislation that do not arise from liberalism as such.

The antecedent agreement to the three ends means that the citizens, as legislators, must not make any rule that would tend to make the state insecure, impoverished, or autocratic. As we have seen, using a majority decision rule to strip a minority of citizenship is an example of legislation that puts the ends of the state at risk. In brief, subsequent (stage 3) rules must meet a constitutional standard: the (stage 1) general agreement and the (stage 2) foundational rules. The entrenched constitutional rules must, in turn, be enforced by the citizens. Constitutional rules must, therefore, be a matter of common knowledge, so that any violation is readily apparent. The agreement on the three ends and on the criteria for citizenship, along with the three stage 2 foundational rules, must therefore be structured so as to have "bright line" features, such that any proposed new rule or action by a state official that poses a threat to one of the three ends is immediately recognized as such. Violations in turn trigger a responsibility on the part of each citizen to participate in resistance against the violation and, when necessary, the violator. Resistance may be both institutional and, if and when necessary, an extra-institutional duty imposed on each citizen who witnesses a violation (Sections 6.5 and 6.6). Effective resistance to constitutional violation requires both laws and behavioral norms. Laws will need to feed into (both leverage and create) habits of civic behavior: Law must be at once a focal point that enables coordinated action and a form of ongoing civic education.[31]

The basic rules adopted by the Founders are meant to be the minimum necessary to achieve the three ends of security, prosperity, and nontyranny. Citizens who embrace various systems of value, including liberals and religious traditionalists, might each prefer a more extensive set of entrenched rules. Liberals may want to entrench separation of church and state; traditionalists may want to entrench respect for divine authority. Each group will have the opportunity to pursue a value agenda in the subsequent stage 3 of rule making. The agreement of the citizens of Demopolis on the three ends of security, prosperity, and nontyranny and the stipulation that Demopolis not be poised on the brink of religious or ethnic war allow for decisions on matters of great importance to various groups within the society to be deferred, until after the political foundation has been laid.

Per above, the Founders intend to leave much to the future, not only fraught moral issues but also salient questions of procedure. They need not, at the founding stage, decide on how authority will be delegated to representatives. While the basic rules ensure that the gray box of public goods and civic engagement leaves space for the black box of socially valued

---

[31] On law as a form of civic education in the classical Greek tradition, see Plato, *Laws*; Teegarden 2014 on tyrant-slaying laws in the classical Greek world; Ober 2001 (= Ober 2005a: Chapter 6). Cf. Machiavelli *Discourses* 1.18.

goods, the black box has not been legally defined as an inviolate sphere of rights, as it would be in a liberal regime. The Founders do intend the basic rules they choose in the stage 2 foundation process to be stable (revisable only by a cumbersome process), in that the rules must allow individuals and groups to make plans for the future and to negotiate the rest of the rules for their state. The entrenchment of the stage 1 agreement and stage 2 rules is meant to offer assurances to citizens about the benefits they can reasonably expect in exchange for the costs they are required to assume. The entrenchment of the rules reduces the danger of destructive civil conflict by creating the conditions for agreement about what constitutes a violation and for coordination on resistance to violations. Entrenchment of the rules, along with responsibility for participation in resistance to violation, pushes up the likely costs to potential violators: Those who choose to violate must, in short, believe that they can win a civil war. To the extent to which the rules are generally accepted and internalized as norms by the citizens, violators will find themselves outnumbered and ideologically isolated. The incentives are thus stacked against casual revision of fundamental rules, and against their violation.[32]

3.6 EXIT, ENTRANCE, ASSENT

The basic rules governing participation, legislation, and entrenchment, once formulated, must be ratified by a process that is consistent with the rules – all participate in the process of ratification as politically free and equal citizens, in recognition that they are limiting their own authority to make new rules that would block the ends for which the state exists. The "Founders" are not just those who drafted the rules but all those who participate, via deliberation and voting, in their ratification. After the basic rules have been ratified, citizens are bound by them, as they (and other residents) are by subsequent rules made in accordance with the basic rules. But as rules are specified, some citizens may decide that the costs of nontyranny outweigh the expected benefits. Perhaps they have come to develop a conception of the good that favors autocracy (e.g., a religious belief that mandates the rule of an individual with a special relationship to the divine order). Or perhaps they worry that government without a master will prove unstable over time. Within the demos, there may, therefore, come to be a minority who are willing to forgo the nontyranny feature of the gray box

---

[32] This situation is exemplified in the history of Athens after the legal reforms of the late fifth century BCE: Carugati 2015.

of public goods in Figure 3.2, in exchange for an anticipated increase in the black box of socially valued goals.

The citizens (now imagined as an antityranny majority) are not required to accommodate the policy preferences of a pro-autocracy minority. Those who choose to remain in the state's territory but decline to participate in the work of sustaining the rules aimed at preserving the state's three ends will not have the status of citizen. These "citizenship-eligible noncitizens" may be subject to special taxes or suffer other disabilities. Although leaving Demopolis remains an option for any resident at any point, the citizenry will prefer, for security (mobilization) reasons, not to see the citizen population of their state decline. So the Founders will seek to accommodate those who are only minimally enthusiastic about nontyranny and who support the participation rule only at the lowest possible personal costs. The same prudential considerations will come into play if the citizens of Demopolis ever choose to establish a state religion or make other value-based rules governing social behavior. But exit of participants, while regrettable, is not an at-any-cost consideration for the citizens. They accept that establishing a new rule may lead to the exit of some individuals – i.e., some may choose to relocate to a rival state, because the cost of remaining in the masterless state has become, for them, higher than the cost of relocating.[33]

Those who elect to remain as citizens after the basic rules are ratified have affirmed their willingness to accept the new state's authority as legitimate by the fact of their participation in its founding. Legitimacy is typically thought of as a matter of consent, but the founding of Demopolis was predicated on affirmative assent, a willed choice on the part of each individual citizen – even those who would have preferred some other set of basic rules. The state that the group establishes is intended, moreover, to persist indefinitely through time. So, even if all adults who remain after the initial rules have been set are citizens who participated in the foundation and thereby agreed to pay some participation costs, they must address the question of how to gain the assent of future citizens. These include immigrants, current subadults, and members of future generations. None of them can be assumed, ex ante, to be willing to pay the costs of nontyranny.[34]

---

[33] This assumes there is another country that will accept them; see below. Shapiro 2016: 65–66 emphasizes the high cost of exit.

[34] Note that the question that must be solved at the level of the basic rules is about admission of new participatory citizens, not about noncitizen immigrants; on the difference, see Song 2017. The question of general immigration policy is among the many matters deferred to subsequent legislation. Immigrants who are unwilling or incapable of political participation will not be citizens; their reduced participation costs may be balanced by lower benefits and/or special taxes. General

The original citizens affirmed in practice their willingness to pay the costs of sustaining coercive rules assumed necessary to preserve security, prosperity and nontyranny (e.g., voting, taxation, public service). Potential citizens may not prefer nontyranny at whatever proves to be the social cost to individuals or to groups to which they belong. So, because the Founders are committed to a secure and prosperous state that can exist indefinitely, and because they believe that continued security and prosperity requires legitimacy, they must have a plan for obtaining the agreement esp of those who enter the community, by birth or immigration. Given the requirement that all citizens participate, the agreement must be in the form of an active affirmation (the equivalent of having participated in the founding) rather than the tacit (Lockean) or hypothetical (Rawlsian) consent that legitimates government in liberal political theory.[35]

These considerations point to the need for civic education as well as for interstate agreements with other states. Civic education will aim at rational persuasion: demonstrating to potential citizens the value of participation in a masterless state that is also secure and prosperous.[36] But it is not necessarily the case that civic education – no matter how rational, fact based, emotionally motivating, and rhetorically well presented – will succeed in persuading potential citizens that the benefits outweigh the costs. The masterless state therefore has good reason to devise incentive-compatible rules governing the civil status of resident noncitizens and to enter into agreements with neighboring communities, so that interstate migration, predicated on regime preference, remains feasible and peaceful and does not threaten security.

immigration policy and citizenship will be entangled, however, if the state's legitimacy is predicated in part on claims about human flourishing that push in the direction of offering most long-term residents the opportunity to become citizens; Section 5.5. On "the problem of generations" and the general problem of the indeterminacy of "the people" over time, see Espejo 2011: esp. Chapter 7.

[35] Establishing ideal conditions that define the substantive content of the rules to which a rational individual would hypothetically consent is the purpose of the "veil of ignorance" thought experiment of Rawls 1971, who sought to improve on earlier ideas of tacit consent (based on continued presence and consumption of public goods within a jurisdiction). Hardin 1999: Chapter 4 rejects all consent theory ("a charade" put on by "a cabal of metaphysicians": 180), in favor of "acquiescence," defined as not coordinating with others to engage in mutiny against the government. Hardin characterizes actual consent as "a dead political theory" (143). He does not consider the sort of affirmative assent that grounds basic democracy but might well reject it along with democratic participation generally (166–169). Among the problems here is that "consent," as willingness to be the recipient of another's activity (whether actual, tacit, or hypothetical) is what a subject gives to a ruler (or a patient to a physician, an experimental subject to an experimenter); it is, as such, ill adapted to the grounds on which a citizen agrees to join in the collective project of self-government. See, further, Section 4.4.

[36] On the content of Demopolis's civic education, see Chapters 4, 5, and 6. On democracy and persuasion, see Garsten 2009, 2011; Ober 1989, 2014.

3.7 NAMING THE REGIME

Considerations emerging from the thought experiment of Founder-citizens setting the basic rules for a masterless, prosperous, secure state have led to the conclusion that the state is predicated on self-government by citizens that is collective (based on active participation by the citizens who constitute the demos), limited (rules cannot violate conditions necessary to achieving the ends for which the state exists), and stably effective in the sense of producing policy that enables the state to be at once prosperous and secure. The Founders of Demopolis give their regime the name "democracy," by which they mean to proclaim that the demos is indeed capable of creating and sustaining the conditions for limited and collective self-governance in a dangerous and mutable world. The theoretical model of democracy emerging from the Demopolis thought experiment is broadly consistent with what "democracy" meant to the ancient Greeks who coined the term and first used it as the name for a form of government by, for, and of an extensive and socially diverse body of citizens. The Founders need not, therefore, worry that the term *democracy* is properly reserved either for the autocratic rule of a majority-of-the-moment or for the conjunction of liberal principles with a majoritiarian decision rule limited by the rule of law.

While Demopolis takes for its regime a name originally coined by the ancient Athenians, Demopolis is not constrained by the historically specific cultural or social norms, beliefs, or practices that characterized the Greek city-states. Demopolis certainly need not be a slave society. It may include women and naturalized foreigners in the citizen body. It may also develop constitutional rules allowing legislation, adjudication, and administration to be delegated to representatives rather than being administered by the directly democratic mechanisms of government employed by the ancient Athenians. And this means that Demopolis need not be limited in scale. The question of how the residents of Demopolis, as participatory citizens, might prevent representatives from devolving into autocratic rulers will be taken up in Chapter 7.

Chapters 2 and 3 have presented the case that basic democracy is, in ancient practice and contemporary theory, a way of achieving security, prosperity, and nontyranny. In the next four chapters, we turn to the question of its legitimacy and to the conditions necessary to sustain the democratic regime. The legitimacy question did not arise for the Founders, who shared an ex ante preference for nontyranny, participated in establishing the basic rules of self-governance, and thereby agreed to obey and to pay the costs of enforcing those rules. But a justification is owed to future citizens of Demopolis. They will be expected to obey and to enforce the rules but were not present at the foundation. They may not share the Founders' ex ante preference for nontyranny. Moreover, if basic democracy is to be plausible as a realistic regime in a context beyond ancient Athens, I must answer some of the questions that have been posed by democracy's ancient and modern critics. Chapters 4–7 elaborate upon the political foundation established in the Demopolis thought experiment to show how a basic democracy, one that does not immediately adopt a liberal superstructure, might address questions of, inter alia, individual motivation, civic identity, and the practical demands of incorporating expertise into public decision making. In Chapter 8, I suggest a theoretical range of modern liberal and nonliberal societies for which the basic democratic constitutional framework sketched in this chapter is, or is not, a plausible political foundation.

CHAPTER 4

Legitimacy and Civic Education

The two previous chapters defined basic democracy "before liberalism," in history and theory, as collective and limited self-government by a large and socially diverse body of citizens. The history of political development in ancient Athens demonstrated the possibility of basic democracy as a viable regime in a complex society far larger than the tiny, face-to-face foraging communities in which participatory self-government was first practiced. A thought experiment set out the fundamental rules enacted by a hypothetical group of persons seeking to found a state able to achieve and preserve the three ends of nontyranny, security, and prosperity. The basic constitutional rules established by the imaginary citizens of Demopolis are relevantly similar to those of the historical "mature classical Greek" conception and practice of democracy, but Demopolis is not beholden to the historically specific circumstances of ancient Greek culture and society.

In this chapter we turn to the question of democracy's legitimacy, in the sense of the justification offered by the state to those subject to its rules, but not present at its foundation, for why they ought to accept, and thus obey, coercive public authority and pay the costs, in time and taxes, necessary to sustain the regime. The argument for democracy's legitimacy – in the sense of how it could be justified to future citizens who may lack the Founders' ex ante preference for nontyranny – is made in the context of a defense of basic democracy against the charge that collective self-governance cannot be at once effective (securing prosperity and security) and limited. My apology (in the ancient sense) will demonstrate how material goods and certain nonmaterial goods provided by democracy can be mutually sustaining, in theory and in practice. That demonstration is imagined as the content of the life-long, formal and informal, civic education offered to potential citizens in Demopolis after the basic democratic foundation. It reveals some of the ways in which, for the purposes of explaining the operation of democracy, the methods and results of positive theory, normative political theory, and history may be tightly and productively interwoven.

4.1 MATERIAL GOODS AND DEMOCRATIC GOODS

If basic democracy is to predicate its legitimacy on being a rationally choiceworthy, as well as psychically engaging, form of social order, when set against plausible nondemocratic alternatives (notably Hobbesian absolutism), it must provide citizens with important goods, and it must do so reliably. Most fundamentally, it must provide security against internal and external threats to individuals' lives and to their welfare. Moreover, to be *robustly* choiceworthy, in addition to these material goods, it must also provide an adequate supply of "democratic goods" – that is, nonmaterial but highly valued goods accruing to citizens from their practice of democracy.[1] This is because, although democracy can shown to be capable of providing prosperity and security at least *as well as* autocracy, it may not be possible to demonstrate conclusively that the most effective democracy can consistently provide material conditions of life that are substantially *better than* the most effective autocratic rival.

A democratic regime necessarily imposes certain costs on citizens, in the form of responsibility for participation. I suggested in Chapter 3 that those costs need not be so high as to preclude the pursuit of a range of socially valued goods (the black box of Figure 3.2). But, assuming that time and energy are limited, and that demands on them are ultimately zero-sum, the participation costs borne by democratic citizens are "opportunity costs" – meaning that they come at the expense of time and energy that might otherwise have been spent pursuing other valued goods.[2] An autocracy, like a basic democracy, will levy taxes upon subjects and a duty to obey, but it may not exact an equally high level of participation costs.[3] A benevolent autocracy might (at least for now, and for the readily foreseeable future) impose on its subjects fewer public duties than does a democracy on its citizens, and consequently allow more space to pursue other projects.

---

[1] In Chapter 5, I argue that natural human capacities provide one standard by which democratic goods may be evaluated. Democratic goods may or may not be "rightly valued" or even morally permissible when measured against other external evaluative standards; see Chapter 8.

[2] The arguments of Hardin 1999: 155–174, against wide participation in politics, recall the complaint expressed in an aphorism attributed (rightly or not) in several forms to Oscar Wilde: "The trouble with democracy (Socialism) is that it takes too many meetings (evenings)." By "socially valued" I do not mean that those doing the valuing are autonomous (in a Kantian or otherwise liberal sense), only that the projects and their ends are different from the responsibilities and goods arising from political participation.

[3] Of course some autocracies (e.g., the former Soviet Union, Maoist China, contemporary North Korea) do impose high participation costs, as well as costs arising from psychic dissonance: not only voting (for the government-approved slate of candidates) but attendance at pro-government rallies and speeches, obeisance to symbols of authority, and so on.

If the material conditions are comparable and the costs of democracy are higher, then a rational future citizen of Demopolis will need some reason to prefer self-government to autocracy. Some future citizens will presumably (for whatever reasons) share the ex ante assumption of the Founders about the relative badness of autocracy. They may need no justification, beyond that offered in Chapter 3, for why they should obey the rules and pay the costs. But other potential citizens may not share the assumption about tyranny's badness. They will reasonably ask whether and how the costs of a regime of self-government are justified.

A given individual may differentially value the goods produced (or made available) by a given expenditure of time and effort. So, for example, I might spend as much time and energy on my dreary job as a widget-maker as I do on my exciting pastime as a painter. I value the paintings more highly than the widgets. I spend time making widgets, because if I do not do so, I will go hungry and will not have the resources I need to pursue my painting. But if I could be assured of my welfare, I would quit my job in order to pursue painting full time. If "political participation" is the dreary job and "socially valued goods" are the pastime, then, assuming my welfare is assured, I will prefer autocracy to democracy. If, on the other hand, I value participation as an end in itself, or if paying participation costs makes available to me goods whose value exceeds the opportunity costs, I will choose democracy over autocracy. The situation is illustrated in Figure 4.1.

Assuming parity in provision of security and prosperity, and higher participation costs for democracy, rational utility maximizers with sufficiently steep future discounts (those who are not concerned about the autocrat someday becoming less benevolent) will choose democracy in favor of autocracy *only* under the following circumstances: (1) There are goods reliably delivered by democracy that are unavailable or less abundant under an autocracy, no matter how benevolent. (2) Those "democratic goods" are available only to those who pay participation costs. (3) The value of democratic goods outweighs the opportunity costs arising from public duties of participation. With reference to Figure 4.1: In order for a rational individual to freely and reliably choose option A (democratic citizen) over option B (subject of a benevolent autocrat), the total value to the individual produced by the gray box (participation costs) and black box (time spent on socially valued projects) in option A must be greater than the value produced by the black box in option B.

The goal of this chapter and the next is to show, first, that basic democracy can realistically be expected to produce competitive levels of

A. Democratic citizen   B. Subject of benevolent autocrat

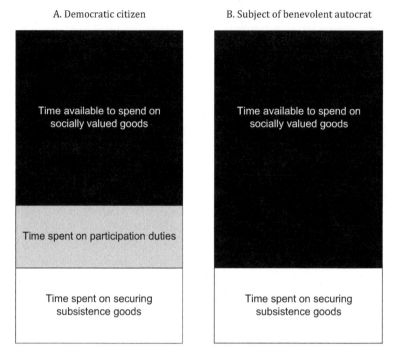

Figure 4.1 Comparison of the value of living as a democratic citizen and as the subject of a benevolent autocrat. In order for a rational individual to reliably choose A over B, the total value to the individual produced by gray and black boxes in A must be greater than the value produced by the black box in B. We assume that the value of the white box is the same in A and B.

security and prosperity (i.e., comparable to the levels produced by an effective autocracy) and, next, that the value of the goods produced by the gray box of political participation does (for people with a plausible conception of their own good) exceed the opportunity costs. Certain of the goods produced by participation are intrinsically available for consumption only by the producers themselves; that is, engaging in production is what makes the good available to the individual producer.

This chapter and Chapter 5 focus on material goods and on democratic goods intrinsic to participation. As we have seen (Section 3.3), some of the goods provided by democracy are nonrival and nonexcludable public goods. Among the goals of Chapters 6 and 7 will be to answer another set of critical challenges by showing that basic democracy can devise mechanisms to defend against two threats: The first threat is that the public goods associated with political freedom, political equality, and civic dignity will be degraded by defection and cheating on the part of those unwilling to pay participation costs. The next threat is capture by a coordinated and self-interested political elite to whom authority has been delegated by the demos. If democracy has no ready means of addressing collective action problems of free riding and commons tragedy, or of revoking delegated authority when representatives fail to fulfill their public duties, it will not long survive in a competitive and mutable environment.

4.2 LIMITED-ACCESS STATES

A standard (historically prevalent) model of nondemocratic social order, made possible by the emergence of agriculture, has been recently characterized as the "limited-access order."[4] In a limited-access order, a relatively few power-holders dominate society, and they expropriate, as rents, much of the surplus (beyond the level of subsistence) produced by capital and labor investments by other members of society. These rent-seeking power-holders have a strong incentive to maintain social order and thus to limit unauthorized internal violence. They have a similar incentive to secure their society against external threats, by organizing military force. The limited-access state is defined by the rational behavior of power-holders in maintaining their monopoly on rents by denying potential rivals entry to the institutions of the state and preventing them from forming new organizations which might create alternative institutions.[5]

The mature limited-access state is stable, in the terms of positive political theory, because it distributes goods according to a "proportionality principle" – that is, goods are distributed to individuals and groups in direct proportion to their capacity to disrupt the social order by threatening violence (Cox et al. 2012). Through proportionality, all those with the capacity to disrupt the order lack an incentive to do so, while those with an

---

[4] North et al. 2009. The "limited-access state" is called "the natural state" by North et al. I do not use "natural state" here, to avoid confusion with Hobbes's "state of nature." Although they muster considerable empirical support for their theoretical claims, the limited-access order described by North et al. remains a general model rather than a description of any given state. In historical fact, the level of expropriation by ruling elites varied considerably. See Milanovic et al. 2011.

[5] Most documented premodern societies, but not classical Athens, fulfill the expectation that in a limited-access state most laborers will live near subsistence: Scheidel 2010; Ober 2017a. Milanovic et al. 2011 offer a method for estimating the "inequality possibility frontier" of a given society, that is, the limits of resource extraction from nonelites that can be sustained without demographic collapse. A robust democratic society will need to be well outside that frontier, both in terms of generating a surplus beyond subsistence, and in leaving much of it in the hands of producers. A Hobbesian absolutist regime, by contrast, may approach the frontier, so long as it does not reach it.

incentive to change the social order lack the power to do so. The limited-access state is typically relatively unproductive (compared to open-access states) because it lacks both incentives for widespread individual invest-ment in human capital and institutions for ensuring fair competition. The rent-seeking rulers rationally calculate, however, that a large, monopolistic rent-share of a relatively small pie is better for them than a smaller and less certain open-market share of a larger pie.

If, compared to the limited-access state, basic democracy is *less* capable of achieving a stable social equilibrium that provides internal and exter-nal security against violence and at least minimal levels of prosperity (per capita consumption safely above subsistence: the white box of Figure 3.2), it may not matter what other valuable nonmaterial conditions democracy might, hypothetically, be able to offer. If democracy cannot provide wel-fare, citizens risk falling below the level of bare existence. In the absence of conditions that allow their survival, most people are unlikely to regard other values as counting for much. Likewise, if democracy is substantially less capable than the limited-access order at providing conditions of inter-nal security against arbitrary violence and external security against threats by external enemies, it is similarly implausible to say that the provision of other valued conditions of life could make up for that lack. The Founder-citizens of Demopolis were not, as we have seen, willing to sacrifice either prosperity or security for nontyranny. The premise of their regime was that the three ends were simultaneously achievable, under the democratic con-stitutional rules that they instituted. But was their premise valid?

As we consider the nonmaterial goods that democracy before liberal-ism delivers to citizens, we must not lose sight of the key question: *Can basic democracy – a regime characterized by the conditions of collective and limited self-government by citizens – reliably deliver security and an adequate level of prosperity?* That question may best be answered by responding to a particularly powerful and influential argument to the effect that limited self-government by citizens can provide neither security nor prosperity.

4.3 HOBBES'S CHALLENGE

Thomas Hobbes argued, in *Leviathan*, that the answer to the question posed in the last paragraph is emphatically no. His argument was premised on the assumption that humans are, by nature, both rational and emo-tional beings.[6] They are self-interested (utility maximizing), proud (they

---

[6] On the role of emotions in Hobbes's account of human motivation, see Foisneau 2016: 123–146.

seek honors that recognize their self-assessed superiority), and, as a result of those drives, dangerous to one another. Humans in the masterless "state of nature" are mutually dangerous because of their primordial equality. We each have a natural claim on everything, a conviction concerning our right to it, and we can and will kill each other in order to get it. Given the availability of weapons and the potential for short-term gang formation, each individual, even the strongest, is vulnerable to the potential for violence inherent in every other member of society.

Given conjoined drives of rational self-interest and emotional self-aggrandizement, Hobbes concludes that the murderous potential of the human race will be realized, and thus all will live in rational fear of violent death, until and unless two conditions are met. First each of us values life over honor. Next, each is mortally afraid of a third party who forbids killing. Given these Hobbesian premises, it follows that without rationally ordered preferences and an adequately powerful and appropriately motivated third-party enforcer, humans cannot make credible mutual commitments to one another. Without the ability to make credible commitments, humans lack the capacity to reap substantial benefits from cooperation. They remain, therefore, in a perilous and impoverished condition. The equilibrium of the state of nature actually prevents both security and prosperity.

Hobbes argued that without Leviathan – the third-party absolute ruler/enforcer that is established by a covenant among rationally self-interested and rationally fearful individuals, a contract in which natural liberty is exchanged for the security provided by a sovereign – humans have no way to escape the state of nature. And thus human lives are doomed to be "poor, solitary, nasty, brutish, and short." Arguing from what we would now call positive political theory, Hobbes claimed that for those persons wishing to live *at all* well or securely – i.e., outside the violent war of all against all that characterizes the state of nature – there is no alternative to submission to the authority of a sovereign, an absolute ruler who is unconstrained by law and unlimited in his scope of action by any separation or balance of governmental powers. The sovereign must remain outside all formal constraints, including law or other "balancing" institutions, because only an unconstrained sovereign could serve as a reliable third-party enforcer of others' commitments. In short, because civilization requires that individuals be capable of credibly committing to one another (e.g., in contracts), to escape from the state of nature requires absolutism.[7]

---

[7] Tuck 2016 seeks to moderate Hobbes's commitment to absolutism by emphasizing "democratic" elements, especially in his earlier works (*Elements of Law*, completed 1640, and *De Cive*, published

This line of argument has serious consequences for what people can reasonably expect from social order. If Hobbes is right, subjects can expect that the sovereign will enforce a regime in which subjects are secure in respect to the danger they pose to one another. The sovereign will suppress unauthorized internal violence. Moreover the sovereign can be expected to mobilize forces to resist external threats to his own sovereign authority. The subjects of the sovereign can also expect that when people are freed from the threat of endemic violence, the level of aggregate welfare arising from social cooperation will exceed the miserable conditions of the state of nature. Yet, apart from the guarantee that our lives will not be perpetually at risk, and the expectation of marginally superior material conditions of existence due to enhanced opportunities for social cooperation, Hobbes does not give his readers reason to assume that we will live very well.

Under the rule of Leviathan, we will not securely possess *any* goods, other than those necessary to ensure the maintenance of our lives, because the sovereign may at any point choose to appropriate surplus goods. Although we can expect the sovereign to enforce the contracts we make with one another, there is no contract between ourselves and the sovereign. So long as he does not actually threaten my life, the sovereign may confiscate my property (*Leviathan* 29.169–170) and may humiliate me at will (*Leviathan* 10.43). Indeed, the ruler may demand anything of me short of my life. He may not demand my life because it was to preserve my life that I entered into the covenant in the first place. If the sovereign threatens our lives, the covenant is terminated, and we return to the state of nature.

Sharing the aversion to the state of nature felt by all rational persons, a sane sovereign will choose not to threaten the lives of subjects. In addition to preservation of life, subjects may *hope* for benevolence and rational respect for their property and dignity from an absolute ruler. Honor seekers may hope for suitable recognition of their merits. But there is no guarantee of the sovereign's fairness or benevolence: The ruler may be like Hadrian – a "good emperor" who is either altruistic or has a long time horizon – and thus has good reasons not to expropriate or humiliate in ways that might impoverish his subjects or hurt his own revenues. This is indeed what Hobbes hopes for (*Leviathan* 30.175). By the same token, however, the sovereign may be a (nonmurderous) Caligula or Agamemnon (of Books 1–2 of the *Iliad*) – a ruler with short time horizons, who takes what he wants

---

1642, 2nd ed. 1647), and his account of freedom as noninterference. Here I focus on *Leviathan* (published 1651) and follow what I take to be the conventional view that, in that work at least, Hobbes is deeply committed to absolutism: The Leviathan, ideally a monarch, must be outside the law and unconstrained by any balancing institution. See, recently, Foisneau 2016.

when he pleases and takes pleasure in humiliating his subjects (*Leviathan* 18.94).

In sum, Hobbes claims that if and only if we establish Leviathan, we can avoid the constant fear of imminent death that is our fate if we do not submit to an absolutist government. But we will not have secure rights to property or standing beyond that necessary for subsistence. We will be free in the "silence of the law," but only in the sense of not being physically restrained from acting when the law does not forbid it. We cannot expect to live with dignity unless it is in the sovereign's pleasure that we do so. The absolute ruler will (through his agents) be the sole source of law and the monopolistic enforcer of the laws. Standards of justice, in respect to distribution of the benefits of social cooperation, will be determined by the sovereign. Although Hobbes's ideal ruler will treat his subjects without undue partiality for the great and wealthy (*Leviathan* 30.180), nothing guarantees that fairness standards will be maintained consistently over time.[8] If we take positive political theory seriously, Hobbes's claim that we cannot reasonably hope to have minimal security and prosperity unless we are willing to establish a lawless third-party enforcer is not readily dismissed (Hampton 1988).

Hobbes poses a second challenge, one that the framers of any political order aspiring to stability must confront: The potential for social disruption of individuals driven by love of honor. Any given society is likely to have at least some persons who are confident in their own powers, who seek to be recognized for their own superiority over others, and who are provoked to anger (and thus rule breaking) by what they regard as the contempt of those who do not grant that recognition. Under Leviathan, these people will be systematically frustrated, insofar as they are rendered equally *without* honor, like servants before a master, in the presence of the sovereign. Because grants of civil honors are entirely at the discretion of the sovereign, similar circumstances may result in either honors or dishonor depending on the sovereign's whim. Hobbes hopes that education of subjects concerning the rights of the sovereign, and the sovereign's distribution of civil honors to worthy (but not ambitious) men, will address the problem. But in extreme cases, an honor lover (think of Homer's Achilles) may rank the chance to gain great honor above life itself. This poses a

---

[8] In contrast to contemporary neo-Hobbesian scholarship that emphasizes the value for long-term aggregate welfare of strong, highly-centralized "Leviathans" (e.g., Morris 2014), Acemoglu and Robinson 2016: 32 point out (with special reference to the history of modern Rwanda) that, "contrary to what Hobbes argued, a Leviathan is just as likely to make life 'nasty, brutish and short' as it is to remove such threats."

serious problem for any equilibrium theory, like Hobbes's own, that is predicated on agents rationally choosing life itself over all other goods.[9] We will consider the problem of how basic democracy addresses honor seeking and egregious self-aggrandizement in Chapter 6. Here I focus on Hobbes's rationality-based argument for the necessity of an absolute and unitary sovereign.

Luc Foisneau (2016: 25–47) has pointed out that Hobbes bases his own thought experiment in *Leviathan* on what might be called a "democratic moment." It is by a majority decision that the populus first establishes the sovereign. It cannot be a consensus decision, because it is not the case that all of those in the state of nature are rational enough to recognize that establishing Leviathan is the unique way out of their miserable circumstances. But, as Foisneau rightly emphasizes, the democratic moment is just that: Once Leviathan is established, democracy drops from the agenda. Following the classical framing of the question, "who rules?" Hobbes offers three options: an individual (monarchy), a small coalition (aristocracy), or a mass of ordinary people (democracy). But, as we will see, Hobbes rank-orders these options, and he is decidedly antidemocratic in his account of a sovereign mass. While Hobbes holds that, in principle, a demos unconstrained by law could be an absolute sovereign, he seeks to show that the demos necessarily does less well as a ruler than an individual or a small coalition.

Given Hobbes's premises, democracy (of a sort) is a way out of the state of nature only so long as democracy is understood as the (nonmurderous) tyranny of the majority. The demos can be a Hobbesian sovereign *if and only if* two conditions are met. The demos must be unconstrained by law and it must be personified as a fictive person whose unitary will is unambiguously expressed by its majority vote. It is certainly possible to personify a demos, in iconography or literature, as a fictive person. The Athenians famously did so in publicly displayed document reliefs, as did Aristophanes in publicly performed comedies. Yet, even without reference to impossibility theorems and voting cycles, the reality of diversity and subgroup identity formation within a community of participatory citizens (who must,

---

[9] Hobbes on education: *Leviathan* 30. The rights of the sovereign must be "diligently, and truly taught; because they cannot be maintained by any Civill Law or terrour of legall punishment": 30.175. Honors dispensed by the sovereign: 10.43–44; but it is dangerous to grant honors to the popular or ambitious: 30.183. Before the sovereign, all are, like servants, "equall, and without any honour at all in the presence of the Master": 18.93. Honor and dishonor at the sovereign's whim: 10.43 (example of the King of Persia). Vainglory as confident overvaluing of oneself, its relationship to perceived contempt, anger, and crime: 6.27, 8.35, 13.61, 27.155. My thanks to Alison McQueen for pressing me on these points.

for Hobbes, also be subjects) renders problematic the conceptualization of a nonunanimous vote as the expression of a unitary will. For Hobbes, the question is whether the citizens, as a natural multitude (with diverse wills), could act effectively, in an assembly, as an artificial "people" with a unitary will to which all would then be subject. The basic answer is no, if there is (as in any real democracy) a need for deliberation before decision, or if the people in assembly must (as in a basic democracy) take an active role in government, rather than standing by, passively, as a "sleeping sovereign."[10]

The problem inherent in a hypothetical Hobbesian Leviathan-demos is clarified by Carl Schmitt's (2007) friend–enemy distinction. A majority vote publicly reveals the fact that the sovereign is divided; reasons that persuaded citizens in the (eventual) majority were rejected those in the minority. The unpersuaded minority, naked before the power of the majority, may be presumed to oppose the outcome and to be potentially ready to fight. The ex post hostility of the minority is not a problem for the vote that brings about Leviathan, *so long as the contracted sovereign is not the demos*. A monarch or elite coalition, once established, is expected to overawe all subjects equally. All should obey out of mortal fear, regardless of how they voted.[11] But if the demos establishes *itself* as sovereign, it is not a matter of subjects equally in awe of a unitary sovereign. In the hypothetical case of a newly established Leviathan-demos, the victorious majority may choose to disenfranchise the members of the "No Leviathan" minority, as potentially dangerous enemies. Subsequent votes might likewise disenfranchise other "enemy-minorities." This civic regress will end up at war, if and when the violence potential of the remaining citizens is insufficient to overawe the disenfranchised others.

The burden of Chapters 6 and 7 will be to show that this regressive friends-enemies logic, which threatens the lawless Leviathan-demos with self-destruction, need not emerge in a basic democracy. A law-bounded demos can solve Hobbes's challenge by employing entrenched rules as a coordination device that both motivates and enables many individual citizens to cooperate in disciplining rule-breakers. The approach in those

---

[10] The "sleeping sovereign" is the subject of Tuck 2016. On the distinction between the multitude and the people in Hobbes, and the problem of deliberation and government, see Tuck 2016: 99–103. Anderson 2009 argues that in ancient Athens the demos was personified in a Hobbesian manner, and finds support for this in Aristotle's arguments for parts and wholes in the *Politics*, but see Ober 1996: 117–120, 2013b.

[11] Hobbes, *Leviathan* 18.90: "Because the major part hath by consenting voices declared a Sovereigne; he that dissented must now consent with the rest, or else justly be destroyed by the rest." See further Tuck 2016, esp. 104n40.

chapters will be to examine several local democratic equilibria, rather than try to model the entire system as a single game.

Hobbes's account of "demos as sovereign" furthermore includes a "poison pill" in that democracy in classical Greece, which was his best historical example of majoritarian tyranny, *failed*, as he supposed (wrongly: Ober 2015b), to deliver the goods of living at all well or securely. Indeed it degenerated into something resembling a war of all against all. Hobbes's conception of democracy was borrowed, in the first instance, from Thucydides. Hobbes authored the first English translation of Thucydides's *History of the Peloponnesian War* (published 1629) before writing *Leviathan* (published 1651). Thucydides was, by Hobbes's own account, a primary source of Hobbes's conviction that real-world majoritarian tyranny works badly and is inherently unstable.[12]

For Hobbes, as for many other ancient and early-modern political theorists, the proof of the incapacity of majoritarian democracy to deliver even minimal security and prosperity was to be found in the history of the Greek city-states. This meant, in the first instance, the history of democratic Athens, with a strong emphasis on Athens's failures in the Peloponnesian War. But majoritarian tyranny's failure was also highlighted for Hobbes in Thucydides's (3.81–85) nightmarish account of the actions of the democrats, as well as the oligarchs, in the civil war at Corcyra. Thucydides's narrative of the collapse of social order in Corcyra provided the model for Hobbes's description of the state of nature in *Leviathan*. Hobbes further assumed that the idea that a stable democracy *did* provide welfare and security over time was illusory: Such a "democracy" actually would be so only in name. In fact (cf. Thucydides 2.65.9: on Pericles as crypto-monarch) it was the rule of one man or a few men.[13]

The question we are faced with, if we take positive as well as normative approaches to political theory seriously, is how basic democracy answers Hobbes's challenge. That is: How can we (each of us, as individuals, and all of us, as citizens of a collectivity) live securely and prosperously without ceding authority to a sovereign ruler in the guise of an autocratic individual or elite coalition? If democracy is collective and limited self-governance by

---

[12] On Hobbes's translation of Thucydides, see Iori 2015, who (Chapter 8) emphasizes that in this work Hobbes is consistently critical of democracy; criticism is clear in Hobbes's Introduction, his design for the frontispiece, and his word choices in the translation itself. Iori concludes that this critical stance conforms with Hobbes's statement in his autobiography that Thucydides had shown him "democratia . . . quam sit inepta." My thanks to Paul Demont for alerting me to Iori's book and sharing an advance version of his review of it.

[13] For Hobbes's use of Thucydides (not Aristotle) as his model for democracy, see Hoekstra 2007 with Skinner 2007, contra Tuck 2007.

citizens, we will need to explain how that sort of political order could also be stable over time and deliver security and at least minimal welfare. If we can show that basic democracy is able to meet each of these conditions, we will have answered Hobbes's challenge. That answer, as I will suggest, can be developed by a consideration of the goods that democracy delivers, *before* admixture of the goods provided by liberalism. These democratic goods arise from the *very conditions* that are required if democracy is reliably to deliver the material goods of security and prosperity.

4.4 CIVIC EDUCATION

Each of Demopolis's Founders had his or her own reasons to prefer nonautocracy; as we have seen, they did not need to agree on *why* having a master was intolerable; it was enough that they agreed that it *was* intolerable. As we have also seen, some future citizens may not have ex ante reasons to reject tyranny. And yet, in the absence of an agreement among citizens that the value of nontyranny justifies the costs of participation, the democratic regime risks losing its basis of legitimacy. The current citizens of Demopolis must, therefore, be prepared to offer future citizens convincing reasons for valuing nontyranny.[14] They may do so in the form of a civic education that proposes arguments for the high intrinsic and instrumental value of collective self-governance. The civic education of Demopolis, in common with that of any regime that treats its citizens as rational (as well as emotional) persons, is, in short, a fairly presented argument for the regime's legitimacy. That education may be delivered, in part, as a structured school curriculum. But it cannot be limited to formal schooling. To achieve the end of rationally persuading and psychically motivating citizens to assume the responsibilities of participation, the education of citizens must be a lifelong affair, a matter of grasping and internalizing the logic of the basic rules and associated political norms, and developing the corresponding behavioral civic habits.

Demopolis's education will not be predicated on strict value neutrality. The civic education of Demopolis aims at producing citizens with a distinctive social identity: men and women who have embraced a democratic set of values and who have embraced those values because they saw good reason to do so. The argument for choosing democratic citizenship is not definitive, in the sense that no reasonable person could do otherwise. But in

---

[14] This requirement of justification is what Williams (2005: 4–6) calls the "Basic Legitimation Demand."

light of democracy's necessary condition of dignity as noninfantilization, the argument for citizenship must rise above paternalistic claims for the inherent value of tradition: Demopolis's educators must offer potential citizens persuasive and motivating reasons for the way we do things around here, rather than asserting, as one might say to a child, "that is just how things are done."[15]

The rules that were established, both by the imagined Founder-citizens of Demopolis and by the real citizens of Athens, were devised, as we have seen, to meet the imperatives of sustaining security and prosperity in a masterless regime. In devising the civic curriculum, Demopolis's educators can appeal to the results of contemporary natural and social science. They can point to a body of literature that strongly supports the correlation between democracy and economic development. Contemporary social science offers no reason to believe that autocratic states outperform democratic states on standard economic measures. Likewise, they can point to the relative stability of at least some democratic states, ancient and modern, and to the relative instability of many autocratic limited-access states. They can cite studies that establish a positive correlation between mass democracy and military success. Thus, on the fundamental question of whether democracy can support welfare and security, the evidence of contemporary social science suggests that Hobbes was wrong on the empirics.[16]

There is also reason to believe that nontyranny, insofar as it reduces hierarchy and equalizes the chance to exert control over one's own destiny, is good for human health. Michael Marmot's "Whitehall II Studies" used the methods of social epidemiology to study the health of British civil servants. His highly robust result was a "health gradient": The lower in the status hierarchy an individual was situated, the worse was his health. By controlling for differential access to health care or poverty Marmot (2004) made a strong case that health differences are caused by status inequality. It is, he concludes, status inequality itself that drives inequalities in healthiness. The mechanism of "status syndrome" appears to be the relative level of control people have over their own destiny: Persons with low control experience greater levels of chronic stress. Notably, a correlation among lower

---

[15] Demopolis's education is certainly not liberal, but neither is it "didactic in intent in [the] exclusive and authoritarian way" that is rejected by Shklar 1989: 33. On the question of whether a liberal society could be built on a foundation of a democracy that requires for its legitimacy a civic education for citizens, while allowing free exit for those who do not accept the tenets of that education, see Section 8.4.

[16] Correlation between democracy and economic growth: Ober 2015b with literature cited. Democracy as a primary cause of growth: Acemoglu and Robinson 2006; Acemoglu et al. 2014; democracy as an effect of growth: Boix 2003, 2015. Democracy and military success: Reiter and Stamm 2002.

status, higher stress, and worse health outcomes is observed among other social animals. Robert Sapolsky (2004, 2005) has traced the ill effects of hierarchy and status-induced stress in various nonhuman species. It seems a plausible hypothesis that insofar as democratic society reduces the kind of strong status/control hierarchy associated with autocracy, it will, all things considered, be good for human welfare.

There is also some empirical evidence that the proximity of a boss is negatively correlated with reported, subjective happiness. Daniel Kahneman (2011: 394) reports that in a study he carried out with colleagues about social factors affecting subjective happiness in the workplace, "the immediate presence of a boss" was strongly correlated with unhappiness. Indeed, it was "the only thing that was worse than being alone." This result seems plausibly related to the finding by Bruno Frey and Alois Stutzer (2000, 2002) that studied the effect of directly democratic institutions across Swiss cantons on reported happiness. One of the most surprising results was that, *ceteris paribus*, individuals were happier the better developed were the institutions of direct democracy in the local region (canton) of residence. A second, related, finding was that reported happiness was increased by the degree of government decentralization (federalism) in the region of residence. Notably, although Frey and Stutzer claim that, in material terms, noncitizen residents actually benefit more from the outcomes of Swiss direct democratic institutional mechanisms (initiatives and referenda), they show that citizens gain more happiness from living in direct-democracy regions. Frey and Stutzer suggest therefore that it is actually opportunity for participation in democratic practice, not better material outcomes, that produces the enhanced happiness result.[17] All of this makes sense, insofar as collective self-governance is the "natural human default," the standard mode of human social organization for thousands of generations before the development of agriculture.

The educators of Demopolis will not, however, depend entirely on causal arguments explaining empirical correlations between democracy and economic growth, security, health, or subjective happiness in making the argument for the value of nonautocracy to future citizens. They want to be able to say not only *what* democracy is good for, but *why* and *how*. Their answer links goods of material welfare to what I characterized above as democratic goods. The educators can claim that the basic rules they devised reliably provide the conditions that give citizens access to certain democratic goods.

---

[17] But on the dark side of Swiss direct democracy, in respect to systematically biased immigration decisions, see Hainmueller and Hangartner 2013.

They can show that people have reason to value those goods highly, whether as ends in themselves or as instruments for gaining other valued ends. And they can show that the conditions are sustained through specifiable democratic mechanisms. The reasons for valuing the free exercise of constitutive human capacities, political freedom, political equality, and civic dignity, along with the specification of mechanisms for their provision, may be imagined as the substantial content of the civic education that may be offered to "potential citizens" of Demopolis – to those who were too young to be active citizens at the founding moment, to subsequent generations, and to immigrants.

The "value proposition" of Demopolis's civic education is that the intrinsic value of certain goods produced by participation in democracy, along with their instrumental role in sustaining welfare and security, justifies accepting the coercive authority of a democratic government and paying the relatively high costs of civic participation. The civic curriculum of Demopolis is not ideological (in the negative sense of indoctrination predicated on falsehood) insofar as the arguments for the value of the various goods are valid, in the sense of being logically derived from facts (or plausible postulates), based on the findings of natural and social science and supported by history. Some of those findings concern human nature and conditions that promote human flourishing.[18] I suppose (unsurprisingly) that the pedagogic method of Demopolis's civic education will be similar to the methodology of this book. That is, it conjoins the approach to positive political theory that underpins contemporary social science, with analytic normative political theory, history, and some aspects of natural science.[19]

In predicating the persistence and legitimacy of the state on civic education, I am following the lead of classical Greek theorists. Both Plato, in the *Republic* and *Laws*, and Aristotle in the *Politics* were deeply concerned with the form and content of civic education. Education in Demopolis is certainly not to be premised on the *Republic's* Noble Lies. It agrees, instead, with Aristotle's conviction (*Politics* Books 7 and 8) that predicating

---

[18] Note that the curriculum need not be based on an exhaustive account of human nature, or on an exhaustive list of conditions promoting human flourishing. The curriculum will be adequately reality-based if it accurately (that is, in accord with natural and social science) presents aspects of human nature that promote flourishing given conditions pertaining "now and around here" (Williams 2005: 8). If other aspects of human nature and other conditions promote the flourishing of others, elsewhere, that is not a refutation of the reality-based nature of the education offered to the potential citizens of Demopolis.

[19] My Stanford undergraduate course on "Inventing Government" represents my own imperfect attempt to boil down the "formal instruction" part of that sort of civic education into a ten-week term.

education (and thus the regime) on falsehoods (no matter how noble) is abhorrent, and that the citizens-in-training must have rational reasons, in line with their actual natures and interests, to embrace the values that they are taught. But unlike the civic education of Aristotle's "polis of our prayers," Demopolis need not teach a single standard of general virtue, because basic democracy is not committed to a single, unitary conception of the human good. The citizens might eventually agree on a single conception of the good (and establish it as a state religion). But a basic democratic regime may instead aim at providing ample opportunity for citizens to pursue a diverse array of individually chosen projects. These alternative pathways are discussed further in Chapter 8.

Perhaps the closest classical model for the civic education of Demopolis is Christopher Bobonich's (2002) rationalistic interpretation of the persuasive prescripts attached to each of the laws of Magnesia (an ideal state to be established in Crete) in Plato's *Laws*. According to Bobonich, the prescripts to Magnesia's laws are meant to persuade the citizens to obey, by appealing to their rational interest in obedience to laws that actually conduce to their true welfare. Likewise, so I have argued elsewhere (Ober 2005a: Chapter 6), the practical experience of "working the machine" of Athenian democratic governance provided an effective civic education to Athenian citizens. Through civic participation they came to understand, not only how their government worked, but why democracy was, in fact, good for themselves – as individuals, and, collectively, as the citizen body.[20]

This book may, in sum, be imagined as a synopsis of the justificatory civic education offered to each generation of future citizens of Demopolis. If they rationally accept the arguments made in the course of their education and are psychically motivated by them, if they come to embrace a social identity that is (in part) grounded in their activity as citizens, then the state will have justified to its citizens why it may fairly require them to pay the relatively high costs of democratic self-governance. The requirement will have become a preference, and the preference will be based on individual and common interests. In that case, we may suppose that the potential citizens will willingly, indeed gladly, assume the role of law-abiding and participatory citizens. The social fact of citizenship is reasserted by the speech act of each citizen's affirmative assent, and thus Demopolis is sustained for

---

[20] Civic education is equally important for Hobbes's Leviathan state (*Leviathan* 30, with n. 9, above): Hobbes calls for the sovereign's laws to be expressed in simple language, to be universally known, and for the reasons for the laws to be made clear to all who are subject to them.

another generation. Basic democracy is, in short, robust if and when it is recognized as choiceworthy and actively chosen.[21]

In Chapters 5 and 6 we turn to the psychically motivating arguments that the educators of Demopolis could make that might persuade a rational, skeptical resident to adopt the social identity of citizen, and thus willingly to take on the duties of citizenship. We begin, in the following chapter, with the idea that civic participation is not only a cost that must be paid because of its instrumental value in securing the democratic regime, but is also of substantial and intrinsic benefit for each individual citizen.

---

[21] Social facts and speech acts: Austin 1975; Searle 1995. I do not seek to specify the form or content of the affirmative assent of the post-Founder-generation citizens, but it might be in the form of an oath, taken at any point in an adult's life at which he or she feels ready to take up the responsibilities and privileges of citizenship. Civic oaths are, of course, part and parcel of modern democracy; they are required of, for example, jurors and members of the armed forces. Naturalized American citizens are required to take an oath that, among other things, obligates them to support the Constitution: www.uscis.gov/us-citizenship/naturalization-test/naturalization-oath-allegiance-united-states-america (accessed July 26, 2016). It is unclear why the accident of born in the US should absolve natives from the responsibility of making a similar declaration. On the civic oath of the ancient Athenian ephebes, and its modern reincarnation on some American university campuses in the twentieth century, see Hedrick 2004.

CHAPTER 5

Human Capacities and Civic Participation

If we accept that "history proves possibility," then it appears that Hobbes's argument that only absolutism can deliver security and prosperity is adequately refuted. We now know, as Hobbes, did not, that there are well-documented examples of nonabsolutist governments, ancient (before liberalism) as well as modern (after liberalism) that, on the face of it, fit the criteria of stable collective and limited self-governance by citizens (whether directly or through their representatives), and that have enabled residents to live relatively securely and well.[1] But, as noted in the previous chapter, empirical refutation is not enough. Citizen self-government must be legitimated by justificatory arguments offered to those who remain unconvinced that democracy's past historical performance is an adequate guarantee of future returns to civic effort, or who are willing to consider autocracy as a low-cost solution to social order. So we still need to explain *how* and *why* limited citizen self-government delivers the material goods of security and welfare before the addition of the special features unique to liberalism. And we need to decide what, beyond the provision of material necessities, basic democracy might be said to be good for.

I will argue in this chapter and the next that democracy's ability to deliver the necessary material conditions is intimately bound up in democratic goods – that is, goods that are made available to individuals through their participation in collective self-government. These include (but need not be limited to) free exercise of constitutive human capacities and the conditions of political liberty, political equality, and civic dignity. Rather than being an impediment to the achievement of materially adequate conditions of

---

[1] Ancient: Ober 2008a: democratic Athens and its relatively high performance in provision of security and material welfare for citizens. Modern: Doucouliagos and Ulubaşoğlu 2008: literature review and meta-regression on modern democracy and economic performance; Cox et al. 2012 present data on regime stability. Here I am assuming that there are modern representative democracies that fit my definition of basic democracy; see further, Section 8.1. But, since the empirical refutation requires only one counterexample, the refutation does not hang on that claim.

life, or luxuries made possible by the prior achievement of adequate material conditions, these democratic goods fill out the positive political theory of basic democracy. Considerations from normative theory will, therefore, help to explain how it is that democracy answers Hobbes's positive-theory challenge.

By establishing the background conditions common to a wide range of forms of social organization (from Hobbesian absolutism to Aristotelian civic order), we can show how basic democracy achieves its historically demonstrable ability to deliver favorable material conditions for human existence in a way that is relatively stable and reliable, and how its ability to do so relates to democratic goods. We can answer Hobbes's challenge in the terms of positive political theory, and we can address doubts about whether democracy before liberalism is good for anything in the terms of normative political theory, if we make a few fairly simple assumptions. Those assumptions concern (1) humans' inherent and distinctive capacities, (2) methodological (rather than ethical) individualism, (3) interdependence as an imperative for cooperation, and (4) the mutability of the environment in which societies exist.

Calling the assumptions I will make "simple" invites agreement on the part of my readers. But that invitation may not be accepted by everyone. One way of moving beyond the untested presumption that "our intuitions" (analytic political theorists' favored term of art) about preconditions of social order are valid is to base arguments for democracy's value on those preconditions on which Hobbes and Aristotle might have agreed. I will attempt to show that there is limited but meaningful overlap in their positions concerning certain human capacities. This is significant because Hobbes saw his normative and positive theoretical enterprise as (among other things) a refutation of Aristotle's views about the natural relationship between human sociability and politics, views that Hobbes bluntly characterized as absurd, repugnant, and ignorant.[2] The point is not to blur the sharp differences between Aristotle and Hobbes on questions of moral psychology, ethics, and political theory. Indeed, their differences come into sharper focus once we recognize the limited ground that they do share. But because Hobbes did disagree so vehemently with Aristotle about so many things, any ground they share has a strong claim to intuitive validity. That

---

[2] See, for example, *Leviathan* 4.46: "And I believe that scarce any thing can be more absurdly said in naturall Philosophy, than that which now is called *Aristotle's Metaphysiques*; nor more repugnant to Government than much of that hee hath said in his *Politiques*; nor more ignorantly, than a great part of his *Ethiques*." Laird 1942 remains a very useful summary of Hobbes on Aristotle's *Politics*.

claim is further strengthened when that ground is also shared by contemporary social and natural scientists.

The limited agreement between Aristotle and Hobbes is only on certain preconditions of social order, not on the implications of those preconditions. I readily acknowledge that they would *not* agree on what their shared ground means for democracy and human flourishing, and that the partial overlap in their positions on preconditions is easily overshadowed by their disagreement on other substantive matters. But once we step away from the debate between them concerning the nature of effective political authority and its relationship to the making and enforcement of law, their limited agreement on human capacities, which does track certain findings of contemporary social and natural science, provides the basis for an answer to the question of how the costs that must be paid to sustain basic democracy might be justified to skeptical future citizens by the educators of Demopolis.

My primary assumption in what follows is that humans, like other animals, have inherent characteristics and distinctive capacities. The relevant human capacities are sociability, rationality, and communication. These capacities are detailed below, with reference to Aristotle's and Hobbes's arguments in respect to each. The free exercise of those capacities is, I will conclude, an intrinsic good that is fully realized only in a democracy. The three secondary assumptions concerning individuality, interdependence, and mutability follow from this primary assumption and will be taken up in more detail in the next chapter. Those secondary assumptions will in turn provide the basis for the other democratic goods listed above.

5.1 SOCIABILITY

"Sociability" is the claim that living in norm-structured groups of epistemically diverse individuals (i.e., no "hive mind") is both typical of humans and, as a practical matter, necessary for our well-being. Aristotle emphasized this point as a matter of moral psychology in the *Politics* and elaborated upon it in his *History of Animals*.

Aristotle divided the kingdom of animals into two primary categories. In the first category Aristotle placed those species whose members lived essentially solitary lives, without need for complex forms of intraspecies cooperation – we may think, for example, of orangutans, many wild felines, bumblebees, or spiders. In the second category are those species whose members always live in groups – for example flocks of birds, schools of fish, herds of herbivores, and bands of primates. Within the second category of the social, group-dwelling animals, Aristotle observed that the individuals of some species gained an essentially passive benefit from their sociability. Many herbivores, for example (think of antelope, bison, or zebra), benefit from the multiplication of individual senses. If a single antelope in the herd sees, hears, or smells the approach of a predator, and therefore takes flight, all the rest in the herd may take her flight as a signal and flee to safety. But antelope do not create or share public goods. So there is mutual advantage, but not active cooperation in producing that advantage.[3]

Aristotle's second subcategory of group-dwelling animals is made up of species whose members live more actively social lives, in that they cooperate in the production of some tangible good that is publicly shared by all members of the community. The behavior of these public-good-producing creatures was designated by Aristotle as "political." Social insects provided Aristotle with his prime examples of nonhuman political behavior. In the *Politics* he singled out honey bees, but in the *History of Animals* (1.1.20) he includes ants among political animals, along with bees, wasps, and cranes. He notes that, of these species "some submit to a ruler, others are subject to no governance; so, for instance, the crane and the several sorts of bee submit to a ruler, whereas ants and numerous other creatures are every one his own master." Aristotle erroneously thought that each beehive had a "king" who directed the other bees' activity. But he was right to believe that the ants of a given nest cooperate to produce public goods without a master. Like honey bees, harvester ants process and store food that is shared by all individuals in the nest. All creatures that live in clearly defined communities, producing and sharing public goods, are, in Aristotle's behavioral taxonomy, "political animals."[4] Humans, according to Aristotle, fall into this public-good-producing subcategory of social creatures, which is the basis of his famous claim that "the human being is a political animal" (*Politics* 1.1253a1–3). Indeed, for Aristotle, humans are the *most* political of animals – that is, we are, in behavioral terms like social insects, only more so.

Hobbes engaged directly with Aristotle's characterization of humans as political animals, taking the comparison to social insects head-on: "It is true, that certain living creatures, as Bees and Ants, live sociably one with

---

[3] The situation is more complicated in at least some herd-dwelling species, in which herd members share, via rotation, pro-social "duties" in assuming the costly role of serving as "sentry" and may cooperate (again potentially at cost to the individual) to repel predators – but the principle is, I trust, clear enough.

[4] Aristotle's king bee (*History of Animals* 5.21) was actually the queen, i.e., the common mother of all bees in the hive; but queen bees no more direct the activity of a hive than do queen ants in a nest. On the surprisingly complex forms of cooperation achieved by honeybees, notably in the vital project of finding a new nest site, see Seeley 2010.

another (which are therefore by *Aristotle* numbered amongst Politicall creatures), and yet have no other direction than their particular judgements and appetites; nor speech, whereby one of them can signify to another, what he thinks expedient for the common benefit." Hobbes acknowledged that "therefore some man may perhaps desire to know why mankind cannot do the same" (*Leviathan* 17.86).

Hobbes's answer was, he supposed, decisive: (1) Humans, unlike social insects, were "continually in competition for Honour and Dignity"; (2) for social insects common and private goods were identical, "But man, whose Joy consisteth in comparing himselfe with other men, can relish nothing but what is eminent"; (3) social insects, lacking reason, do not find fault with the administration of government, whereas men habitually do; (4) lacking language, social insects cannot misrepresent reality to one another, as men do; (5) social insects make no distinction between injury and damage, as men do; (6) "lastly, the agreement of these creatures is Naturall," whereas humans can have agreement only by artificial covenants between them, and thus they require a third-party coercive enforcer of agreements: an absolute ruler, standing above and outside the law (*Leviathan* 17.86–87).[5]

Hobbes certainly opposed Aristotle's strong version of human sociability, which had allowed for bootstrapping a stable and potentially virtuous and eudaemonic public order from norms arising from natural interactions among the members of the community. For Hobbes, humans in the state of nature despise social interaction, as both dangerous and harmful to their pride (*Leviathan* 13.61). The question for Hobbes is why humans, by nature antisocial, nevertheless live together in societies (Foisneau 2016: 121–122). While rejecting Aristotle's assumption that human society is naturally aimed at the conjoint achievement of our highest ends, Hobbes's seems to agree with the basic point made by Plato in the *Republic* (2.369b–372a), that humans are interdependent in that they cannot live at all well unless they form an extensive system of social cooperation. Humans must find a way to live in a society if they are to enjoy an acceptable level of material existence.

If we take seriously the adjective "solitary" in Hobbes's famous five-word characterization of lives in the state of nature we might suppose that humans lack the capacity to cooperate in society before the establishment of the sovereign. But, as Kinch Hoekstra demonstrates in detail (Hoekstra 2017: Part 1), the condition of "solitary" existence in Hobbes's state of nature is a rhetorical exaggeration, contradicted by his allusion to

---

[5] The preceding four paragraphs are adapted from Ober 2015b: Chapter 3.

small-scale group formation ("confederacy") in the state of nature. Indeed, the human capacity to form groups capable of cooperating in the formulation and execution of common goals is essential to the Hobbesian state of nature, in that it ensures that even the strongest individual has reason to fear others (*Leviathan* 13.60).

Hobbes certainly thought that living in norm-structured social groups is essential to human well-being: It is to enable that sort of life that the social contract creating Leviathan is made. The agreement that leads to Leviathan assumes that humans know that, under the right conditions, they are capable of social cooperation. So, we may conclude that, while firmly rejecting natural sociability as the impetus to the achievement of the necessary social conditions, Hobbes agreed with Aristotle that humans had an inherent *capacity* for social cooperation and that the exercise of that capacity was necessary for human flourishing.

In the real world, it is the case that humans live in norm-structured groups and always have.[6] Based on the evidence of archaeology and anthropology, it is certain that biologically modern humans (like their hominid ancestors and relatives) lived in small bands of, at the outside, several dozen individuals. These bands made their living by foraging – hunting and gathering natural foods. Such groups are invariably norm-structured. In the foraging communities studied by anthropologists, norm-violation incurs sanctions from other group members.

Notably, the norms of foraging groups, although decidedly *not* liberal are, in political terms, democratic. The higher primates most closely biologically related to humans (chimps, gorillas, bonobos) also live in bands. But human bands are different from those, in that a band of human foragers typically has neither an "alpha" leader nor a strict hierarchy among the group's membership; there is no king or boss of the band. The lack of an alpha leader is the result of active resistance to attempts at dominance by would-be alphas (Boehm 1999). That resistance ranges from expressions of disapproval through ostracism to execution. As a result of the resulting "negative dominance hierarchy," decisions about matters of public import tend to be made more or less consensually, rather than being dictated by the will of an individual or a small coalition.

After breaking off from the "common primate ancestor" (shared by chimps, humans and bonobos), the distant ancestors of modern humans evolved in the context of living in small groups over millions of years,

---

[6] Even hermits depend on the background conditions produced by sociability among others, at a minimum by using tools invented and developed in the context of cooperative social organizations.

eventually achieving our modern biological form. At some point in that evolution, human sociability diverged from the strict hierarchy typical of other primates. We subsequently lived in essentially democratic small groups for at least tens of thousands of years – the great majority of all human history – that is, until after the development of arable agriculture about 12,000 years ago. It is, therefore, reasonable to conclude that democracy is the "natural" (that is, genetically chosen by evolutionary adaptation) form of human sociability; just as strong dominance hierarchy is the natural form of, for example, chimpanzee sociability.[7]

Evolutionary and social science aside, there appears to be general agreement between Aristotle and Hobbes about the baseline human capacity for small-group cooperation. Hobbes might, moreover, be willing to concede that such groups were capable of devising norms that allow them to pursue common ends, although he would surely emphasize that prominent among those ends were potentially murderous plans that exacerbated the fearfulness of life in the state of nature. In addition to the insecurity arising from murderous threats, he would also emphasize the relative poverty of foraging communities. Aristotle, following the lead of earlier Greek "anthropological" thought, from Protagoras and Democritus to Plato, likewise supposed that very small natural human groups, those organized according to kinship, were endemically at risk from one another and from natural forces.[8] Aristotle and Hobbes could, therefore, agree that the sort of cooperation that leads to small-group existence is both a natural human capacity and insufficient to elevate humans to a condition that could reasonably be described as flourishing – even in the most basic sense of reasonable security and prosperity. For those baseline material conditions to be fulfilled, human communities must become bigger and more complex. And with the growth in scale and complexity, as we have seen (Chapter 3) come the problems of collective action analyzed by Mancur Olson and by a subsequent generation of social scientists.

5.2 RATIONALITY

When we turn to the second domain of distinctive human capacity, strategic rationality, we are on ground that is congenial to Hobbes and that might seem foreign to Aristotle. With his emphasis on human pride and honor

---

[7] Foraging communities, "negative dominance hierarchy," and nonautocratic politics, with contrast to chimpanzees and other primates: Boehm 1999, 2012a, 2012b; Harari 2015; Turchin 2015.

[8] Well-known examples of pre-Aristotelian Greek anthropology include Democritus (DK B 252); Plato, *Protagoras* (the "Great Speech of Protagoras"); Plato, *Statesman*.

seeking, Hobbes did not conceive of humans simply as the coldly analytic utility calculators assumed in the strongest versions of rational-actor theory, the imaginary (or at any event rare) agents Richard Thaler (2015) has dubbed "Econs." The passion for honor and desire for acknowledged superiority that characterizes some, if not all, humans complicates any simple picture of rationality. But Hobbes predicated his argument for the social contract on the assumption that ordinary adult, healthy humans have rationally ordered preferences – ranking life itself, security, and welfare above other goods – and that we employ strategic reason to pursue our interests, public and private. Moreover, Hobbes knew that humans recognize the capacity for rational preference ordering and strategic reason in others, and that we make our plans and act accordingly. Hobbes's central argument in *Leviathan* is that strategic rationality, under the conditions of primeval equality and mutual threat, precludes the possibility of mutual commitments that are general and credible enough to bootstrap humanity out of the state of nature. Thus, without a third-party enforcer in the person (or personification) of a lawless sovereign, the social equilibrium delivers little in terms of the primary goods, and humans cannot achieve the scale and complexity of social organization that is adequate to lift them into conditions of security and relative prosperity.

Aristotle's strong emphasis on the potential for social order and public good provision inherent in human sociability might seem to suggest that he would have rejected the thought that humans were, by nature, rationally strategic in the sense of seeking their own utility in constant competition with other self-interested utility seekers. In Book 1 of the *Politics* (1252b14–30) Aristotle describes the development of human society as moving naturally from the simplest form of the nuclear family (plus slaves), through the small kin- and locality-based community composed of several family groups, to the relatively large and complex society of the polis – the natural end (*telos*) of human social development. But, based on a number of other passages in the *Politics*, Aristotle appears to have agreed with much of Hobbes's assessment of the ways in which strategic rationality distinguishes humans as social beings from bees, ants, or other inherently "political" animals.

In the passage cited above on social insects (*Leviathan* 17.86–87), Hobbes's basic point is that individual ants and bees lack personal interests or preferences that could bring their behavior into conflict with the common interest of the nest or hive. Moreover, even if an individual ant or bee did, counterfactually, have individual preferences, ants and bees lack the kind of strategic rationality that would allow them to formulate plans for pursuing those individual preferences. Social insects in a given nest or hive cooperate "all the way down" – they are not in competition with one another for scarce resources; they have no conflicts with one another that do not arise from error (e.g., misrecognizing a nest-mate for a stranger). By contrast, humans, Hobbes asserts, have strong reasons, based in their ready identification of individual interests – in life itself, in honor, in self-aggrandizement – to compete rather than to cooperate with one another in ways that would conduce to the common good. And we have the resources, in the form of strategic rationality, for pursuing our private goals.

Hobbes meant to refute Aristotle, but Aristotle's account of human social behavior in the *Politics* frankly acknowledges the many ways in which the individual "parts" of a community – individuals and subgroups with preferences much more narrowly conceived than "the common good of the community" – identify interests that are not aligned with the common interest. "Parts" may act strategically to seek their private advantage at the expense of the advantage of the whole community. Much of the discussion of Books 3–6 of the *Politics* is directed at the problems that arise when social parts (individuals, groups) fail to align their interests with that of the political whole that is the state.

In his consideration of the emergence of the natural community of the polis in Book 1 (*Politics* 1252b14–30) Aristotle asserts not only that the polis is the natural end of human sociability, but also that that "in general to live together and share all our human affairs is difficult" (1263a15–16, cf. 1286b1). And so, although "there is in everyone an impulse to live in a political community, nonetheless he who first brought men together (to live in a polis) was the cause of the greatest of goods" (1253a29–31). The essential roles played by the lawgiver and by formal rules recurs in Book 7. Here Aristotle sketches the most perfect achievable form of the natural polis: the "polis of our prayers." Aristotle strongly emphasizes that formal rules, established by human agency and coercively enforced, are required in order for the polis of our prayers to persist over time in a flourishing condition. These rules would not, of course, be necessary if humans were, like ants or bees, by nature incapable of being other than cooperative all the way down. As with Hobbes, the source of the problem of potential noncooperation is, for Aristotle, inherent human strategic rationality – the very marked human capacity to identify and pursue individual and subgroup preferences in the recognition that rivals for scarce goods were doing likewise.[9]

---

[9] On the relationship of the natural polis of Book 1 to the best achievable polis of Book 7, see Ober 2015a. See further Ober 1996: Chapter 11, esp. 169–170; Ober 1998: 295–297, with literature cited 297n19.

Aristotle, unlike Hobbes, supposed that the problem of cooperation was soluble in the absence of a lawless sovereign so that rules could be devised enabling a community of citizens to govern themselves. In an Aristotelian "best possible" polis, as in real Greek democracies of the classical era, citizens rule over one another (as judges and civic magistrates) and are ruled over by fellow citizens, in turns. Citizen self-government is, for Aristotle, sustainable, productive of security and prosperity, and limited by the laws. But Aristotle did not suppose that achieving that happy condition was a simple matter; in the middle books of the *Politics* he details the many ways in which real-world citizen-governed Greek poleis fell short of optimum flourishing, as a result of parts identifying their interests in contradistinction to the interests of the whole – the political community of a city-state. He certainly did not suppose that the best possible human community, one in which each member would flourish to the extent allowed by his or her nature, could ever come into existence through the manifestation of natural human sociability alone.

While there is a range of views on the role of strategic rationality in human behavior and social organization among contemporary social scientists, a broad mainstream of scholarly opinion grounds social explanation on assumptions about human strategic rationality. Human rationality is inherently imperfect. As a result of the development of experimental psychology, behavioral economics, and neurological studies of the role of emotion in judgment, it is now widely acknowledged that there are substantial limits on rationality understood as expected utility maximization. Yet by the same token, the point of the new work is to show how and to what extent rationality is limited, not that rationality as pursuit of self-interest is nonexistent. Strategic calculation is widely acknowledged by social scientists as a standard feature of human interaction. The role of rationality in explanation has been conditioned, not replaced by the insights of contemporary psychology.[10]

The ground on which Aristotle and Hobbes appear to agree is, I believe, well within this contemporary social-scientific mainstream. Hobbes and Aristotle both regarded humans as fundamentally concerned with their own well-being. Each reserved a substantial role for emotion in human behavior, but each supposed that among the distinctive traits of humanity is a high-order reasoning capacity. Rationality allows individuals to order their preferences so as to pursue their desired ends in more or less coherent

---

[10] Simon 1955; Kahneman 2011; Thaler 2015. Constrained strategic rationality was also understood in a "folk" sense by Greek writers: Ober 2009; Ober and Perry 2014, and by Greek institutional designers: Ober 2008a. For "social science" read, in the first instance, political science and economics.

ways. It enables us to form strategic plans for pursuing our ends, in recognition that others are acting in a similarly rational manner. Both Hobbes and Aristotle saw cooperation at scale, in relatively large (above face-to-face) and complex societies, as essential to human flourishing. Both saw that obedience to rules was a prerequisite for cooperation. Both predicated the legitimacy of a given regime on the rational acceptance of the rules on the part of those subject to them. That is, both believed that in order for the regime to be legitimate, obedience must be voluntary, and given in recognition of the fact that each individual will do better if each and all obey the rules.

5.3 COMMUNICATION

The third fundamental and distinctive human capacity is high-order interpersonal communication – the use of language among persons with some need of one another to deliberate (offer information and reasons for belief and action) and thereby make consequential decisions on matters of substantial import to the parties involved. Hobbes and Aristotle both recognized the development and instrumental use of language as a fundamentally important and distinctive human trait. Both supposed, correctly, that language use/symbolic system development is universal among human groups. Aristotle (*Politics* 1253a8–18) makes the point that, along with reason, the use of language, for communicating about means and ends, advantage and justice, was what made humans the "most political" of animals:

> the human, alone among animals, possesses the faculty of language (*logos*) . . . Language is designed to indicate the advantageous and the harmful, and thus also the just and the unjust. It is in this respect that the human is distinguished from the other animals; only the human has a sense of good and evil, just and unjust, and the other moral sensibilities.

As we have seen, Hobbes (*Leviathan* 17.87) thought that language use distinguished humans from (among other animals) social insects. Both Hobbes and Aristotle were extremely well versed in, and made contributions to, the field of rhetoric. Both Aristotle and Hobbes were, therefore, very well aware that language could be used to pro-social ends, as deliberation aimed at promoting higher forms of cooperation among larger bodies of persons. But they were each also very well aware of how persuasive speech could be used for strategic ends in the pursuit of narrow self-interest. Both knew that strategic communication, in the form of deception and manipulation, could corrupt politics and undermine the bases of social cooperation. Both were concerned, in one way or another, with education as a pro-social form of communication: Individuals teach (disclosing what they know) and learn via communication with others.[11]

Once again, the apparent agreement between Aristotle and Hobbes on the distinctiveness of human communicative capacity, and the purposes to which that capacity is put, is well within the contemporary mainstream of scientific opinion. There is continued scholarly controversy over exactly how and when speech and language evolved, relative to the development of the human brain, other physiological traits, and the social organization of human groups. But it is certain that speech and language use, both for strategic purposes and in pursuit of cooperative ends, is a universal feature of human society. Neither the potential value of communication for enabling sophisticated forms of cooperation at scale, nor the danger to common-interest outcomes that is represented by deceptive and manipulative speech is in doubt.[12]

5.4 EXERCISE OF CAPACITIES AS A DEMOCRATIC GOOD

The human capacities of sociability, rationality, and communication seem to be closely related and interactive, both in origin and function.[13] Together, these three capacities rank high among primary attributes that distinguish humans from other animals and they are plausibly considered as preconditions of human social order. Other mammalian species are strongly social, pursue individual as well as collective ends, and engage in communication that enables them to achieve those ends. And yet, when compared with humans, other animals have limited capacity to employ language and reason. The distinctive conjunction of sociability, rationality, and communicative capacities may be said to be (nonexhaustively) *constitutive* of humanity.[14]

As we have seen, that conjunction is a problem for advances in large-scale social development, in that the employment of strategic rationality by free riders initially sets limits on the size and complexity of functionally effective human communities. Yet the same conjunction of attributes is what has historically enabled human communities to devise and implement

[11] Aristotle *Art of Rhetoric*, with Kennedy 1963; Hobbes *Leviathan*, with Skinner 2008.
[12] Language origins: Harari 2015; framing: Lakoff 2003 [1980]; rhetoric in contemporary political theory: Garsten 2011.
[13] Origins and function of sociability, rationality, communication: Harari 2015, with literature cited.
[14] Other candidates for constitutive human capacities are not hard to come up with, e.g., Williams 2005: 99 on ability to feel pain (physically, as other animals, but also virtually) and a responsiveness to affection (again, virtual as well as physical) and pain at its loss.

mechanisms that promote credible commitment to common ends on the part of many persons not individually known to one another. The primary mechanisms are adequately well-enforced rules (norms, laws) that reliably identify and punish defectors while rewarding cooperators. The conclusion that human sociability (despite our capacity for mutual harm), rationality (despite the limits on human reason), and communication (in potentially pro-social and antisocial ways) are (nonexhaustively) constitutive of humanity provides one possible answer to the question of what democracy is good for beyond security and material welfare: *Democracy is good for the free exercise of constitutive human capacities.*[15]

Hobbes would surely have disagreed with that conclusion, even if I am right to say that he would have agreed with certain of its premises. Aristotle would have regarded it as problematic at best. It is, in any event, only one among a range of claims that might be made in arguing for the value of democratic participation. The democratic good I defend in this chapter is meant to be independent of liberalism's familiar basket of goods and independent of goods based on religious belief. Other independent-goods arguments could, I assume, be devised. Moreover, my account of basic democracy is intended as a potential framework for either a liberal or a traditionally religious state (Chapter 8). So, depending on how one imagines Demopolis's future development, a variety of more familiar moral claims might also be advanced for why and how citizens benefit from participation in government. I offer the following argument for the free exercise of constitutive human capacities as a democratic good *exempli gratia*. It is one way to answer the normative question of what democracy before liberalism is good for and one argument that could be made by Demopolis's original Founders for why future citizens should abhor tyranny and how they would benefit, psychically as well as materially, from public activities that might otherwise be thought of only in terms of costs.

The free exercise of these fundamental human capacities, through participation in democracy, is good for human flourishing, in a sense that exceeds simple material welfare, on the following argument. Under the conditions

---

[15] The argument of this section is adapted, in part, from Ober 2007b; I discuss there why the being-kinds with which I am concerned here are limited to healthy adults, and what I mean by nonparasitic exercise of capacities. By "freedom" I mean here nothing more than the primitive freedom defined by Williams 2005: 79, "the simple idea of being unobstructed in doing what you want [here: what you want because it is good for you as a type of being] by some form of humanly imposed coercion." My argument is in some ways similar to the "capabilities approach" in economic and ethical theory (e.g., Sen 1993; Nussbaum 2011), but, per above, my argument remains minimalist: unlike Sen and, a fortiori, Nussbaum, I do not seek to specify all of the various capabilities that might be necessary to sustain a human life that would be recognized as fully flourishing in contemporary liberal terms.

of basic democracy, citizens freely and openly employ reason and communication in making, together, decisions of primary importance to themselves. They take responsibility for the implementation of those decisions
and bear their consequences. Democracy, unlike other forms of political
organization, not only permits, but requires, for its continued existence,
the conjoint exercise of these three fundamental capacities by participatory
citizens. Joint political action at scale, through the pro-social exercise of
reason and communication, is just what it is for citizens to govern themselves. Moreover, because participation in democratic culture and institutions requires the reiterated and active exercise, at scale, of reason and
communication to achieve social ends, the practice of democracy refines,
broadens, and deepens inherent human capacities of sociability, reason, and
communication.[16]

That argument can be developed either on the basis of subjective experience of value or, alternatively, on a more demanding quasi-Aristotelian
ground. The latter assumes that, for any given being, certain things are
objectively good – i.e., that their goodness is (for that being) independent
of that being's subjective experience.[17] Both the subjective and objective
versions of the argument assume that every type of animal (human being,
cat, etc.) possesses certain distinctive *constitutive capacities* – that is, natural
capacities that constitute that type of animal *as* a distinctive being-kind.
The opportunity properly (in a healthy, nonparasitic way) to exercise constitutive capacities is good for that type of being. It is good (for that type
of being) either because it is subjectively experienced as good (because it
satisfies desires to exercise the capacity, fulfills a preference to do so, brings
pleasure in so doing, etc.), or, on quasi-Aristotelian grounds, because exercise of the capacity objectively is good (for that type of being). In either
case, the exercise of capacities is a good independent of, and supplementary to, the products of their exercise.[18]

---

[16] Social insects (e.g., bees, ants) cooperate at scale without resort to human-like reason, but ants and
bees are not relevantly to be thought of as individuals. The mechanisms by which social insects gain
security and welfare, while involving communication, are very different from those employed by
human communities: Ober 2015b, Chapter 3.

[17] It is Aristotelian in being predicated on the kinds of arguments made by Aristotle, not in the sense
of being his own argument. For the distinction, see Ober 2013b. Note that the general idea that
the exercise of natural human capacities is essential to human flourishing is decidedly not *peculiarly*
Aristotelian. In "The Metaphysics of Morals" Kant, stated that "the highest purpose of man" was
"the development of all natural capacities" (Kant 1991: 133, cited in Starr 2007: 72). But, as Williams
(2005: 102) notes, Kant is not concerned with *empirical* capacities, which are the sort of capacities
that did concern Aristotle and do concern me in these chapters

[18] A number of capacities, e.g., to eat and to reproduce, are shared by all animals. Eating is an essential
precondition for flourishing, but it is not (in and of itself) *constitutive* of a particular being type. The

The argument that free exercise of constitutive capacities is an intrinsic good may be illustrated by the example of a domestic cat. Domestic cats as we know them are descended from genetically near-identical wild ancestors. Those ancestors were "designed" by the ordinary, random, unintelligent processes of evolutionary natural selection to be highly specialized hunters of small prey (e.g., mice). Prey is caught with the cat's paws, which are furnished with retractable claws and may be thought of as highly specialized hunting tools. A hunting cat stalks and leaps: pouncing upon its prey with its paws. The pounce is, as anyone who has spent any time around a cat knows, among the most striking and most typical of cat behaviors. Pouncing is typical of kittens, adult cats, and even some old and infirm cats. Whereas the pouncing instinct clearly arises from the material necessity of acquiring food by hunting, it is not reduced, in domestic cats at least, to food acquisition. An ordinary, healthy cat will eagerly and repeatedly pounce upon objects simulating prey, and will do so without any reward other than (it appears) the activity itself.[19]

Pouncing (leaping upon an object taken as prey) is *ex hypthesi* a constitutive capacity of cats. A cat can exist, on a material plane, without the opportunity ever to exercise its capacity for pouncing – it can be kept alive, for example, in a small cage, provided with adequate food, etc. Yet to say that a cat that lived out its life in a cage had lived an adequately a good cat life would be, I believe, simply and horribly wrong. It would require denying that an opportunity for pouncing (among other activities) is intrinsically and necessarily part of what makes a cat's life good for the cat – whether it is subjectively experienced as good or objectively good.[20]

The intuition that animals suffer if they are denied any opportunity to exercise their constitutive capacities (as well as if they are deprived of food, shelter, etc.) is, I suppose, at the core of many people's beliefs about acts constituting cruelty to animals. If that intuition is correct, a cat possessing

---

free exercise of constitutive capacities must, in my argument, be added to the exercise or potential exercise (an animal may, in my view, flourish without actually reproducing) of these other commonly held capacities in the definition of flourishing.

[19] Cat evolution and behavior: Bradshaw 2013. I choose the cat example not only because I happen to have a lot of experience with cats but because domestic cats are closer to their wild progenitors, in behavior and morphology, than are dogs or other animals likely to be familiar to most readers.

[20] I appeal here to the nonexpert observations of one who has lived with a number of cats. Nagel (1974) famously asked "what it is like to be a bat," as a way of pointing to the fact of the existence of subjective consciousness in nonhuman animals, and the impossibility of knowing what that consciousness is like, other than in imaginative terms. My argument depends on a cat having a subjective consciousness (i.e., it makes sense to say something is good for a cat, as opposed to, say, a rock, or even a plant). I cannot, of course, claim to know, objectively, what the act of pouncing is like for a cat. I do not believe that my "good for" claim requires that I have "is like" knowledge.

all other goods (food, shelter, etc.), but denied any opportunity to exercise its capacity to pounce, whether on prey or prey analogues (toys, teasers, etc.), could not reasonably be said to have flourished over the course of its life as a cat. Those responsible for keeping cats in small cages over the course of their lives are blameworthy, in that they do harm to those cats. The cat that lives out its life in a cage suffers a deprivation that ought not, under ordinary circumstances, be suffered by any cat. There may be some consequentialist justification for someone to keep some cats in small cages. But the fact remains that the cat in a cage lives a *fundamentally* less good life than does the cat with an opportunity to pounce, all other things being equal.

Adequate human flourishing, on this line of argument, is likely to require the opportunity for exercising the basic human capacities for exercising reason and communication within a social milieu. Reasoning and deliberating (communicating via language about salient matters of common concern)[21] are distinctive and constitutive human capacities – they are human social capacities appropriately used to pro-social (common good-compatible) ends.[22] The exercise of these capacities is subjectively experienced as good by most people: We constantly engage in the use of language and the employment of reason in social settings (among family, friends, voluntary associations of many kinds) in ways that seem, on the face of it, to show that the exercise of those capacities is subjectively valued by us.

It is possible, but unnecessary, to suppose that the exercise of their capacities is also objectively good for humans – that is, that even those persons who do not experience any desire satisfaction, preference fulfillment, or pleasure from employing language and reason in social settings nonetheless gain value from so doing. In any event, free exercise need not be imagined as the *highest* objective human good, or the *most* subjectively desirable human experience. Some people, for example, may follow Aristotle (in Book 10 of the *Nicomachean Ethics*) in regarding contemplation as the most choiceworthy human activity. Others may suppose that the value associated with exercising the three capacities derives from some higher source of value (e.g., God or rights) and that the intrinsic value of free exercise is of less moment than its instrumental value in fulfilling other, higher, ends (e.g.,

---

[21] I employ "deliberation" in an ordinary language sense here, to include debate, argument, and even rhetorical manipulation, rather than in the special sense of "reciprocal justification through giving and taking reasons that might reasonably be accepted by all parties," in which it is used by deliberative democrats.

[22] This is at least one primary reason why lying, cruelty, cheating, etc. – which certainly do lie within human capacities – are ordinarily blamed, whereas use of reason and speech to promote pro-social ends is ordinarily praised.

worship or justice). But they might, nonetheless, agree that when a human being is deprived of the chance to communicate, using reason, to pro-social ends, she experiences deprivation. This is at least one reason why, for example, solitary confinement is as an especially severe form of punishment for a prison inmate.

However subjectively or objectively, intrinsically or instrumentally valuable it is, the exercise of the conjoined capacities of sociability, reason, and communication is insufficient, in and of itself, for human flourishing: A starving and vulnerable human is not in a flourishing condition whatever his opportunity to reason and communicate with his fellows. Basic democracy is predicated on its capacity to provide both security and welfare. In Section 5.6, I argue that it does so *through* the employment, by citizens, of their constitutive capacities. Collective self-governance is the joint activity of citizens in the exercise of their constitutive capacities for reason and communication to pro-social ends, and doing so at the highest level: in regard to the most consequential decisions and outcomes, including security and welfare.

5.5 FREE EXERCISE AND PARTICIPATORY CITIZENSHIP

Just as the cat in a cage suffers a harm, insofar as it has been denied the chance to live an adequately flourishing cat's life, so too the human who, over the course of his or her life, is denied the opportunity to employ reason and communication to pro-social ends suffers deprivation and fails to live a completely flourishing human life.[23] Anyone responsible for systematically denying others the opportunity to engage in the conjoint exercise of the three constitutive capacities does harm to his fellows – regardless of whether it is by depriving them of subjectively valued experience or of an objective good. But it might be thought that constitutive capacities could be freely exercised, and thus the subjective or objective good involved in that exercise is fully gained in social situations that have nothing to do with collective self-government, for example among family, friends, and in voluntary associations. On what grounds might free exercise of constitutive capacities be said to be a specifically *democratic* good in itself (as well as an instrument in gaining other goods), and thereby serve to justify the costs of participation in a basic democracy?

---

[23] I suppose that this inherent capacities argument is compatible with some religious conceptions – a religious individual may say (albeit, in my view, incorrectly) that humans were made that way by God, thus the "design" is not Darwinian but "intelligent."

A benevolent tyrant could allow deliberations on the level of civil society (say, in religious associations), or in a jurisdiction beneath that of the state (say, at a town meeting), while forbidding consequential political deliberation at the level of the state. If someone objects to the restriction, the tyrant could point out that she is excluded from deliberating in many social situations: in another's family circle, in a voluntary association to which she does not belong, and so on. But in response, the objector can point out that those excluding her from sharing in deliberations within their family or association can give her convincing reasons for the exclusion: She does not *belong to*, is not *a member of*, the group in question. By contrast, she *does* belong to and *is* a member of the state. Why, then, is she excluded from exercising her capacities for reason and communication in pro-social ways at the level of state policy? Why must she be only a subject and not a participatory citizen?

The obvious answer is paternalistic: The tyrant knows best what is good for her. That answer is inherently infantilizing, and thus an affront to her dignity (Chapter 6). Anyone who is a member of a state but is denied the chance to participate in government lives out her life beneath a "glass ceiling," above which her capacities *could* be exercised, but may not be, because the ruler forbids it. Life may be otherwise satisfying beneath the ceiling. But the very existence of the ceiling is a constant affront, denigrating the very capacities that constitute her as human. Moreover, the tyrant's monopoly on public authority casts a shadow on all the other social situations in which she is permitted to exercise her capacities: That permission is revocable by the tyrant, and thus her exercise is not truly free: She must always consider whether what she communicates, or the reasons behind her statement, might provoke the tyrant's ire. Hobbes would tell her that she is free in the "silence of the law," but the tyrant's shadow takes the form of the bars of the cage that is always ready to enclose her. We need not accept Aristotle's teleological account of the state's priority to say that, like the literally caged cat, she is thereby harmed. As in the case of the caged cat, there might be some consequential argument offered by the tyrant for why others are forbidden to deliberate on public policy. A primary point of the set of claims developed in this book (and by the imagined educators of Demopolis) is that there is no adequate justificatory argument to be made, because there is no prima facie reason to believe that security or welfare requires autocracy.[24]

---

[24] Note that on this argument, simply serving as a dictator (irrespective of any other wrongs committed as a dictator) could be grounds for sanction. If the inherent capacities argument is correct,

Moving back into history: It is important to remember that the political system devised and sustained by all-male, mostly native, slave-owning participatory citizens of Athens excluded many adult long-term residents of Athenian territory from political participation as citizens, with the authority to make and enforce policy on matters of common interest. Noncitizens in Athens were certainly not just the human equivalent of "cats kept in cages." They undoubtedly did reason and communicate on grave matters of common concern. It is very likely that at least some of their information, ideas, and opinions were influential, via the citizens with whom they were socially involved, in the making of Athenian public policy.[25] But Athenian women, slaves, and most resident foreigners were officially excluded from the institutionalized forums in which policy was debated and made by empowered citizens: Noncitizens had no vote in the Assembly, no share in public offices, no place on juries. By denying women and other long-term residents subject to Athenian authority a full role in freely exercising their human capacities for reason and communication about the most consequential matters and in the most decisive political settings, the Athenians were, we are now in a position to say, blameworthy. The blame arises from a contemporary point of view that is inescapably informed by liberal thought, but it does not arise within a liberal conception of the sources of human rights.

Were the Athenians also blameworthy from within the perspective of their own culture? Arguably, they were. The Athenians *did* have a sense of political participation as a human good and they *did* employ something like a free exercise argument in defending the legitimacy of their democracy.[26] *Pace* Aristotle (below) here is no reason to suppose that most Athenians actually believed that women, slaves, or foreigners were fundamentally different from native men in regard to their human capacities of sociability, reason, and communication. Athenian men did *not*, therefore, have a reasoned justification for why the good arising from political participation ought to be limited to native males. That is to say, they lacked a reason that was better than, "that's the way things are done around here – and, given our cultural imagination of citizenship, the exclusion does not threaten the security of the state." The second part of that claim (were it to have

benevolence of dictatorial behavior does not eliminate the wrong done to the dictator's subjects. My thanks to Charles Girard and Huw Duffy (among others) for pressing me on the constitutive capacities argument.

[25] See, for example, the essays collected in Taylor and Vlassopoulos 2015; Tiersch 2016.

[26] Ober 1989 discusses the background of Athenian ideas about the inherent value of participation to citizens, and the relationship of the free exercise of a widely distributed capacity to reason and to communicate to ancient Athenian defenses of democracy against elitist critics.

been made), might not, in any event, be correct. I have argued elsewhere (Ober 2008a: 258–263) that the exclusion of women and long-term residents (including slaves) from political participation denied the Athenian state full access to vital human resources that might have enabled Athens to more fully realize its potential as a state and society.

As we have seen, a basic democracy must justify its legitimacy by reference to its provision of democratic goods, as well as material goods. Those democratic goods may or may not be provided in ways that are defensible. It is difficult to escape the conclusion that, in light of the ethical considerations arising from the free exercise of human capacities, the ancient Athenians were blameworthy in respect to denying women, slaves, and other long-term nonnative residents the chance to exercise their constitutive human capacities of reason and communication at the highest social level. And that blame arises even when we remain within the classical Greek cultural frame.

It appears that insofar as a basic democracy employs free exercise as an argument in support of its legitimacy, it must justify *any* exclusion from political participation to long-term residents of the state territory. That is to say, in Demopolis all long-term residents of the state's territory ought to be presumed, *ab initio*, to be candidates for the civic education that is the path to entering the status of participatory citizen. This strengthening of the principle that "all those culturally imagined as citizens are citizens" arises from what Bernard Williams (2005: 3–6) called the "basic legitimation demand." The demand that the state provide long-term residents with ample opportunity for free exercise, or justify to them why it does not, resembles a rights claim. It is, however, independent of (although not, I believe, incompatible with) the sort of natural or human rights appealed to by liberal political theorists. Justification for participatory exclusion by a basic democracy must be made in terms of the ends for which the state exists.

Given his strong emphasis on the good of political participation and his grounding of human goods in a conception of human nature that included the idea of constitutive human capacities, Aristotle ought to have seen that exclusion of long-term residents from citizenship required a special justification. Arguably he did. But the result was, regrettably, a moral-psychological Band-Aid rather than a worked-out philosophical argument. Ignoring free foreign residents (like himself), Aristotle sought to justify the exclusion of women and slaves from active political participation in the state by reference to his bald assertion that women and slaves were, in ways that he did not bother to specify, deficient in respect to their capacities for deliberative reasoning (Ober 2015a).

If Aristotle's reason for excluding entire large categories of long-term residents from the possibility of full political participation was painfully inadequate, is it nonetheless possible that an argument for exclusion could be sustained within the framework of a basic democracy – if, certainly, not within liberalism? The question of whether, in the contemporary world, a large and otherwise diverse demos might legitimately exclude some extensive category of persons, for example religious nonconformists, from political participation is taken up in Section 8.5.

Returning to the issue of civic education: The argument that the exercise of human constitutive capacities is good for human flourishing and that democracy is the form of social organization in which those capacities are most fully exercised is buttressed (although not, of course, proved) by the empirical results about health and subjective happiness discussed in Section 4.4. If, counterfactually, Marmot's Whitehall studies had shown that being a low status individual in a strict hierarchy reduced stress and increased health outcomes, the argument that relatively nonhierarchical political order promotes human flourishing would need to engage in a good deal of special pleading. Likewise, if Frey and Stutzer's study of the effects of direct democracy on subjective happiness had shown that more democracy reduces reported life satisfaction, it would be a problem for the democracy and flourishing argument. Although it seems to me to be inadequate simply to equate flourishing with physical health or reported subjective happiness, there ought to be a positive correlation; the fact that the correlations between conditions associated with nonautocracy and health and happiness can be demonstrated therefore count in favor of the capacities/democracy/flourishing argument.

The opportunity costs of participation remain real and substantial. But those costs are, in light of the constitutive capacities argument, now seen to be benefits that are similarly real and substantial. Because the benefit accruing from freely exercising constitutive capacities is intrinsic to that exercise, the benefit to the individual of participating as a citizen in a democracy (i.e., employing reason, and communication in a social milieu in order to make the most highly salient choices about the most important issues of common concern) is realized intrinsically through participation. That intrinsic benefit is not available to nonparticipants, even though they may exercise their capacities in other social situations and may benefit (or, of course, suffer) from the outcomes of others' participatory decision making. Free riders on the democratic order are, in the scolding phrase beloved of teachers at all levels, "cheating themselves," as well as their fellow citizens. Punishment of free riding may, therefore, be regarded as correction, as well as deterrence, and need not be construed as mere retribution.

5.6 FROM CAPACITIES TO SECURITY AND PROSPERITY

As I suggested above, one argument that could be made by the absolute ruler in favor of denying his subjects the opportunity to deliberate on matters of common interest is that the gain in security and welfare, on a consequentialist calculus, makes up for the "free exercise" harm so that there is a net gain in total well-being. The consequentialist argument is strengthened, moreover, if that gain can be achieved in no other (less harmful) way. That is, of course, the core of Hobbes's argument in favor of absolutism. As we have seen, Hobbes's argument fails empirically, since at least one (albeit ethically blameworthy) basic democracy can be shown to have provided security and welfare at levels at least comparable to those provided by autocracies. It would fail catastrophically if basic (ergo participatory) democracy could be shown to be, on the whole, more likely than absolutism to provide security and welfare.[27]

A tight inferential argument, drawing a causal arrow unerringly from the free exercise of human capacities by citizens to increased material well-being at the level of the individual and the state, is beyond the scope or ambition of this book. But it is not difficult to explain why, in theory, the exercise of the human capacities for sociability, reason, and communication in an extensive and diverse society is plausibly associated with security and prosperity as well as increased subjective happiness. Reason and communication, freely exercised within a community, should enable individuals to identify their relative advantages in skills and talents. Free exercise should, therefore, promote more efficient economic specialization via rational investments in human capital. The growth of specialization and human capital in turn should tend to increase aggregate prosperity via developing comparative market advantage.

Moreover, free exercise of reason and communication by all relevant members of a society can, under the right circumstances, lead to better (more effective in terms of producing and sustaining public goods) judgments about matters of common interest, and thereby to relatively more

---

[27] For a historical argument along those lines, based on the experience of the ancient Greek city-states, see Ober 2015b.

productive policies. Finally, free exercise is, all other things being equal, likely to promote relatively fairer policies insofar as the gains in welfare are distributed across the society (as common goods) rather than concentrated in the hand of a small rent-seeking elite (as private or club goods), as is the case in the typical limited-access state (Section 4.2). There is considerable (if not incontrovertible) evidence that more open societies are also more secure and more prosperous. Free exercise of the relevant human capacities requires open access to the relevant public institutions. Insofar as open-access orders can be shown empirically to outperform limited-access orders, the case for equating democracy with flourishing receives further support.[28]

As noted above, the inherent and instrumental value of the exercise of constitutive capacities hardly exhausts the justificatory claims that might be made on behalf of participation as a democratic good. Other claims for the value of participation might be offered that are independent of liberal or religious convictions. Moreover if a liberal or religious superstructure were to be built onto the basic democracy foundation (per Chapter 8), different values-based justifications for democracy could be employed in the education of citizens. The point of developing the free exercise argument is not to provide a unique solution to the problem of how to justify democracy to future citizens. Rather it is to show that civic educators in Demopolis *could* offer potential citizens reasons for preferring democracy to autocracy, and for the fairness of the requirement that citizens pay relatively high costs to sustain democracy through their participation. And they could do so without reference to either liberal or religious values.

The next set of reasons that Demopolis's educators might advance concern the conditions of democracy, the status of those conditions as democratic goods, and their relationship to material well-being. Certain conditions are required in order for a democratic community to increase the stock of human capital; to apply, through effectively organized interpersonal communication, the exercise of reason by individuals with diverse talents and perceptions to solving problems relevant to the provision of common goods; and, thereby, to increase security and welfare. The relevant conditions are political liberty, political equality, and civic dignity.

---

[28] The basic argument was made by Thomas Paine, *Rights of Man* II (1995 [1792]: 227–233), extending arguments made by Adam Smith in *Wealth of Nations*. See also Aristotle *Politics* 3.11 with Ober 2013a, 2008a; Landemore 2012, on epistemic democracy. I argue in Ober 2015b: Chapter 5 that the conditions described above explain the economic and cultural efflorescence of the classical Greek world. Lower inequality drives prosperity: Milanovic 2011; Dabla-Norris et al. 2015. Open access outperforms limited access: North et al. 2009.

Considered together, assumptions about individuality, interdependence, and mutability, introduced above, help to explain how and why liberty, equality, and dignity arise in a basic democracy, and how they may be reliably sustained in a robust social equilibrium. We turn to those conditions and assumptions in the next chapter.

CHAPTER 6

Civic Dignity and Other Necessary Conditions

Chapters 4 and 5 began to develop an argument, in the form of the civic education offered to the future citizens of Demopolis, for the legitimacy of basic democracy. Along with the basic legitimation demand that the coercive power of the state be justified to each resident, the question that potential citizens should ask, and that the program of civic education must answer, is why a rational person would choose to accept the comparatively high opportunity costs associated with political participation. Basic democracy's legitimacy rests on the claim that it provides both material and nonmaterial goods sufficient to compensate for those costs. Sustaining that claim requires answering "Hobbes's challenge," by showing that collective and limited self-governance by citizens can provide both adequate security and welfare without a third-party enforcer of rules and agreements, and reasons to value nonmaterial democratic goods. I suggested that democracy can meet the challenge through its credible commitment to free exercise of the constitutive human capacities of sociability, reason, and communication. If the argument holds, material goods are provided via the provision of a democratic good.

It remains to explain *how* democracy before liberalism solves the fundamental problem of social cooperation, and how far a basic democracy can be scaled up. If ancient Athens, with its citizenship in the tens of thousands, represents the upper bounds for the citizen population of a basic democracy, the political theory developed in these chapters will be of very limited application, at least at the level of the state.

6.1 CONDITIONS AND VALUES

Long before liberalism ancient Greek democracies delivered prosperity and security without autocracy. But just how did they do it? And how might a city-state sized government be scaled up to the size required by a modern state? The value of addressing those questions extends beyond the intrinsic interest of discovering a mechanism for fitting normative and positive theory to observed facts about the world. In the absence of a satisfactory theory to explain how it is that democracy reliably and robustly solves collective action problems and produces good policy, democratic institutions remain vulnerable to challenges by supporters of autocracy. Since antiquity, democracy's critics have claimed that government by citizens is unreliable in the face of complex problems and severe crises.[1] The apparent advantage offered by "strong and centralized government, in the competent hands of a few true experts" appears more compelling if democrats can offer no answer better than "somehow, we always muddle through," in response to pressing questions about how democracy deals with high-stakes challenges.[2]

How can potential citizens be assured that the "outcome variable" of the historical successes experienced by democratic states arose from the "explanatory variable" of the merits of the system itself, rather than from some unobserved factor (e.g., luck) that may not persist into the future?[3] In addition to demonstrating the intrinsic value of democracy, for example, in the terms of free exercise of constitutive capacities, a basic democracy must include in its civic curriculum a satisfactory explanatory account of how it is that democracy provides security and prosperity under changing conditions. It must explain why the democratic social equilibrium is robust to shocks – both those that arise exogenously and those that emerge endogenously, from ongoing social development.

To answer those "how and why" questions, we return to the four "simple assumptions" sketched in the introduction to the previous chapter. I have so far addressed only the first of these, which concerned human capacities of sociability, rationality, and communication as preconditions of social order. In order to answer the question of how democracy robustly provides material goods, and to fill in the account of democratic goods, we now turn to the other three assumptions: methodological individualism, interdependence as an imperative for cooperation, and mutability of the environments in which societies exist. In the functioning of democratic institutions, the conjunction of these three assumptions is closely related

---

[1] This is the core claim of Schmitt 2004 on "the exception," but also of "civic incapacity" theorists, such as Achen and Bartels 2016.

[2] Runciman 2013 points out the dangers associated with the overconfidence that may attend the demonstrated capacity of a democracy to muddle through various crises – thus leading democrats to believe that all crises can be similarly muddled through.

[3] Of course, a system of policy making and implementation that worked well in the past may not be adequate to address the problems of the future. But the potential future inadequacy of existing approaches (and thus the possibility of productive institutional change) can only be addressed within the framework of a democratic process when citizens understand how the system works. Finding the balance between learning and innovation is a primary challenge for democracy: Ober 2008a.

to basic democracy's necessary conditions, briefly alluded to in Section 3.4: political liberty, political equality, and civic dignity.

This chapter focuses on civic dignity as the condition of being socially accepted as fully worthy of political participation and thereby immune from the disabilities of civic humiliation and infantilization. Civic dignity is a fundamental condition of democracy that, like the free exercise of constitutive capacities to which it is closely related, tends to be obscured within mainstream liberal political theory. Once civic dignity is recognized *as* an independently necessary condition (rather than being subsumed under the rubric of either liberty or equality), it can be seen to do a great deal of work in sustaining democracy. Dignity provides an answer, lacking in Hobbes's theory, for how a government can induce pro-social behavior from individuals who, as a matter of ingrained character (aka, the ordinal ranking of their preferences), gain greater utility from asserting their own superiority and having that superiority acknowledged by others than they do from other aspects of life. Such persons – in Hobbes's terms, those devoted to honor and motivated by "vainglory" – are a serious problem for Leviathan if they value the expression of self-assessed superiority and contempt for others over life itself. The imperative to defend dignity also provides a compelling justification for democratic rules mandating equality in respect to voting and other forms of political participation. And it provides a principled means to reject the claims in respect to distributive justice made by extreme egalitarians and extreme libertarians alike.

Personally, and in agreement with Kantian liberals, among others, I regard dignity, liberty, and equality as intrinsically valuable ends, rather than merely as necessary conditions or instrumental means to other ends. I assume that some of the citizens of Demopolis share that conviction. Others of the citizens may not share that conviction; as we have seen (Section 3.1), Demopolis's Founders had various reasons for rejecting autocracy and diverse value commitments. But my personal value judgments, and those of Demopolis's original citizens, are beside the point.

Basic democracy is, I will argue, good for producing and sustaining the lived conditions of dignity, freedom, and equality, and also likely to increase their value in the eyes of citizens, even if they are *not* highly valued intrinsically or ex ante. That is because, so goes the argument of the civic educators of Demopolis, in light of the assumptions about individuality, interdependence, and mutability, democracy is sustained in a high-performing equilibrium – i.e., will reliably produce adequately high levels of security and welfare – *only* under the political conditions of liberty, equality, and dignity. As such, liberty, equality, and dignity are not *epiphenomenal* conditions that may be optionally and ex post added to democracy if and when they are widely enough recognized as independently valuable. They are *fundamental* practical conditions that are required for sustaining a democratic social equilibrium. The reasons for that dependency arise from a consideration of the implications of individuality, interdependence, and mutability for the organization of knowledge within a democratic community.

6.2 INDIVIDUALITY, INTERDEPENDENCE, MUTABILITY

Individuals with differing and potentially competing interests are *interdependent* because they must cooperate if they are to flourish in a *mutable* environment. This compound assumption follows from the primary claim, defended in the previous chapter, that human capacities prominently include sociability, rationality, and communication. As we have seen, both Hobbes and Aristotle recognized each of those capacities as necessary for human flourishing – although their recognition arose from very different accounts of moral psychology, placed very different emphases on each of the elements in the capacity tricolon, and drew different conclusions from their conjunction. Hobbes argued that the practical interdependence of individuals in a mutable environment yielded a unique solution to the problem of flourishing (or even tolerable) human existence, in the form of the unlimited political authority of a lawless sovereign. That argument proved vulnerable to refutation by reference to history. In this section we consider the three features of individualism, interdependence and mutability to establish *how* a nonautocratic social order might reliably produce security and welfare through mechanisms requiring certain forms of freedom, equality, and dignity.

The methodological individualism with which I am concerned here is a descriptive, rather than a normative, conception of human motivation. It is not to be confused with the *ethical* individualism that contrasts an autonomous will with external motives, and that underpins Kantian liberalism (Williams 1993: Chapter 2). The individualism that matters to me here is not moralized, but it is opposed to sociological or epistemic holism. It assumes that every human group (including ancient Greek city-states: Murray 1990), no matter how apparently culturally and socially homogeneous, is a composite, consisting of diverse individuals, multiple minds, pluralistic identities, and thus, at least potentially, conflicting interests. Social identities are profoundly important to any descriptive account of social order, and no human can ever be uniquely self-invented. But, unlike ants or bees, individual humans are quite capable of identifying their interests as other than those of the community as a whole.

The inherent pluralism of every human community produces disagreement. As we have seen (Section 5.2), this fact was central to Aristotle's, as well as to Hobbes's conception of the problem that political order must solve. Under the right conditions, specified differently by Aristotle and Hobbes, the employment of the human capacities for reason and interpersonal communication will allow for those conflicts to be negotiated peacefully, and common interests to be identified. Hobbes regarded the "differences among private judgments" problem as solved by the unitary will of a sovereign – ideally an individual monarch. Aristotle supposed that it was solved by convergence among many virtuous citizen-rulers (as natural parts) on justice as the common good of the state (as a natural whole). Both regarded education, as a path to social identity formation, self-consciously organized as such by wise rulers, as essential to the goal of gaining agreement.

As Michael Bratman (1999: 93–161; 2014) has shown, joint action can be explained philosophically as a complex shared cooperative activity. Bratman presumes that intentions are held by individuals: Saying that "we intend" to do something, together, means, first, that intentions held by two or more individuals are shared by those persons: X intends to *phi* and Y also intends to *phi*. Shared intention, unlike Rousseau's conception of a "general will," allows for legitimate debate and potentially for substantial disagreement. But in order to act jointly, individuals must not only share certain intentions, they must mesh certain of their subplans, manifest at least minimal cooperative stability, and possess relevant knowledge in common. Bratman's model is predicated on positing a minimal-sized (2-person) face-to-face group undertaking a simple task (painting a house together). But, as Anna Stilz, Emilee Chapman, and other political theorists have recently argued, Bratman's approach to joint action can be scaled up to help explain the collective self-government by citizens of a large democratic state. Voting, for example, is a form of joint action that, when it is properly organized, manifests each of Bratman's conditions.[4]

---

[4] Application of Bratman's theory of joint action to democratic politics: Stilz 2011; to voting: Chapman 2016. I discussed the application of Bratman's joint action model to ancient Athenian democracy in Ober 2008a: Chapter 1, with special reference to the elaboration of Bratman's theories by List and Pettit 2011. See further Ober 2013a. Pettit's complex "dual aspect model" of democracy (Pettit 2013: esp. 285–292), which emphasizes the centrality of the influence and control exercised by a demos, seeks to resolve the ambiguity between the actions (intentional and otherwise) of many individuals in "constituting" a political order, and the resultant "constituted people" as a state-agent that can

The next assumption is that humans are interdependent, and that, under high-stakes conditions, this produces a motive for cooperation. The interdependence with which I am concerned here is a minimum condition, the need that people in a community have for one another if they are to secure the conditions for human existence. Under the right conditions, networks of interdependence can broaden, extending well beyond the bounds of the political community and sustaining conditions far beyond mere survival. But survival comes first. The premises on which this assumption rests have already been discussed (Section 5.1), in reference to Aristotle and Hobbes on the question of the human capacity for social existence. The imperative of cooperation, for the kind of interdependent beings we are, is predicated on the need to create a workable society based on the exchange of credible commitments among its members. If a society is faced with intense competitive pressure or some other existential threat (e.g., severe climate change) and fails to find effective ways to secure an adequately high level of social cooperation, it faces potential elimination (see, further, Ober 2008a: 80–84).

High-stakes conditions, i.e., those involving the existential question of individual and collective survival, increase the imperative to cooperation and thereby increase the likelihood that the members of the community will recognize a common interest in public goods essential to security. Both Aristotle and Hobbes predicated their respective discussions of the origins of human community on high-stakes assumptions. The relatively low-stakes conditions that apparently persisted for much of the post–World War II "end of ideology" era, for the relatively affluent citizens of developed countries, arguably blunted the urgency, for liberal political theory, of the relationship between survival and interdependence.[5] Now, in an age characterized by climate change, economic disruption, religious and ethnic violence, and mass migration, the fundamental "first question" of politics, so obvious to both Aristotle and Hobbes, may be returning to the forefront of theoretical attention.

---

be imagined as having a sovereign will. Pettit distinguishes this constituted agent from Rousseau's notion of a unitary general will and from the related fictive public person that is Hobbes's political sovereign. I have avoided the language of unified wills and popular sovereignty (as a term applied to the locus of authority within a state, as opposed to the legal standing of a country in an ecology of states), on the grounds that those terms obscure more than they explain about the democratic political processes with which I am concerned here. See, further, Espejo 2011: esp. Chapters 2–3.

[5] Of course international relations in the age of nuclear weapons are very high stakes, and yet seemingly lay outside the realm of mainstream political theory, outsourced, as it were, to realist international relations theorists and a few, marginalized, pacifists. On twentieth-century realist political theory in the shadow of nuclear holocaust, see McQueen 2017.

The final assumption is that the environments in which human societies function are typically mutable. Changes in the environment come about via exogenous shock (new rivals, technological change, war, climate change, and so on). Change also comes about endogenously, through the ongoing development of institutions and norms. As rational and communicative human agents gain experience with institutions, both the attitudes of the agents and the institutions they create will change. Some changes may be subtle, others dramatic.[6] The success or failure of a society to innovate promptly and effectively in response to changes in external and internal circumstances directly affects the society's capacity to preserve the security and welfare of its members over time. It must be capable of revising the terms of social cooperation in ways that can respond effectively to new challenges, without crashing the cooperative social order.

The conjoined assumptions of individuality, interdependence, and mutability underline the point that in order to survive in a high-stakes environment, the citizens of a basic democracy must at least meet Hobbes's challenge, which means achieving and sustaining relatively high levels of social cooperation. When compared to absolutism, democracy lacks the resources of centralized command and control, and of unitary third-party enforcement of contracts – that is to say, democracy lacks the Hobbesian sovereign's devices for ensuring a level of social cooperation adequate to provide security and prosperity.

How, then, do democracies, composed of many diverse, interdependent, and masterless individuals, secure public goods substantial enough to meet high-stakes challenges in a mutable environment? Seeking to mimic the advantages enjoyed by a unitary sovereign in regard to centralized command and control is unlikely to be successful. Hobbes was right that a socially diverse demos, and especially a demos that is limited by law, makes a relatively poor showing at centralized command and control. Hobbes was not wrong to claim that, under the right circumstances (e.g., contemporary China) a sovereign unconstrained by law (in this case a small and cohesive group of rulers) can, at least for a while, provide security and increase the welfare of a large society of self-interested individuals. Hobbes's error (the

---

[6] Arresting the process of endogenous change is the fundamental goal of political conservatives, ancient and modern; examples include Plato's *Republic*, in which all change, after the establishment of the ideal state of Callipolis, is degenerative, and *Statesman*, a "second-best" approach to government in the absence of a true expert, predicated on law that will ordinarily be resistant to change. William F. Buckley's mission statement (November 19, 1955) for the conservative *National Review*, stated that, "It stands athwart history, yelling "Stop." By contrast, democrats typically characterize democracy as receptive to change; democratic change may, but need not necessarily, be described as progress toward justice or some other moral goal.

source of his false prediction that no basic democracy could long escape the miserable conditions of the state of nature) was to suppose that the centralized command and control associated with the unitary sovereign is the *unique* solution to the problem of achieving social cooperation at scale in the face of individualism, interdependence, and mutability.

6.3 KNOWLEDGE AND COLLECTIVE ACTION

The rules by which a society is organized bear directly on that society's adaptive capacity. A well-organized basic democracy is able to confound Hobbes's prediction because, under the right conditions, diversity among the judgments of the membership is an asset rather than a liability. Diversity comes into play on the benefit side of the ledger if and when the problems of collective action are solved by a system of limited and collective self-government by citizens (as Aristotle argued that they could be). Under such circumstances, individual citizens possessing diverse knowledge and skills have an incentive to invest in themselves (by deferring short-term gains in favor of more education or training), thereby increasing their own comparative advantages, their community's store of aggregate human capital, and the joint stock of potentially useful knowledge. Once they no longer have reason to fear suffering a "sucker's payoff" (sacrificing utility by naively cooperating with a strategically uncooperative player) in a game with a potentially exploitative autocrat, citizens likewise have good reason to cooperate in solving problems bearing on their common interests in security and welfare by sharing what they know. Democratic conditions of freedom, equality, and dignity promote both rational human capital investments across diverse domains of endeavor, *and* the rational disclosure and exchange of useful knowledge that is made more valuable by those investments.

Because the total membership of a large and diverse society in which individuals have invested in their own education has ready access to a wider array of useful knowledge than any small and relatively homogeneous subset of that society (e.g., a ruler and his elite coalition), and because opening access to knowledge does not endanger the collective rulers of democracy as it does the ruling coalition in a limited-access, autocratic regime, a well-ordered democratic society may potentially be able to solve problems arising from a mutable environment more effectively than an autocrat. The growth of the stock of knowledge useful to problem solving can, at least potentially, offset efficiency gains associated with the autocrat's hierarchical chain of command, and any loss of efficiency inherent in the participation of many individuals in the processes of democratic government (Ober 2008a). Realizing that potential, which requires managing available knowledge such that it is effectively deployed in problem solving, is a matter of institutional and mechanism design, to which we return, below.

But addressing the collective action problem comes first. In order for a democracy to gain the potential to solve major problems of common concern by employing the knowledge resources of a diverse society, the rules and associated cultural habits must give each citizen reason to invest in herself and then to cooperate in sharing what she knows without worrying about a sucker's payoff. Moreover, even after the collective action problem has (*ex hypothesi*) been solved, the relevant rules and habits must be structured so that the right sort of knowledge gets to the right place in the "solution space" and at the right time. A massive and indiscriminate "data dump" of "everything everyone knows" into a problem-solving context may be worse for the goal of devising the best available solution than a shortage of useful knowledge.

The answer to the conundrum of how to achieve masterless social cooperation that is reliably capable of producing public goods at levels adequate to sustain security and welfare through the management of deep, diverse, and dispersed knowledge resources is not simple. It requires each of the three interrelated conditions of liberty, equality, and dignity.

6.4 POLITICAL FREEDOM AND EQUALITY

The political conditions of liberty and equality are strongly associated with democracy as collective self-governance by citizens. For many people, freedom or equality (or both) is the *point* of nontyranny. But even if liberty and equality are not regarded as democracy's ends, when citizens are not free to communicate with one another, speaking their minds and disclosing relevant information on matters of public import, it is hard to say in what sense governance is *by citizens*.[7] If citizens are not in meaningful ways political equals, it is likewise difficult to say in what sense they are *self-governing*.

The close relationship of conditions of political freedom and equality to democracy is confirmed by the historical record: Liberty and equality were

---

[7] The distinction between the civic duty of free speech for a citizen and the duty of an autocrat's subject to suppress his speech is underlined by a passage from Kant: In reference to a command by King Frederick William II to cease writing on the topic of religion, Kant opined, "Repudiation and denial of one's inner conviction are evil, but *silence* in a case like the present one *is the duty of the subject*; and while all that one says must be true, this does not mean that it is one's duty to speak out the whole truth in public." (*AA* 12.406, cited in Kant 1991: 2; emphasis added).

widely recognized as among democracy's core practices, as well as its values, by ancient Greek writers on politics. Both critics of democracy as it was practiced in Athens and other Greek states (e.g., Plato and other political philosophers) and those sympathetic to democracy (e.g., Demosthenes and other political orators) regarded a conjoined commitment to both liberty and equality as preeminently characteristic of democratic states. Liberty, in democratic city-states took the form of freedom of speech and association, as well as freedom from fear of unauthorized intrusion or arbitrary expropriation by powerful state magistrates or by powerful private individuals. Equality was exemplified by having an equal vote, an equal right to speak out in public, and equal access to law, offices, and other public institutions.[8]

Political liberty and equality, shared by members of a diverse community of interdependent individuals who participate regularly and actively in common enterprises, can promote the production of public and private goods at high levels. Under the right institutional conditions, free individuals who need not fear expropriation by a tyrannical government or by rent-seeking elites will rationally invest in the development of their own special skills and talents, thereby increasing the collective return to specialization and comparative advantage, and growing the joint stock of human capital. Equal access to institutions (e.g., dispute resolution procedures) and to public information (e.g., laws governing commercial exchange) drives down transaction costs, by reducing both informational asymmetry and the tendency to partiality (judging similar cases differently) on the part of officials. As the costs of transactions decline, the volume of transactions and the mutual gain from each transaction increase, growing the aggregate wealth of society. Moreover, free and equal citizens who share a common interest in remaining so will, again under the right institutional conditions, rationally share useful information and specialized knowledge when jointly making policy on matters of their common interest. When dispersed and diverse technical and social information and knowledge are disclosed and shared it enables the community to devise better, more innovative solutions to challenges in a changing environment.

As the store of human capital grows, as transaction costs drop, and as better public policy is made on the basis of better information and shared knowledge, the aggregated benefits of social cooperation increase. If a significant part of the benefit is invested in public goods, and insofar as private benefits are distributed broadly (rather than monopolized by elites as

---

[8] See the essays by Ostwald, Hansen, Raaflaub, and Cartledge in Ober and Hedrick 1996.

rents), the community becomes, over time, more secure and more prosperous. This sequence of development is amply documented in the histories of Athens and other democratic Greek city-states.[9]

We will return in Chapter 7 to the question of designing mechanisms that might enable knowledge to be effectively aggregated by a democracy, so as to produce overall better policy. The key to the design solution will be finding ways to employ expertise without risking elite capture of the government, and by paying proper attention to policy failures, as well as to policy successes. The prior question is, however, how a collectivity of masterless citizens can create conditions in which, first, each individual credibly commits to obeying rules requiring costly personal investment in practices that sustain public goods, and, next, each participates in costly punishment of those who break the rules.

6.5 CIVIC DIGNITY AS LIVED EXPERIENCE

Security and prosperity are reliably provided by a democracy only when liberty and equality are reciprocally supportive and when neither principle is maximized at the expense of the other. Under such circumstances, citizens live without fear of expropriation or exploitation and can plan their lives accordingly. Their *equal* political standing is matched by a *high* social standing, so all "stand tall," rather than cowering, either in mutual fear (in a Hobbesian state of nature), or in awe of an unconstrained ruler (under a Hobbesian sovereign). Democratic citizens are simultaneously secure in their political liberty, and in their legal and political equality, when majoritarian power and the powers wielded by individuals and groups are limited by constitutional guarantees ensuring immunity against arbitrary threats to persons or their property.

But, as was foregrounded by the American civil rights movement of the mid twentieth century, and as the experience of police harassment by vulnerable African-American communities makes painfully clear, constitutional guarantees are of practical value only when they pay off in people's lived experience. The post–Civil War amendments to the US Constitution promised freedom and legal equality to all citizens. That promise was belied by the system of indignity sustained by "Jim Crow" rules and racist norms in many American states. In order for freedom and equality to be meaningful, and thus in order for democracy to deliver the basic goods of

---

[9] See Ober 2008a, 2010, 2013a, 2015b for more detailed discussion of how and why liberty and equality increase human capital, drive down transaction costs, and enable effective aggregation of useful knowledge.

security and prosperity, even the weakest and most vulnerable citizens must also be experientially secure in their dignity – in their worthiness as participatory citizens and their daily lived immunity from the disabling burdens of humiliation and infantilization.[10]

I suggested in the first chapter that basic democracy has an implicit ethics. It is in the realm of dignity that the ethical demands of democracy become especially clear, and where the line between political and interpersonal behavior becomes most permeable. A citizen subject to humiliation by the powerful, whether it is a powerful public official or a powerful private individual or syndicate, is not free in the sense required of participatory citizenship. An adult citizen who is subject to having his speech or action treated as if it were that of a child is not in the relevant sense equal. And, as we have seen, without free and equal citizens, it is meaningless to speak of democracy.

The democratic imperative of securing the dignity of each citizen creates rules and habits of enforcement that push back against the demands of right-libertarians for maximizing personal freedom in ways that would effectively disenfranchise the weaker among the citizens. It likewise resists demands by left-egalitarians for maximizing social justice in ways that would endanger the security of citizens' possession of personal property. An appropriate concern for dignity stands guard against the threat to democracy that arises from the employment of majoritarian power to maximize either personal liberties in respect to property or economic equality (Section 6.8).

Dignity also serves to fill in the value set of basic democracy. I have claimed that political forms of liberty and equality must be sustained by basic democracy, as conditions necessary for the regime's continued existence. But the political forms of freedom and equality that are required to sustain a basic democracy are likely to appear unpalatably "thin" to liberals of almost any stripe. Liberal projects typically take the form of thickening freedom and/or equality, by adding to their substantive social content, often under the rubric of autonomy, justice, inherent rights and respective moral duties. Attention to the independent requirements of civic dignity likewise adds substantive content – although not specifically liberal or moral content (contrast Christiano 2008: 138–154) – to the lived experience of democratic citizenship. It does so, moreover, in a way that promotes the development of a sustainable, self-reinforcing social equilibrium among a

---

[10] Police harassment as a fundamental violation of rule of law: Gowder 2016. This section is adapted from Ober 2012.

diverse population of rationally self-interested individuals. In brief, dignity makes basic democracy at once deeper and more robust: Democratic institutions defend dignity, while the habits of dignified citizens provide behavioral foundations for defending democracy and for improving institutions over time.

The concept of civic dignity, as a value and as a set of practices, will be prominent in Demopolis's civic education. The argument of this part of the curriculum is predicated on the idea that the rules defending dignity rest on a shared recognition that indignity is experientially bad for those who suffer it, and bad for democracy. Indignity entails, for the individual, suffering harms, or being liable to suffer harms, as a consequence of being treated with contempt or as a child. When I am subjected to humiliation, I am treated as an inferior by those who seek to assert their own superiority. When I am subjected to infantilization, I am assimilated to the category of those presumed incapable of judging and pursuing their own interests. Insofar as an adult life is characterized by humiliation or infantilization, or by persistent fear of being subject to those conditions, it fails to go well. While dignity may not be a sufficient condition for a life to go well, *ceteris paribus*, lives lived with dignity go better than lives lived without it.

Indignity is bad, not only for individuals, but for democracy as collective self-governance. Humiliation is incompatible with the sort of liberty necessary to sustain democracy because the individual who suffers, or is subject to, humiliation is not in a position to speak out or to associate with others in the frank and open manner demanded by participatory citizenship. If I know that speaking out on certain topics, or associating with certain others, will expose me to public humiliation, unless I am exceptionally courageous – as were, for example, many participants in the American civil rights movement in the mid twentieth century, I am likely to restrain my own speech and forgo those associations. I will defer to those in a position to humiliate me, looking for their permission before speaking or associating, cringing and groveling when I fear that the exercise of my formal political liberties might incur their displeasure. If I do enter the public domain with those who humiliate me, I am unrecognized, invisible; my presence is no more acknowledged than that of a servant at an aristocratic dinner party.[11]

---

[11] Humiliation is a social condition rather than an emotion; it is very different from shame and has a different relationship to politics; on democracy and shame, see Saxonhouse 2006; Tarnopolsky 2010. It is also very different from humility or humbleness: There need be no indignity, for example, in an attitude of humility on the part of a devout person in the presence of a manifestation of divinity, or a secular person confronted by the wonder of nature, or a neophyte before a master practitioner. Choosing humility over pride, or humble circumstances over grandeur, is surely compatible with living without humiliation or infantilization.

Likewise, infantilization is incompatible with the sort of equality necessary to sustain democracy. Democracy is a sham if, when I speak in public, my speech is treated as childish babble, if the information and arguments I advance are accorded no respect despite their salience to the topic of public discussion, or if I am denied access to the information necessary to form a reasoned opinion. Democracy is illusory when citizens are kept in a condition of tutelage, such that their votes are limited to choices among options that have been judged risk-free or have been preapproved by a paternalistic elite. Democracy as collective self-government is sustained only when citizens securely share genuine high standing – when they are free not merely from active interference in their chosen actions but from the threat of humiliation, when their voices are heard, their equal votes count in decisions on salient matters, and when they employ their own judgment in choosing among inherently risk-laden options. The twentith-century civil rights slogan, "I am a man," rejected both humiliation and infantilization by demanding the respect and recognition owed to a adult worthy of participating as an equal in civic society.

Living with dignity involves the regard in which we are held by others, and how we are treated by them. Dignity is manifest in how we behave toward others, and in how they behave toward us. The dignity relevant to democracy is, in substantial measure, a matter of the respect and recognition we publicly accord to one another, through our words and our actions, as persons worthy of political participation. Civic dignity is robust insofar as it is sustained by rational self-interest, well-known and well-respected rules, and internalized norms and habitual behavior developed as a result of living according to those rules. Dignity is transformed in the civic realm, from a scarce resource gained in zero-sum contests or by the whim of a master, to an abundant common pool resource sustained by coordination among those with shared interests in its preservation. It is thereby distinguished from honor. While a basic democracy has good reason to recognize extraordinary public efforts with special honors (Section 6.6), civic dignity establishes a high baseline of respect and recognition for all citizens. By building common knowledge among citizens, and providing incentives for individuals to act in the public good, civic dignity resists devolution into a commons tragedy.[12]

---

[12] Social regard and recognition: Hegel *Philosophy of Right*; dignity as visibility: Ralph Ellison, *Invisible Man* (1952), with Allen 2004. Recognition and dignity: Taylor 1994. Dignity, respect, and reciprocity: Gutmann and Thompson 1996. Social bases of self-respect (rather than self-respect as an attitude toward oneself) included among the primary goods required by citizens in a just society:

Recognition that their own lives do indeed go better under a regime of civic dignity, on the part of citizens who are at risk of suffering indignities under an autocratic regime, provides a rational motive for assuming costs in the defense of the dignity of others. Mobilization of citizens in defense of dignity is facilitated by rules (laws and norms) defining behaviors that constitute violations, specifying remedies, and thereby enabling individuals to coordinate their actions in response to violations. The institutions established by the democratic community must provide both well-understood mechanisms and adequate incentives for individuals (public officials and private citizens alike) to come to the defense of those suffering dignitary harms (e.g., the victims of police intimidation or hate crimes). When the rules are properly structured, any member, or group of members, of a civic community suffering indignity can expect aid from their fellow citizens – most obviously in the guise of their civic peers sitting as a jury in a court of law, but potentially in the form of direct action by individual citizens and by the citizenry collectively.[13]

6.6 A CIVIC DIGNITY GAME

A democratic civic dignity-preserving equilibrium can be modeled in a simple 2- or 3-player game. In this game we assume that there is a rule (law or norm) forbidding indignity and that the rule is common knowledge. We also assume that the society includes persons (of the sort Hobbes supposed were motivated by a prideful desire for self-aggrandizement) who seek confirmation of their own superiority through humiliating others. Assume that person 1 (P1) is a powerful individual (public official or elite private person) who is of that kind, someone who takes pleasure in humiliating relatively weak (poor, obscure, ill-connected) persons.

In the simplest 2-player game, P1 moves first, choosing to respect or humiliate a weaker third party, thereby violating the rule forbidding such behavior. If P1 humiliates, person 2 (P2), an ordinary citizen who knows

Rawls 2001: 58–60. Dignity as a social relation and a fundamental condition (along with material welfare and autonomy) of justice: Cohen 1997; Darwall 2006; Christiano 2008: esp. 63, 93.

[13] Rules established by modern states in defense of dignity include laws against hate crimes. Yet hate crimes are also sometimes opposed by coordinated collective action among citizens; see www.niot .org (accessed March 26, 2016) for examples. Beneath, but complementary to, state law, contemporary organizations, public and private, feature a wide range of rules and mechanisms, formal and informal, for addressing threats to the dignity of their members. Such threats need not rise to the level of criminality to require redress. Codes governing appropriate conduct among employees of modern American universities, for example, prohibit a variety of activities that are not punishable under state law.

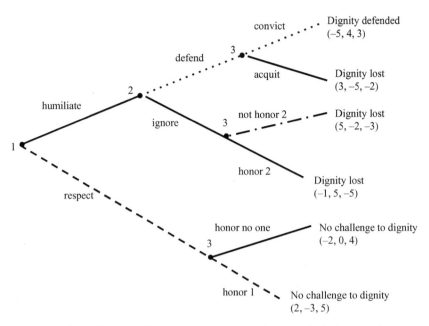

Figure 6.1 Three-player civic dignity game. Players 1 and 2 are rivals for honors. Player 3 is Demos. Preference orderings are shown as quantitative payoffs to each player (1, 2, 3). The dashed line is the equilibrium path. The dotted line is the equilibrium path of the two-person game (played by 2 and 3) if 1 goes off the path by choosing to humiliate. The dash-dotted line is the equilibrium path if 2 goes off the path by choosing to ignore after off-path 1 humiliates.

the rules and witnesses P1's violation, chooses either to defend the third party or to ignore the offense. If appropriately motivated (per discussion, Section 6.5), P2 will choose to defend the third party rather than to ignore the offense. Recognizing that P2's motivation will lead P2 to defend the third party, and that this has blocked P1's most preferred outcome (humiliating without cost), P1 chooses to respect the third party's dignity over paying the high cost of confronting P2's defense. The equilibrium path is thus "P1 respects the third party"; the outcome of the game is "no challenge to dignity" – i.e., no humiliation of the weak third party. The game thus models a dignity-preserving social equilibrium (Ober 2012: 832–835).

The more elaborate 3-player version of the game illustrated in Figure 6.1 adds the chance for special public honors to the equation. This game begins with the same assumptions as the 2-person game about P1 and the third party. As in the previous game, if P1 chooses "humiliate" rather than "respect," P2 chooses whether to oppose the powerful P1. But in this 3-player game P2 requires aid of other citizens if her defense is to succeed. P2 may seek that aid by charging P1 with illegally inflicting indignity in a public trial. P1 and P2 are assumed to be rivals for special public honors (e.g., for reputation or political office), and so they both value public recognition. Player 3 is a Demos with decision authority over cases of illegally inflicted indignity, and over distribution of special public honors. If P1 respects the third party, Demos honors P1 or honors no one. If P1 humiliates the third party and P2 ignores the offense, Demos chooses whether to honor P2 or not. If P2 defends the third party, by bringing P1 to trial, Demos convicts or acquits P1. "Dignity defended" is the outcome if P1 humiliates, P2 defends, and Demos convicts. "Dignity lost" is the outcome if Demos acquits, or if P2 ignores the offense (whether or not P2 is honored). The outcome is "no challenge to dignity" if P1 respects the dignity of the third party (whether or not P1 is honored).

The preferences of each player over the possible outcomes of the game are indicated by the quantities listed in Figure 3.1. The quantity for each outcome represents the value of that outcome for each player (in the order P1, P2, P3: Demos): 5 is excellent; 0 is neutral; -5 is terrible. Each player seeks his highest payoff, in light of the anticipated moves of the other players.

P1's best outcome (payoff of 5) is to humiliate freely *and* see his rival (P2) denied honors; the assumption is that honors for P2 were proposed, but rejected by Demos. Next best (3) is acquittal; this is inferior to his best outcome because of the cost of undergoing the trial. Third (2) is to forgo humiliating but to gain valued public honors; the assumption is that P1, like P2, does desire public honors. Fourth (-1) is to gain the outcome of freely humiliating only at the high cost of seeing his rival honored. Fifth (-2) is to forgo challenging dignity without gaining honors; the assumption is that no honors were proposed. Worst (-5) is to incur the very high cost of a legal conviction.

P2's best outcome (payoff of 5) is to gain honors without cost to herself. Her next best outcome (4) is to defeat her rival and enhance her own reputation by gaining a conviction in the trial. Third, she is indifferent (0) to a world in which dignity is unchallenged and no one is honored. Fourth best (-2) is being denied honors. Fifth (-3) is seeing her rival honored. Worst (-5) is P1's acquittal, meaning that her rival gains his preferred outcome and gains in reputation at P2's expense.

P3: Demos most prefers (payoff of 5) the situation in which there is no challenge to dignity and pro-social behavior by citizens is honored. Demos prefers honoring over not-honoring because honors are expected to enhance the willingness of citizens to pay the potentially high costs of active civic engagement. Next best (4) is no challenge to dignity without granting honors. Third best (3) is convicting a violator: The gains (the spectacle of the trial, public revenue from fines) exceed the costs of mounting a trial. Fourth (−2) is an acquittal in the trial: Although Demos's authority has been asserted by holding a trial, P1 may violate again. Fifth (−3) is for dignity to be lost without a trial and P2 to be denied honors. Worst (−5) is for dignity to be lost and P2 to be honored despite her egregious failure to engage in the pro-social action of defense.

The equilibrium of this game is as follows: Since the ordering of Demos's preferences will lead P2 to defend if P1 humiliates, P1's best option is "no challenge (and being honored)," which is the predicted outcome. The equilibrium path (Figure 3.1, dashed line) is P1, respect; Demos, honor P1. As in the simpler 2-player game on which the 3-player game is based, this game is Nash subgame perfect. But if P1 goes *off* the equilibrium path by choosing to humiliate, in the resulting two-party subgame the equilibrium path (Figure 3.1, dotted line) is P2, defend; Demos, convict; and the predicted outcome is "dignity defended." "Dignity lost" is the predicted outcome only if P2 goes off-path by ignoring the offense when off-path P1 humiliates; in this case the equilibrium path is "not honor 2" (Figure 3.2, dash-dotted line).

This extended game obviously oversimplifies the conditions pertaining in any real society, no matter how democratic. In the real world there will always be "off-path" behavior, because humans do not act as perfectly rational and fully informed agents. But through simplification the game illustrates how democratic institutions (rules forbidding indignity and Demos as collective actor), along with civic norms in which pro-social competition in the form of rivalry for public honors is validated, provide behavioral foundations for defending civic dignity.

As we saw (Section 4.3), persons with a passionate desire for recognition of their self-assessed superiority are likely to be malcontent in a society ruled by a Hobbesian monarch or coalition: The honor lover is reduced to an equality of low status in the presence of the sovereign before whom all are as servants before a master. Honors, when granted, and dishonor are at the sovereign's whim. Moreover, it will be difficult for the sovereign to prevent malcontents from acting on their desire for self-aggrandizement. The sovereign will find it difficult to monitor and thereby suppress the kind contemptuous behavior that will, as Hobbes recognized, lead to destabilization of the regime. The sovereign's agents cannot always be everywhere. Their own tendency to excessive pride may, furthermore, reduce the likelihood that they will loyally fulfill the sovereign-principal's wishes. Thus Leviathan is less stable than would be the case if human behavior were reliably predicted by a universal preference ordering in which fear of death invariably came first. Hobbes's own realism about human psychology threatens to undermine his rational contract thought experiment.

Basic democracy does not suffer those disabilities. The individual honored by the demos for extraordinary public service is thereby elevated, in public esteem although not in civic dignity, above others. The recipient of honors is not belittled by the inherent and unreachable superiority of a monarch or elite ruling coalition. As the game illustrates, the demos has good reason to honor and to withhold honors in a consistent and predictable way. Moreover, ordinary citizens can be virtually everywhere, always, as monitors and first responders to dignitary threats. And they have rational reasons to pay the costs of responding to those threats, if and when they occur. In a real society, of course, people may have reasons to defend the dignity of others that are not based in self-interest. A regime of dignity may be reinforced and extended by motivations of moral outrage or disinterested altruism. But the dignity-preserving civic order modeled by the game does not, in the first instance, depend on that reinforcement.

6.7 DIGNITY AND CIVIC VIRTUES

Because calling to account individuals or corporate bodies that seek to humiliate others entails risk (the possibility of retaliation by the violators and their allies), it demands a certain level of courage. The defense of civic dignity therefore engages a corresponding virtue of civic courage (Balot 2014). Yet civic dignity does not place an extraordinary burden of courage on individual citizens: No one need be super-courageous (in the way that some participants in the civil rights movement so clearly were) so long as other citizens can and will coordinate their actions, by establishing and supporting rules that enable a ready response to dignitary threats. As a citizen of a community with well-structured rules, I can reasonably expect members of my community to act (and to have acted, preemptively, by establishing the right institutions) in defense of my dignity. They do so, in part, because they recognize that it is in their own interest as individuals who (1) may in turn be threatened by the arrogance of the strong,

(2) are concerned with the defense of their own dignity, and (3) recognize that defense of dignity requires the aid of fellow citizens. Civic dignity is thus at once virtuous, reciprocal, and rational.[14]

In a basic democracy the responsibility of a group of civic peers to maintain the dignity of each and all is specified in law and in political culture. The law serves as a focal point (the term is that of Schelling 1980 [1960]) enabling the actions of officials and citizens to be effectively coordinated (Weingast 1997). Because the mutuality of responsibility for responding to dignitary threats is common knowledge, when I choose to act in another's defense I can assume that my choice accords with the preferences and interests of my fellow citizens, and that my actions will be coordinated with theirs. By coming to another's defense I am not, therefore, naively subjecting myself to a sucker's payoff. And so, once again, our collective dignity, as a citizen body, is guaranteed by the rational commitment of each individual to the system that guarantees his and her own welfare.

Sustaining a regime of respect and recognition among an extensive population of diverse individuals entails a second civic virtue: self-restraint (in classical Greek ethics: *sophrosune*). As citizens, we ought voluntarily to restrain ourselves from self-aggrandizing actions that compromise another's dignity. Once again, rationality limits the demands placed on individual virtue. As citizens, although we may each have an impulse to the sort of arrogant self-aggrandizement that Hobbes regarded as endemic, we rationally restrain ourselves from acting upon that impulse for three overlapping reasons: First, because we know the rules, and we know that many others are monitoring our behavior and will respond if we violate the rules: We expect to be punished for infractions. Next, because having been educated by the rules, our time horizon has extended: We have come to believe that it is in our real, long-term interest to deny ourselves short-term gratification at the expense of the dignity of others. And third, having internalized dignity as a motivational norm, acting arrogantly is no longer a simple source of pleasure: We are less likely to be gratified, at least in any straightforward sense, by behaving in ways that humiliate or infantilize others.[15]

The key to sustaining a regime of civic dignity is a joint commitment to, and an agreement on the definition of, right action in respect to dignity and

---

[14] The idea that the weak may coordinate to restrain the strong few was well known in Greek political thought: cf. Plato *Gorgias* 483b–e.

[15] Cf. Plato, *Statesman*, where civic order is predicated on a balance between courage and moderation. Self-restraint/moderation (*sophosune*) is one of the four classical virtues (along with courage, wisdom, and justice), a virtue that was embodied, in democratic Athenian evaluative vocabulary, by the middling/moderate/dignified (*metrios*) citizen. Here, and elsewhere, I draw on Aristotle's (*Nicomachean Ethics*) theory of ethical training by habituation and practice (*askesis*).

threats to it. Mutual recognition of our common interest in sustaining the system of civic dignity leads each of us to assume some responsibility for doing so. Each of us acknowledges that we have some duties to one another and to the community, and we each grasp that doing our duty is also a rational choice, given the established institutional and cultural conditions. If each of us does the right thing, acts correctly, and thus fulfills those duties, then our dignity is sustained in common. If we coordinate our behavior by using legal rules as focal points for aligning choices and actions, then no one is so strong as to be able to break the rules with impunity, and no one is left unprotected – no matter how individually weak he or she may be. Our commitment and agreement are strengthened when we each recognize that our dignity is sustained through coordination that is strengthened rather than weakened by competition on the part of the ambitious over a scarce resource – that is, public honors, rather than the nonrival public good of civic dignity.

The system is reinforced by reputation effects when citizens join in blaming and sanctioning those who fail to do their part in sustaining the regime of dignity, while praising and rewarding those whose service in its defense is outstanding.[16] Civic dignity need not be opposed to the desire to excel or to the expectation that individuals who do excel will be appropriately recognized for achievement. As the three-player game, cited above, suggests, civic dignity creates space for recognizing extraordinary merit and for according special honors to those who both desire and deserve them. An appropriately restrained version of competitive meritocracy may flourish within a regime of civic dignity, so long as the drive to publicly acknowledged excellence remains oriented toward pro-social ends.

Likewise, the concern for defense of civic dignity among a body of citizens need not dull the concern felt by citizens for the dignity of those outside the citizen body. Indeed, citizens have a rational interest in protecting the dignity of noncitizens when their lives are bound up in networks of interdependence and/or intimacy with those of noncitizens, or when citizens are not readily distinguished from noncitizens. In order to defend citizen interests, a basic democracy may extend legal protection beyond the ranks of the citizens themselves (Ober 2005a: Chapter 5). Complacent or vicious forms of localism may emerge within a body of citizens (Kateb 2006). But by the same token, sensitivity to threats to civic dignity may lead to, or sharpen, recognition of the value of human dignity (Ober 2012: 844).

---

[16] On the prosocial role of esteem and disesteem, cf. Brennan and Pettit 2004.

The case of civic dignity demonstrates how democracy is sustained in a self-reinforcing equilibrium (however imperfectly realized) in a population of (more or less) self-interested individuals. The regime rests on the reasonably rational and well-informed choices of citizens who know that they themselves may be faced with threats. Each individual predictably acts in ways that sustain the regime, paying the costs of responding to threats, because each reasonably expects that his own life will go better if he does so. Common knowledge of rules enables coordination among a diverse set of individual social actors, while the opportunity to gain civic honors as a reward for extraordinary service encourages individual initiative.

6.8 BETWEEN LIBERTY AND EQUALITY

The citizens of Demopolis are expected to act, in their role as citizens, as responsible adults, and they expect to be treated accordingly. Thus the rules of Demopolis, and the education that is meant to justify those rules, are nonpaternalistic. To be treated as an adult, without being subject to paternalistic intervention, is to be free to make decisions that entail risks of a sort that a parent would rightly seek to prevent a child from taking, and to access information that a parent might keep from a child. The parent reasonably assumes that the child is likely to make relatively poor risk assessments as a result of an incompletely developed capacity to weigh potential costs against anticipated benefits or to make appropriate use of information. The parent's protective role will often include withholding certain kinds of information that might lead the child to act in ways likely to harm herself (e.g., how to turn on a stove, start a car, load a gun).

The adult citizen cannot be assumed to have an infallible capacity to assess risk or to process information. The government of a democratic state may seek to protect adult citizens against some risks without infantilizing them. It may keep some information secret for legitimate reasons of state security. It may require motorists to wear seat belts. Yet because dignity is a necessary condition of democracy, a democratic state cannot be a paternalistic state; it must as a rule allow citizens to make their own choices and must justify exceptions to that rule.[17]

---

[17] Dignity-based rejection of paternalism does not prevent governments from encouraging pro-social behaviors, e.g., by using "opt out" rather than "opt in" when designing forms by which citizens choose whether to donate their organs in case of accidental death (Kahneman 2011: 373). Nor does it eliminate a government's legitimate authority to discourage some forms of personal risk taking. My dignity is not seriously compromised when I am legally required to use seat belts when driving because the imposition is slight and the joint and several benefit is obvious. But civic dignity does

Making one's own choices in various domains (politics, finance, occupation, interpersonal relations, sport) entails risk. Taking risks, and accepting the consequences of making inherently risk-laden choices, is a basic condition of acting as a dignified adult and as a responsible citizen. If we are to live with dignity we must, therefore, have the opportunity to make, and participate in making, risk-laden choices that affect us, and our community, in important ways. Adults are expected to make generally better assessments than are young children. Yet we can never completely control our environment; everyone is chronically exposed to error (our own and those of others) and the vagaries of fortune. When making choices, we try to calculate risk by reasoning, communicating, and assessing the plans of others. Our assessments are imperfect, subject to bias, and contingency may upset the most careful calculation (Kahneman 2011). But assessments of risk remain fairly rational insofar as they are based on good reasons and good information. They will be better yet, if we learn to recognize sources of systematic bias in our own and others' reasoning. Information comes to agents in various ways; the information needed to assess risk and to control for bias comes from both private and from public sources. In a civic community, important public information includes well-publicized rules and common knowledge of norms and habits.

Civic dignity protects each citizen's authority to make *personal* choices affecting him or herself and, acting as a participatory citizen, to make *public* choices affecting the community. It enables adults to act *as* adults in using information and assuming risks. The role of civic dignity in forbidding the sorts of infantilization that would deny adults the opportunity to make risk-laden private and public choices is what enables democracy's dignity to play a beneficial regulatory role in respect to liberty and equality. Non-infantilization allows for judging between opposing claims of liberty and equality by preventing the hypertrophy of either condition when it threatens to treat adults as child-like wards. The demands of noninfantilization push back against the emergence of an intrusive nanny state bent on eliminating all vestiges of inequality on the one hand, and against the willful perpetuation of gross inequalities in the name of individual liberty on the other.[18]

---

limit the scope of public authority: To the extent that a regulation aimed at limiting risk verges upon infantilization, it threatens dignity.

[18] I follow Williams 2005: Chapter 9 ("Conflicts of Liberty and Equality"), against Rousseau and Dworkin, in supposing that there can (and will) be conflicts between liberty-based and equality-based claims within a state that is accepted as legitimate by its citizens.

Living with dignity means that each of us must be free to make conse-quential choices in various inherently risk-laden domains. We must have the option to decide whether to do something or not and whether to vote for this or that candidate or policy, based on our own assessment of risk and advantage. Our dignity is preserved – we avoid the indignity of being treated as children who must be protected from knowing things that might lead us to take excessively risky courses of action – when each of us has ade-quate access to information relevant to our choices. Given the importance of public information in risk assessment, citizens (especially those serving in public office) are responsible for making relevant information available to one another. Our dignity is threatened by deceptions that trick us into accepting personal risks (e.g., dangerous investment decisions) or collective risks (e.g., dangerous public policies) that we would not have undertaken had we been in possession of better information.

Deception and obfuscation are especially destructive of dignity when perpetrated by public authorities. Officials infantilize citizens when they deny them access to relevant information, or present them with false infor-mation, e.g., when obscuring the risks inherent in a given course of private investment or public policy.[19] Yet, on the other hand, dignity is also threat-ened by public-authority paternalism that purports to eliminate all effects of chance and risk from our lives or choices. A system of public authority that deprives individual citizens of the opportunity to take certain courses of action or to vote in favor of them, based on their individual assessments of risk and chance of gain, assaults their dignity. It does so by treating them as wards, in need of a government-appointed guardian due to a presumed incapacity to employ reason and information when making choices impor-tant to themselves and to their community.[20]

As we have seen (Sections 3.4 and 6.4), liberty (of choice, especially in respect to speech and association) and equality (of standing and opportu-nity, especially in respect to law and public decision making) are necessary conditions for democracy. But how does a democracy choose the correct course when the demands of liberty and equality come into conflict? How ought democratic citizens choose among policy options when freedom and

---

[19] Aristotle *Politics* 1278a24–40, 1297a7–13 objects to public deception of citizens by rulers for similar reasons. His position is, of course, at odds with that of Plato in the *Republic*, where Callipolis is sustained by noble lies. The systematic misinformation that was foisted upon the American citizenry (as well as the rest to the world) by the George W. Bush administration as a justification for the American invasion of Iraq, and the many lies spread by Donald Trump and his administration, are, when viewed in this light, attacks on civic dignity.

[20] See Anderson 2007 on the need to retain some element of risk in establishing distribution ranges in democratic egalitarianism.

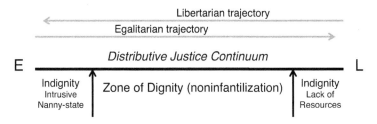

Figure 6.2 Constraints on distributive justice. The continuum of distributive justice ranges from full equality (E) to complete liberty (L). The libertarian trajectory pushes to the left; the egalitarian trajectory pushes to the right. Dignitarian considerations set limits to how far either E or L can be pushed along those trajectories. The impermissibility of indignity for the democratic regime defines the limits to the ambitions of both egalitarians and libertarians. The Zone of Dignity, between the vertical arrows, is the range within the continuum at which noninfantilization is preserved for citizens. That zone thus defines the acceptable range of policy options for democratic distributive justice. The demos of a basic democracy may choose to set its distributive policy anywhere on the continuum within the Zone of Dignity, but not outside it.

equality cannot simultaneously be maximized? The way in which the principle of dignity constrains policy options within the distributive justice continuum by forbidding infantilization is illustrated in Figure 6.2.

The threat that paternalism offers to dignity provides one line of argument against mandatory forms of egalitarianism that seek entirely to eliminate the effects of chance from people's lives, whether by radically limiting the power of individuals to make their own risk-laden choices, or by completely obviating the effects of those choices. Policy that attempts to expunge all effects of chance upon opportunity (e.g., by eliminating all effects of upbringing or educational attainment), or that attempts to enforce perfectly equal outcomes, requires extensive paternalistic interventions in people's lives. Such interventions patently violate noninfantilization. Civic dignity is based on the equal public standing of citizens as members of a political community, but it sets strict limits on the scope of public paternalism as a legitimate means to achieve the end of distributive equality. Looking ahead, to the question of what "democracy before liberalism" can offer to liberals (as well as to nonliberals who prefer nontyranny; Chapter 8), a theory of basic democracy can therefore supplement arguments within liberal theory (notably Rawls's ordinal ranking) for why liberty's claims must sometimes trump those of equality.[21]

---

[21] Rawls 1971, 1996, 2001. See, further, Anderson 1999, 2007. Luck egalitarians seek to avoid the problems associated with equality of outcome by focusing on the value of equality of opportunity, which

By the same token, however, civic dignity requires a government to ensure that all citizens have access to resources adequate to enable them to make consequential public and private choices and otherwise to participate as citizens by taking up demanding and inherently risk-laden political roles in their community. Individuals who are deprived of the basic material goods necessary for them to live decently and to plan for the future are at least as limited in their choices as are the ward-like subjects of a nanny state. Redistributive public welfare policies that ensure that all are provided with adequate food, shelter, personal security, education, and health care promote dignity by enabling individuals to make meaningful personal choices, take calculated risks, and participate in the public domain. Securing the dignity of citizens requires public provision of resources adequate to ensure individual citizens both the opportunity for a reasonable level of calculated private risk taking (e.g., deferring short-term gains by investing in education that may, but may not, lead to greater future gains), and the opportunity for participation in public affairs.

Dignity thus provides a bulwark against excessively strong forms of free-market libertarianism. Dignity limits individual liberty insofar as it is necessary to ensure that all citizens can make consequential choices and participate fully, as citizens, in their community. In so doing, it provides at a minimum the basic material goods (the white box of Figure 3.2) without which lives cannot go even reasonably well.[22]

By resisting extremes of liberty (state neglect) or equality (state paternalism), basic democracy seeks a middle ground in which each individual enjoys at least as much liberty and as much equality as is compatible with a dignified life for all. As noted in the first chapter, democracy before liberalism does not provide a specific conception of distributive justice. But it is provided with a principled mechanism for managing the opposing demands of egalitarian and libertarian conceptions of justice.

As with other aspects of democracy before liberalism, the theory of civic dignity offered here is supported (although not proved) by the historical record. Although the ancient Greek language lacks a fully elaborated

---

is meant to ensure that people have real choices to make. The idea is that all begin at the same point (say, identical genes, upbringing, education, wealth, and income); what they choose to do subsequently is their own responsibility. Yet, as Anderson points out in response to her luck-egalitarian critics, the strict brute luck/option luck distinction fails, since any point on a life path might be regarded as a new beginning, requiring a restart to perfect equality. The result will be that individual choices have no impact, thus confounding the whole point of luck egalitarianism, which was to preserve choice.

[22] A similar argument for an economic minimum and against strong libertarianism is made, on different grounds, by Christiano 2008: 112–116, 261, 272–274.

vocabulary of dignity to match that of liberty and equality, the fundamental concerns regarding humiliation and infantilization, sketched above, are very well represented in democratic Athenian legal discourse concerned with honor (*time*), the act of "dishonoring" (*hubris*), and the appropriate personal and public responses to each. In classical Athens, citizens who actively sought honors through performing prosocial acts of exceptional public courage and generosity could expect to be granted formal public recognition (Whitehead 1993; Lambert 2011; Domingo 2016). On the other hand, acts on the part of empowered magistrates or arrogant individuals that were regarded as threatening to the high civic standing of citizens were subject to legal sanction, and likely to provoke a lively response on the part of responsible citizens.[23]

In the next chapter, we turn to the question of how a direct democracy might sustain the institutions and practices of participatory self-government and civic dignity while simultaneously reaping the benefits of expert inputs into decision making and public policy, and avoiding elite capture. The historical example of classical Athens will, once again, provide a way to frame some of the issues involved in answering that question. But in order to make the argument that a theory of basic democracy is relevant to modernity, I will need to show that it need not be premised entirely on the directly democratic procedures or the small scale typical of ancient city-states.

---

[23] I discuss the Athenian evidence for the discourse and practice of defending dignity in Ober 2000 (= 2005a: Chapter 5), 2012: 840–843.

CHAPTER 7

Delegation and Expertise

The imperatives of civic participation and civic dignity require basic democracy to reject state-sponsored paternalism. The citizens must make their own decisions and take responsibility for them. If the citizens, collectively, act in a childish manner, there is no grown-up to whom they may turn when things go wrong. There is no wise navigator with a firm hand on the tiller of the ship of state (in Plato's famous metaphor), no technocratic elite of bureaucrats ready to take charge of matters in the event of the failure of the political process. Yet, in common with every regime that exists in a mutable and competitive environment, a basic democracy requires expertise if it is to gain and keep security and prosperity.

Basic democracy can hope to leverage the "wisdom of the many," but it cannot make do without deep expertise in many arcane domains relevant to public policy. The counsel of experts must, moreover, be acquired without sacrificing the nonpaternalistic conditions of citizen self-governance. The ancient Athenians devised mechanisms enabling the directly democratic institutions of government to access specialized expertise, but nonpaternalism does not require an Athens-style direct democracy. The citizens of a large-scale modern basic democracy can delegate authority for ordinary legislation to elected representatives. They must, however, establish institutional safeguards to ensure that representatives and experts do not undermine the legitimate authority of the demos. That means the demos must be capable of governing.[1]

7.1 SLEEPING SOVEREIGN OR VIGILANT DEMOS?

If we are to judge by Greek history, in times of crisis the demos's ordinary confidence in its own collective judgment may give way to confusion.

---

[1] Athenian use of experts: Pyzyk 2015; Ismard 2015. Shapiro 2016: 75–78 emphasizes the requirement of recruiting expertise in policy making while avoiding elite capture.

Confusion can open the way for the emergence of a populist leader, one who promises to act in the demos's name, to give voice to its deepest desires, and to provide the paternal authority that democracy had previously lacked. In the *Republic* (Books 8–9) Plato warned that democracy breeds tyrants. He described a cycle of regimes in which the characteristic habits of freedom- and equality-loving democrats ended in the most vicious and repressive sort of tyranny. Plato's hypothetical scenario did not play out in real-world Athens (the brief tyranny of the Thirty after the Peloponnesian War was imposed by Sparta, not chosen by the Athenians), but tyranny has often been a successor to democracy, in antiquity and modernity.

Fear that an incompetent demos will make very bad public policy, and/or that democracy will give birth to tyranny, motivates theories that require delegation of authority by citizens to a representative to be a once-and-forever choice. As Luc Foisneau (2016) has emphasized, this was Thomas Hobbes's position in *Leviathan*. The thought experiment that establishes Hobbes's lawless ruler starts with a binding majority decision by those who will be the sovereign's subjects, as soon as the contract is made. At the decisive moment, the demos surrenders its decision authority in a final and irrevocable manner. Only if a sovereign (whatever its form) irrationally demands the death of otherwise obedient subjects are they freed from their contract; at that point they return to the anarchic state of nature.

Richard Tuck (2016) draws on early-modern political theory to argue that modern democracy was invented by conceiving the demos's delegation of authority as creating a "sleeping sovereign." The idea is that the people retain sovereign authority, but are completely removed from the activity of government. A participatory democrat will regard this demos-sovereign's sleep as a coma that is, in all relevantly political respects, indistinguishable from death. Yet even if the demos should awaken from its slumber, on Hobbes's account rational self-interest will dissuade the citizens from interfering with the government of any but a murderous ruler. Contemporary liberal political theory likewise seeks to separate government from the people's ultimate sovereignty by appealing, variously, to the role of constitutional checks and balances, independent judicial and regulatory agencies, and the Burkean ideal of competent representatives governing without interference from their constituents in the intervals between elections.[2]

The original idea of the sleeping sovereign arose, as Tuck (2016) shows, in monarchical regimes struggling with the fact of the king's individuality and mortality. An individual sovereign must sleep but does not

---

[2] For example Hardin 1999; Shapiro 2016: 2–16; Achen and Bartels 2016.

relinquish his monarchical authority while unconscious. More problematically, an individual sovereign may be an infant, or captured and imprisoned, and thereby lack the capacity to issue orders to subjects. Conceptually separating the monarch's legitimate authority from the process of governing the state solved the dilemma.

A demos is a collectivity; the problem of the monarch's troubling individual liability to the vicissitudes of ordinary mortality does not arise in a democracy. Because a demos is, in Aristotle's terms, "many-footed and many-handed and possessing many sense-capacities" (*Politics* 3.11.1281b5), it is not subject to the ills that gave rise to the sleeping sovereign metaphor. A participatory demos can remain vigilant and it must be able to revoke delegated authority without incurring the costs of anarchy. Indeed, it is that vigilance and readiness to respond that defines the duty of participation in a basic democracy in which legislative authority has been delegated to representatives. The demos, like the many-eyed guardian giant of Greek mythology, Argos Panoptes, can and must remain ever-watchful. The myth, in which the giant was bewitched into slumber and then killed in his sleep by the trickster-god Hermes at the behest of tyrannical Zeus, reminds the citizens of Demopolis that they must not be lulled into sleepy inattention by rhetorical incantations, no matter how divine. Moreover, as in the case of civic dignity, when a violation of the terms of delegated authority is observed, the citizenry must be ready to respond.

In light of the demos's unsleeping invigilation of its representatives, the question arises of how the citizens of a basic democracy can make use of experts, or of expertise that is not codified in ways that would make it readily available to ordinary citizens. Why does the shadow of the demos's constant watchfulness not drive experts, along with their tacit, embodied expert knowledge, from the political system? Without access to expertise, democracy will suffer from a fundamental sort of ignorance. And suffer it does, as we will see, in the opinion of critics of citizens' epistemic limits. How can basic democracy answer that damning charge?

The question of expertise is related the issue of participation. The first rule of Demopolis is that all citizens participate in the work of sustaining collective self-government (Section 3.3). The citizens of Demopolis assent to paying basic democracy's participation costs because they view those costs as essential to the preservation of the three ends for which their state exists, and because they view participation as a benefit. But because they also demand adequate opportunity to pursue projects far removed from their civic life, the burdens of government on citizens must be limited by an opportunity cost constraint. In a small state, like classical Athens, a limited level of direct participation in government by citizens, in legislative assembly, on juries, and in allotted offices, enabled the democracy to achieve the ends of security and prosperity. Athenian citizens had space to pursue their own projects and democratic Athens did well, compared to its city-state rivals, without the need to delegate jurisdiction to elected representatives and without an elaborate government bureaucracy. It is, however, difficult to imagine that regular and direct participation by all citizens could provide an effective day-to-day government for a large, complex, modern nation state. If it is to meet the challenges of scale and complexity that come with modernity and make use of specialized expertise, basic democracy must be able to delegate authority.

7.2 SYSTEMATIC CORRUPTION AS A TYRANNY THREAT

Suppose that, during or subsequent to the establishment of the basic rules sketched in Chapter 3, the constitution of Demopolis has been elaborated so as to allow for delegation of political authority from the demos to representatives. I do not specify the form of representation. Representatives might be chosen in competitive elections (by one of the voting methods employed by modern states or proposed by decision theorists) or by some form of random sampling (as has been suggested by reformers seeking to make democracy more effective). Nor do I specify the extent to which representatives track the preferences of an electorate, as opposed to exercising independent judgment. Suffice it to say that the representatives will exercise delegated authority to establish, execute, and to enforce public policy and that the ends for which the state exists remain those specified in the first chapter: prosperity, security, and nontyranny.[3]

The nontyranny requirement means that exercise of authority by representatives is subject to the condition that the representatives do not violate the terms under which administrative jurisdiction was delegated to them. Those terms will have specified, at a minimum, that representatives do not establish policy that is against the demos's interests. Some public policy made by the representatives will benefit only a part of the demos. But representatives may not make and enforce rules that advance their *own* interests, unless doing so is in the interest of the demos as a whole, as expressed in the three ends of the state. That is to say, a representative who acts as a self-interested part, seeking to satisfy its own partial interests at the expense of the common interests of the whole of the citizenry, will have violated the

---

[3] Political theory of representation: Pitkin 1967; Manin 1997; Urbinati 2006.

terms under which authority was delegated by the demos. If that violation goes unchallenged, the state will, in effect, have a master, and the end of nontyranny is forfeit.

Under some circumstances, representatives who violate the terms of their appointment may be removed through familiar electoral processes, by retrospectively "voting the bums out." Competitive party politics is a common mechanism that facilitates removal of unsatisfactory representatives from office by a citizenry. Under other circumstances, a constitution designed to balance the various powers of government against one another may be adequate to address violations; for example, judicial process that serves to remove a corrupt legislator.[4] But neither electoral competition nor constitutional checks and balances will be effective if an entire political class has come to identify its own interest, as a class, as other than the interest of the people. This circumstance can be regarded as a special case of systematic corruption. I leave to one side the question of whether systematic corruption of this sort of is an actual feature of contemporary democratic systems (as some critics assert), or only a theoretical possibility. In either case, the possibility that a political class might coordinate to capture the government, becoming a de facto tyrant, must be addressed by basic democracy.[5]

To prevent elite capture arising from systematic corruption, the demos must be in a position to revoke its delegation of authority to representatives. That revocation need not be comprehensive or permanent. Here we consider the case of legislative representatives who have failed to act on some matter of pressing public concern. In some such cases, legislative authority might be re-delegated to another part of the government (e.g., judicial commission, executive order, or competent government agency). But in order to make the threat of revocation credible, the demos itself must be able to make the decision of what to do about legislative or other governmental malfeasance that threatens to devolve into tyranny. And this means that the citizens must be vigilant and able to function, at least for a limited time, as a collective ruler. The regime must live up to the original

---

4 Majoritarian competition: Shapiro 2016. In Shapiro's Schumpterian theory, governing is the job of competent and competitive elected elites, who are rewarded or punished in periodic elections. This assumes accurate retrospective voting, which Achen and Bartels 2016: Chapters 4–7 seek to show is uncommon in modern democracy. Starr 2007 offers a survey of the familiar republican processes of balance of powers and checks and balances.
5 Systematic corruption is generally defined as the corruption of the economic system by politics, or vice versa: Wallis 2008. Here I abstract from any particular mechanism that might allow a political class to coordinate in its own partial interest against the common interest of the demos as a whole.

meaning of democracy as "the capable demos" (Section 2.2). The people must be ready to make and enforce their own rules.[6]

7.3 A DELEGATION GAME

The requirement for the demos to retain direct self-governing capability if the democracy is not to be vulnerable to capture by a self-interested representative is illustrated in a simple 3-player game. The players are Nature (N), Representative (R), and Demos (D). Nature here is understood as a prior history of institutional design and civic education. Nature is put in the game as a player only for convenience of illustration; Nature has no preferences over outcomes and does not make choices based on the expected moves of other players in this game. The choices made by Nature are determined by the history of the democratic state before the beginning of the game.

The four possible outcomes of the game are the status quo of representative democracy, tyranny (elite capture), direct democracy (following a revocation of authority delegated to representatives), and an anarchic Hobbesian state of nature. The game form and the payoffs for each outcome to Representative and to Demos are illustrated in Figure 7.1. The game has two starting points, depending on whether Demos is capable or incapable of self-rule. In either case, we assume that Demos has delegated authority for the conduct of government to a Representative (say, an elected body of legislators), conditional on the Representative not violating the terms of delegation. The players' preferences over outcomes, in the order Representative, Demos, are indicated in Figure 7.1.

R's preferred outcome is tyranny, i.e., to rule without constraints. This outcome requires that R violate without D revoking R's authority. R's second-best outcome is the status quo of representative democracy, in which R retains government authority contingent on D's approval. R's third best is direct democracy; the individual members who make up R are citizens, and (assuming they have not been stripped of their standing as a result of violation) they stand to gain the same benefits as other citizens.

---

[6] Shapiro 2016: Chapter 4 argues that republican "balancing institutions" will not get the job done. Liberals may, legitimately, be concerned that the revocation of delegated authority to representatives could result in decisions that are less respectful of human rights. Hainmueller and Hangartner 2013, for example, show that naturalization decisions made by directly democratic municipal assemblies in Switzerland were more likely to discriminate against individuals on inadmissible grounds (ethnicity and national origin) than were decisions by judicially accountable representatives. Whether civic education could eliminate the discriminatory variance is an open question.

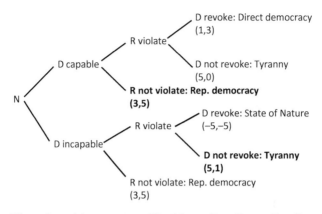

Figure 7.1 Three-player delegation game. N = Nature. D = Demos. R = Representative. N's choice sets up two parallel subgames. Payoffs for Representative and Demos are in the order R, D. The predicted outcome for each subgame is in boldface.

R's worst outcome is the state of nature, which is assumed to be bad for everyone for the reasons specified by Hobbes.

D prefers representative to direct democracy, but the preference is not overwhelming. D recognizes that the status quo gives D somewhat more opportunity to spend time on socially valued goods and D supposes that an able R will embody a degree of governmental experience and policy expertise. But D is willing to legislate directly, at least on an occasional basis, because D not only disfavors tyranny, but also values political participation for its own sake, for reasons discussed in Chapter 5. While there are other forms of participation open to D under a representative democracy, direct legislation is a particularly strong form of civic participation. D's third-best outcome is tyranny. D's worst outcome, like R's, is the anarchic state of nature.

R moves first, deciding whether to violate or not to violate. If R chooses not to violate, the game ends and the outcome is the status quo of representative democracy. If R violates, D chooses whether to revoke or not to revoke R's authority. If D chooses not to revoke, the outcome is tyranny – R can now rule the state in its own self-interest. If D chooses to revoke, the outcome will depend on whether Nature has rendered D as capable or incapable of governing. If D is capable of ruling, the outcome is direct democracy. If D is incapable of ruling, the outcome is an anarchic, Hobbesian state of nature.

If D is capable of ruling, the equilibrium path is R does not violate, and the expected outcome of the game is the status quo of representative democracy. Confronted with a capable D, R's most preferred outcome, violating without D revoking, is not available because D prefers direct democracy to tyranny. If D is incapable of legislating, the equilibrium path is R violates and D does not revoke; the expected outcome is tyranny. In this case R can violate with impunity because D prefers tyranny to the anarchic state of nature, which is the expected outcome if an incapable D revokes R's authority. If D is capable, and R goes off-path by violating, the equilibrium path is D revokes, and the predicted outcome is direct democracy. If D is incapable, and goes off-path by revoking after R's violation, the outcome is the state of nature.

The delegation game illustrates the importance, to persons for whom nontyranny is highly valued, of the demos's capability in respect to ruling through the mechanisms of direct democracy. A capable demos retains a credible threat of revoking authority, so that rational representatives, who prefer the status quo to direct democracy, will not violate the terms under which they assumed authority. In the real world, a capable demos will not need to revoke delegated authority so long as representatives stay "on path" – that is, so long as the real-world behavior of representatives tracks the full-information, rational-actor framework assumed by the game. If the representatives do go off-path, by violating, and if their violation is recognized as such by the capable demos, they must expect the demos to intervene by switching (presumably temporarily) from a procedural norm of representation to the exceptional expedient of direct democracy.

So long as representatives remain competitive with one another (within and between branches of government), and so long the demos is the judge of their competition, the constitutional order will be sustained without revocation of delegated authority. The demos may, in that circumstance, gain from the skill, experience, and expertise of representatives and the various agencies of government that support their legislative efforts. But faced with an ambitious and *cohesive* body of representatives – a systematically corrupt political class capable of coordinating its actions on the goal of usurping the demos's authority – a demos incapable of actually governing, as well as abstractly "ruling as sovereign," is dependent on the "paper barriers" of constitutional rules to restrain the representatives. Should representatives come to understand themselves as a collective agent, with preferences that diverge from those of the demos, the constitutional barriers are likely to prove flimsy. In that case, a democracy lacking a capable demos, if it avoids the state of nature, will predictably devolve into a tyranny. That tyranny may be of the benevolent kind; the autocratic rulers may provide high levels of security and welfare. But their government has no warrant to call itself democracy.

7.4 CITIZEN SELF-GOVERNMENT

The upshot of the delegation game is that a demos that values nontyranny has good reason to establish institutional mechanisms and to educate citizens in ways that will enable the people to rule directly if and when they need to do so. This may be thought of an instance of the general "right of resistance" that has been a mainstay of nonabsolutist political theory since John Locke's *Second Treatise of Government* (1988 [1690]) and that has antecedents in ancient Greek laws encouraging tyrannicide (Teegarden 2014). The return to direct rule of the demos (assuming that the establishment, via ratification, of the basic rules at the foundation was the original act of direct democracy) need not, however, entail a popular revolution in which all existing agencies of government are abolished, or a new constitution is adopted. Rather, it may be enough for the citizens to have an existing constitutional option of initiating and enacting a legislative referendum, if and when the legislative representatives violate their mandate by making a rule against the common interest, or fail to act on some vital matter in the common interest.

The practice of direct self-government by citizens is hardly unknown in modernity. Legislation in the form of direct voting on referenda is common in some of the western states of the US and is sometimes employed to decide highly consequential matters by modern European states; the UK's "Brexit" referendum of 2016 is a case in point.[7] Likewise, norms of direct citizen responsibility for rule enforcement, in the form of bystander intervention and community watch organizations, are familiar features of modernity.[8] By the same token, there is no guarantee that direct democracy will work well. Citizen activism in rule enforcement can devolve into vicious forms of vigilantism. Referenda can be captured by special interests and may result in consequences unintended by the majority of the voters.

There are certainly historical instances, ancient and modern, in which practices of direct democratic self-governance have failed. But anecdotal evidence does not prove that such practices *necessarily* fail. If the citizens

---

[7] Referenda in the US and Europe: Cronin 1989; Kaufmann and Waters 2004; Achen and Bartels 2016: Chapter 3. Direct democracy and public policy: Fung 2015.

[8] Bystander intervention and social norms: Burn 2009; Gidycz et al. 2011. Citizen watch organizations and intervention: Fung 2004.

of a democracy have reasons to want to be capable, and if they are willing to pay the costs of becoming capable, then it is a question of *how* the demos can become capable without incurring unreasonable costs. That is, in turn, a question of design – devising cost-effective educational systems and institutional mechanisms. Of course it might be the case that under the conditions of modernity there is no design solution that can solve the problem of creating a capable demos at a reasonable cost. But making that possibility into the premise of a theory of government (as do some contemporary advocates of epistocracy: Brennan 2016) seems at best premature.

To be a democracy in the original or basic sense, a constitutional democracy must develop and sustain the people's capability of governing directly. This suggests one reason that democracy before liberalism is relevant to a modern theory of democracy. We may concede that it is unlikely that any modern large-scale democracy will be governed by its citizens full time, as a purely direct democracy. But any modern democracy that cannot resort to decision making by the people if and when necessary remains vulnerable to capture by a political elite. That sort of capture is readily imaginable under specifiable conditions of systematic corruption. If citizens demand a democracy that is robustly resistant to elite capture, they must seek to design their institutions and to educate themselves such that their own collective capacity to govern is robustly sustained and a matter of common knowledge.

It is often supposed that modern states could not be governed, even temporarily, by a direct democracy, because of their size and the complexity of the issues that they must address.[9] As we have seen, representation remains the preferred option for the day-to-day government of a large-scale basic democracy, in which citizens have interests in other socially valued projects. But we have also seen that the citizens must be able to suspend representative government in favor of direct self-government if they are to preclude elite capture arising from systematic corruption. Can a modern demos get there from here?

If the issues that government must address are actually so complex that they simply cannot be addressed by citizens acting in their own name, then the demos cannot be capable and the state is inherently vulnerable to tyranny via elite capture: The best that a democrat can hope for is virtuous or otherwise benevolent representatives. But that conclusion would be too hasty. It remains an open question how much of the problem of

---

[9] Assumption that size and complexity of government precludes effective direct democracy: Dahl and Tufte 1973; Achen and Bartels 2016.

governing in the face of complexity is inherent in the *issues* presented by modernity, and how much is a matter of systems of government that have become more complex than is strictly necessary to address vital issues. If a basic democracy is to defend all three of the ends for which the state exists, the government must be tractable enough to be managed by a capable demos until authority can be re-delegated to new set of representatives. So it seems, on the face of it, worth asking to what degree the complexity of modern government can be disaggregated from the complexity of the issues that government must address. Issue complexity need not be reduced to the point that every citizen can understand every issue for herself. Per discussion below, a regime governed directly by the people, can, with the right institutional design, make use of high-quality expertise in rendering judgments on matters of great public import.

Might it be possible to invert the usual story about the relationship between size and complexity and democratic decision making? Rather than viewing size and complexity of government as a constraint on democracy, we might choose to see democracy is a constraint on the size and complexity of government. That constraint would affect the form (but perhaps not the substantive content) of legislation made by the people's representatives, because it introduces a legislative design incentive lacking in contemporary liberal democracies: Insofar as the constraint on size and complexity is common knowledge and taken as an essential feature of democracy, the citizenry will reward representatives who sponsor legislation elegantly designed to accomplish public ends in the simplest possible fashion. They will punish those whose policy proposals are seen as unnecessarily complex. As in the case of the civic dignity constraint on strong forms of libertarian and egalitarian distributive justice (Section 6.8), the revocation constraint means that the conditions necessary to sustain a basic democracy pushes back against versions of liberalism that depend on steady, unconstrained growth of government.

Modern state governments are inherently large and complex. But if, in order to sustain the ends for which a liberal state exists, a system of liberal government must be *so* large and complex as to preclude even the most capable demos from governing on an occasional basis, directly and in its own name, then there is an inescapable trade-off between liberalism and democracy – at least in the sense of a basic democracy that requires an active response to the threat of tyranny arising from systematic corruption. On the other hand, there is, on the face of it, no reason that the government of a liberal democracy *must* be huge and cumbersome, rather than right-sized and elegant. Libertarians have long advocated ways to reduce the size of government in the name of individual freedom. Meanwhile, mainstream liberals with more egalitarian conceptions of social justice have urged institutional reforms aimed at reducing unnecessary governmental complexity.[10] A democratic constraint on the size and complexity of government need not be seen as an impediment to the realization of fundamental liberal values. Rather, it should be understood as presenting an institutional design challenge for democrats, liberal, and nonliberal alike.

7.5 INTERESTS, KNOWLEDGE, EXPERTS

In a basic democracy, capable citizens, secure in their civic dignity, equality, and liberty, are ultimately responsible for public decisions.[11] Democratic legislative process maintains the end of nontyranny by pushing back against elite capture. It must also maintain the ends of security and prosperity. All other things being equal, decisions will be better aligned with desired outcomes when they are predicated on actionable knowledge about relevant features of the world. Since antiquity, political theorists have asked whether a political regime can be at once *democratic* and *epistemic*. Can policy-making processes express and defend democracy's core commitments *and* serve citizen's interests when decisions are based on well-justified beliefs, rather than ill-founded popular opinions? Can democratic process be employed as a system for making relatively wise collective *judgments*, as well as a system for determining and enacting majority *preferences*?

How a democratic community might employ knowledge in choosing wisely among alternatives is a question of institutional design that long antedates liberalism and remains highly relevant today: It concerned classical Greek political theorists and lawmakers and is a central question for contemporary political scientists (Callander 2011). It is a pressing issue, not least because it exceeds the bounds of the state. Universities, business firms, NGOs, federations, and transnational agencies all confront the question of how many individuals, who share certain interests in common, can choose wisely among available options.[12]

---

[10] Somin 2013, with Ober 2015c, discusses some approaches to shrinking government size within the frame of an epistemic theory of democracy. Sunstein 2013 offers proposals for government simplification from within the perspective of mainstream liberalism.

[11] This section is adapted from Ober 2013a.

[12] Important work on epistemic democracy includes Cohen 1986, 1996; List and Goodin 2001; List 2005; Bovens and Rabinowicz 2006; Anderson 2006; Page 2007; Estlund 2008; Furstein 2008; Fischer 2009; Schwartzberg 2010; List and Pettit 2011: Chapter 4; Landemore and Elster 2012; Landemore 2012. A realistic theory of epistemic democracy ought to be incentive compatible (Ober 2008a: 5–22) but no formal model is offered here.

Plato, along with other ancient and modern critics, argued that democracy's commitment to liberty and equality necessarily leads citizens to pursue arbitrary desires rather than real interests, and to make choices based on false opinion rather than knowledge. The critics conclude that democracy is inherently anti-epistemic and that only a nondemocratic regime could make policy favorable to people's real interests.[13] If democracy's critics are right – if, in contrast to a well-ordered epistemic autocracy, basic democracy's irreducible commitments to participation, freedom, equality, and dignity render a self-governing collectivity inherently incapable of effectively employing useful knowledge to make policies leading to favorable outcomes – we must ask whether sustaining democracy justifies the cost of less security and less welfare. It obviously would be better for those who hope to live under a regime that is at once masterless, secure, and prosperous if that question were moot.

The minimal promise of an epistemic approach to democracy is that, under the right conditions, a process of decision making that sustains collective self-government can do better than making random choices among policy options – and thus can promote the interests of citizens by achieving relatively favorable outcomes. If that is the case, and if no nondemocratic epistemic process can be shown to do better, the presumptive benefits associated with the democratic good of free exercise of constitutive capacities, and the goods arising from conditions of political liberty, political equality, and civic dignity, need not be traded off against the expected costs of inferior policy. Temporarily revoking legislative authority delegated to representatives in favor of lawmaking by the people themselves need not result in a degradation of state performance.

One enabling condition for epistemic democracy is participation in decision making by citizens who attend to relevant sources of knowledge, to true expertise and genuine experts. Yet how can attention to experts avoid devolution into rule *by* experts, thus leading to the eclipse of political equality, and at least potentially, to the eclipse of liberty and civic dignity as well? The question of whether a democracy can make appropriate use of diverse forms of expertise, while preserving each of its core commitments, has concerned political theorists and practitioners since antiquity. Like the general question of whether a democracy can ever be wise, it remains an issue for contemporary theorists. Philip Pettit, for example, once argued (in work that seems now to be superseded by Pettit 2013) for a constitutional order

---

[13] Ancient critics are surveyed in Roberts 1994; Ober 1998. Modern epistemic critics of democracy include Caplan 2007; Somin 2013.

in which "authorial" power to legislate lies with depoliticized deliberative bodies possessing appropriate professional expertise, while ordinary citizens are reduced to an "editorial" role that kicks in only after the experts have done their legislative work.[14] Democracy's relationship to expertise is a live issue in current policy debates, with some critics contending that democracy's putatively anti-epistemic character renders it unequal to, for example, the challenge posed by long-term climate change or a globalized economy (Shearman and Smith 2007; Caplan 2007; Somin 2013).

What is the proper design for a democratic process capable of making good decisions about important (even existential) matters, thereby promoting citizens' common interests, while sustaining democracy's core commitments? One influential answer is to aggregate the preferences (concerning representatives or policies) of free citizens by counting their equally weighted votes. Robert Dahl (1989, 2015), among others, has argued, against Plato and other epistemic regime theorists, that democratic values are preserved, and citizens' interests advanced, when policy is set by a majority of voters whose preferences express their own opinions about their own best interests. Dahl's approach preserves liberty, political equality, and dignity by asserting (1) that each individual voter is the best (even if necessarily imperfect) judge of his or her own interests and (2) that a majority of such individually chosen preferences, expressed as equal votes, deserves to be established as state policy. As we have seen (Chapter 3), majority voting will indeed be a necessary feature of a basic democracy, and voting is among the fundamental responsibilities of citizenship.[15]

Yet a majority's *preferences*, even if those preferences do track the real *interests* of the majority, may fail to reflect the *common* interests of citizens, much less the interests of *all* citizens.[16] It is because the preferences of a majority might ignore or harm the most basic interests of individuals or of a minority that, in liberal democracies, certain interests are legally protected as fundamental rights. Rights-based decision procedures are not, however, necessarily efficacious in addressing common interests in the face of existential threats. Indeed, the extent to which a regime of inviolable individual

---

[14] Pettit 2004: 57–62; contra Urbinati 2012. Pettit's position seems to have changed in his more recent work (Pettit 2013), in which the authorial and editorial roles are merged.

[15] The standard democratic norm of "one person one vote" (1p1v) is not the only way preferences could be expressed. Posner and Weyl 2015, for example, propose a form of voting that would allow for differential weighting of individuals' preference intensity and that avoids some of the problems of 1p1v votes. But it is not clear that their approach respects political equality in a way that would sustain democratic legitimacy: Ober 2017b.

[16] Per Chapter 3, I do not follow Rousseau in supposing that, in a basic democracy, the common interest must be the interest of all.

rights is predicated on Kant's doctrine of *fiat iustiitia, pereat mundus* ("let there be justice, though the world ends"), it is deliberately maladapted to furthering common interests on existential matters.

Classical theorists, before liberalism, approached the matter of pre-serving values and fostering interests quite differently. Aristotle regarded advancing the special interests of a majority in a democracy (or of an empowered minority in an oligarchy) as fundamentally unjust, insofar as it came at the expense of promoting common interests. He supposed that a just community would seek to identify common (rather than par-tial/factional) interests and, by appropriate use of practical wisdom (*phrone-sis*), would select policies most likely to advance those interests. Politi-cal decision making, for Aristotle (as, on different grounds, for Plato), was an epistemic endeavor in that it was meant to discover and then implement the best available answers to questions of appropriately shared concern.

If we are willing to accept the common (although not universal) thoughts that (1) people do have real interests (and not *merely* preferences) and (2) that some interests are in fact shared by many members of a com-munity, there is, by extension, no reason to reject a priori the possibility that certain interests (e.g., in security and prosperity) could be so widely shared as to be reasonably described as commonly held. Moreover, one need not embrace Aristotelian eudaemonism to regard pursuing certain common interests as a normatively choiceworthy political goal, or to suppose that practical wisdom is *not* the preserve of a tiny elite and *is* equal to the task of identifying certain interests as shared. For the purposes of this book, a superior common-interest choice is one that selects the available option that, all things considered, best advances an interest commonly shared by the members of a civic community.

We need not follow Aristotle in assuming that politics can or ought to be reduced to a search for the best answers about common interests and their advancement: Many political matters in a pluralistic commu-nity will involve hard choices among conflicting social values and concep-tions of just distribution; many other matters concern the interests only of certain persons. So there will be plenty of room for political disagree-ment, debate, and even conflict. Yet it seems implausible to say that politics *never is*, and *never ought to be*, concerned with interests that are reasonably held to be shared. Democratic politicians, in antiquity (Ober 1989) and modernity alike, frame proposals as promoting the common interest; their rhetoric is not empty insofar as it acknowledges a shared conviction that addressing common interests is one part of what politics ought to be about.

Common interests might, hypothetically, be identified by consensus, but, for my purposes, consensus is unnecessary.

Majoritarian mechanisms may be employed to identify and advance a common interest, so long as the majority decision actually represents a superior common-interest choice, as defined just above. It is implausible to suppose that majority votes always (or even often) accurately identify and advance common interests; many votes will legitimately be concerned with the preferences of some part of the demos. It is sufficient for my argument that certain interests are commonly shared and, in such cases, there is such a thing as the better policy, and that it is conceivably discoverable by an epistemic process. Although common interests and partisan preferences can never be fully disentangled, focusing on shared interests limits the subjectivity of decision making and thereby allows the performance of decision-making groups to be evaluated (Yates and Tschirhart 2006).

To be plausible on the face of it, any approach to epistemic democracy must address the challenges of transitivity (and thus of cycling), collective rationality, and elite control. Options, in order to have stable outcomes, must be transitively ordered, such that if A > B and B > C then A > C.[17] Judgments by a collectivity will avoid cycling among options only under the right conditions (List and Pettit 2011). Deliberation (rule-structured exchange of opinions and justifications for those opinions among decision makers) and independent guess aggregation (e.g., the Condorcet Jury Theorem) are the two most often cited epistemic approaches to democratic decision making. I will hope to show that relevant expertise aggregation, the democratic decision-making process described below, addresses the challenges of collective judgment as well or better than the rival epistemic approaches of deliberation and independent guess aggregation (at least in their conventional forms) and thus is appropriate for decision making in Demopolis.[18]

Insofar as democratic politics is a means for choosing which available option best serves a shared interest, it involves the use of knowledge (accurate information, true beliefs) for discovering the best option. Given indeterminacy and contingency, this cannot mean "identifying the approach that infallibly achieves a common interest." It must mean instead, "choosing the option among available alternatives that has the best chance, all things considered, of advancing a common interest." Two fundamental premises of epistemic approaches to democracy are that (1) there *are* better

[17] On cycling as an issue in epistemic democracy, see List and Goodin 2001; Dryzek and List 2003; List 2011; Elster 2011, with work cited.
[18] On deliberation and independent guess aggregation, see, further, Ober 2013a.

options, in that the chances of a good outcome are better if that option is chosen, and (2) decision makers can, under the right conditions, identify better options.[19]

Options are likely to be better insofar as they take fuller account of relevant facts about the world. Reality-tracking is valued (in this context) because of its consequences: All other things being equal, options that take account of the relevant facts are more likely to lead to a better outcome, all things considered, than those that do not. Because I am concerned, here, with democracy rather than liberalism, I am not concerned with assessing the moral status of the interests pursued by a democratic community (e.g., by weighing the shared interests of a community against global interests or universal human rights). Nor am I concerned with the normative value of epistemic democracy relative to, e.g., agonistic pluralism (Honig 1993; Lacau and Mouffe 2001); as noted above, there is plenty of space for disagreement and contestation within the basic democracy envisioned here. Nor, finally, am I concerned to show that epistemic democracies will invariably outperform autocracies. I am concerned, instead, with the design of institutional mechanisms that would enable citizens in a basic democracy to make decisions that are overall, at least as good as those likely to be made by a well-functioning autocracy. Those mechanisms must advance common interests (in Demopolis: the three ends of the state), while sustaining democracy's necessary conditions.

Epistemic decision making must be concerned with expertise. Experts in a given domain (say, chess masters) are more capable than others at producing a desired outcome (winning) and the probability of achieving the outcome is increased by better choices (good moves). The Callipolis of Plato's *Republic* is an example of an ideal epistemic regime in which rulers are political experts. Their choices accurately track the Form of the Good and thereby produce a just and high-performing (prosperous and secure) society. Callipolis is, however, neither realistic nor democratic. It is undemocratic because a few experts rule without consulting the other citizens and because it is based on systematic deception (the Noble Lies). It is unrealistic because it assumes the existence of general political experts.

---

[19] As Callander 2011 notes, decision makers can never be sure, ex ante, that they have chosen well, nor can they be sure, ex post, that an outcome came about because of their choice But, as he demonstrates, this need not obviate the hope of identifying better options. Hawthorne (und: 5) argues that "for a wide range of philosophically respectable views [on the public good, citing Aristotle, Locke, Rousseau, Mill, Rawls] there is such a thing as the better policy in at least some cases and . . . that such views may find aid and comfort from what Jury Theorems imply about the ability of majorities to find the better policy."

The philosopher-kings are "architect-like" in their master knowledge of a blueprint that perfectly directs the actions of all those whose work (and subsidiary expertise) is necessary to create and sustain a just society.[20] One premise of basic democracy (per Chapter 3) is that there are no general political experts. The problem is not only that, per Dahl's argument, the autocrat cannot be a better judge of others' preferences than they are of their own, it is that no individual or small coalition possesses all the knowledge relevant to securing the common interests of the civic community.[21]

Politics is unlike well-studied domains of endeavor in which individuals achieve true expertise (say, chess or violin playing: Ericsson 2006) in its level of complexity. There are, *ex hypothesi*, no general experts in politics because, lacking access to the Form of the Good (or some similar metaphysical resource), such experts would need to master a range of hard-to-acquire specialized expertise that exceeds the bounds of human cognitive capacity. This is an argument that can be advanced by the civic educators of Demopolis in favor of the masterless regime. It is, however, highly plausible to suppose that there are true experts in many domains relevant to political decision making (Ericsson et al. 2006). Well-intentioned domain experts, along with delusional political leaders, may come to believe, wrongly, that they are general experts. The catastrophic results that can follow, when unlimited political authority is ceded to domain experts and delusional leaders, are well documented (Scott 1998). But this ought not be a reason for excluding expertise in relevant domains from democratic decision making. The goal of relevant expertise aggregation is to bring domain-specific expertise into the process of decision making without ceding political authority to experts or autocrats.[22]

---

[20] Architectonic model: Plato *Statesman*. In his early work, *Protrepticus* (fragment cited in Iamblichus, *Protrepticus* 10.54.12–56.2), Aristotle uses the architect as a model for the ideal legislator. Aristotle likewise applies an "architectonic" frame to political science (*Nicomachean Ethics* 1.2.1094a26–b7), as well as to philosophical foundations (*Metaphysics* 1.2.981a30–982b7), but in these later works he does not suggest that there is a master "architect." My thanks to Monte Johnson for calling to my attention these and other key passages in Aristotle.

[21] Estlund (2003, 2008), who coined "epistocracy" as a term for rule by experts, develops a moral argument against it. My argument, in agreement with that of Shapiro 2016 33–34: suggests that the argument for epistocracy goes wrong at the outset because it wrongly supposes that, because there *are* experts in domains relevant to politics, there are *also* general experts in politics (as opposed to relatively competent political leaders).

[22] Dividing an issue into domains in which expertise is identifiable is described in the literature on decision expertise as "the process-decomposition perspective": Yates and Tschirhart 2006: 426–32. See ibid., 435 on how the multiple factors involved in complex decisions will presumably render "true across-the-board decision-making expertise" in any individual "exceedingly rare." Economics is a field in which domain experts sometimes seek the role of general expert: Caplan 2007.

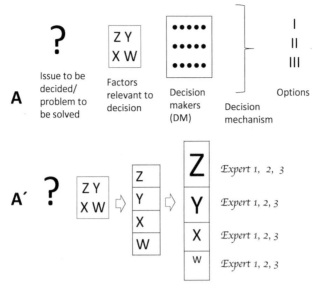

Figure 7.2 Epistemic decision process and relevant expertise aggregation. The first sequence (A) illustrates a generic epistemic process: To address a given issue (?), decision makers (DM) assess relevant factors (Z, Y, X, W) then, via some decision mechanism, identify a range of options (I, II, III). If the process succeeds, they choose the best option. In relevant expertise aggregation (sequence A′), the relevant factors are divided into domains, the domains are weighted, and expert testimony is sought on each weighted domain. The decision mechanism then aggregates votes of DM on weighted domains to arrive at the best option.

7.6 RELEVANT EXPERTISE AGGREGATION: AN ATHENIAN CASE STUDY

In earlier work, I have described several approaches by which a group might aggregate expertise relevant to making a judgment among multiple options on matters of common interest. Based on variations in decision rules, these approaches range from nondemocratic, in which unaccountable experts make decisions, to democratic, in which the final decision is made by voting citizens who have been advised by experts in multiple domains. The core features of relevant expertise aggregation (REA) are as follows; the process is schematically illustrated in Figure 7.2: The issue on which the decision is to be made is divided into a limited number of specifiable parts, or domains, relevant to the issue. So, for example, a decision of how to manage a dam across a river might address, inter alia, economic, environmental, and societal impacts.[23] Reliable experts, who have been given good reasons to disclose their true opinions, are identified in each domain. Domains are ranked and weighted (say, from 0 to 1, with the sum of domain weights adding up to 1) according their relevance to the decision. A limited number of options (choices, understood as solutions to a problem to be solved) is specified, and voted upon, by domain. Each domain total is calculated by multiplying the number of votes by the domain's relevance weighting. The final score is the sum of the domain totals. That final score either determines (in nondemocratic versions of the method) or helps to guide (in democratic versions) the choice of option.[24]

Here I focus on the most democratic variant of relevant expertise aggregation, a process in which the rules for determining domains of expertise and policy options remain unspecified ex ante, and which culminates in a direct vote by citizens on options. It is meant to illustrate the way in which a direct democracy can incorporate valuable expertise in making an existential decision. The case discussed in this section is based on the historical Athenian response to the threat of Persian invasion in 481 BCE, as described by the historian Herodotus (*Histories* 7.140–144) and recorded in the "Themistocles Decree" (an ancient document detailing the Athenian response). While Athens was a full time direct democracy, I discuss below (Section 7.7) how the approach might apply to a democracy in which government is ordinarily carried out by representatives, thus answering the question of how basic democracy functions at scale. Some aspects of the following narrative, meant to illustrate how an epistemic decision-making process in a basic democracy may be parsed into discrete stages, are hypothetical. The actual process employed in 481 BCE was certainly messier, but the process described here accords with the known facts about decision-making procedures in the ancient Athenian council and assembly (Rhodes 1985; Hansen 1987; Missiou 2011).

The structure of the case is as follows: A democratically appointed citizen council prepares an agenda for a larger legislative assembly. The assembly is open to all citizens and is empowered to make binding decisions on matters of common interest. Procedural rules specify deliberation and voting in both council and assembly. Domains of expertise (along with experts in each domain) and policy options are freely chosen in early stages of the decision process. Certain background conditions, common to other

---

[23] Options might include leaving the dam as is, rebuilding it to better achieve some purpose, or removing it entirely.

[24] For a more detailed discussion, see Ober 2013a.

non- or semidemocratic forms of REA, are presumed to hold: The decision-making group seeks the best option in addressing a matter of common interest; issues are divisible into parts, each with a specifiable relevance to the issue in question and each part is explicable as a domain of expertise. These background conditions are common knowledge. The group making the decision exists over time, and group members update their judgments based on new information.[25]

In 481 BCE, as a massive Persian military force prepared to advance west into Europe, the Athenian state was confronted by an existential threat. The issue of how to respond to the invasion would ultimately be decided by a vote in a citizen assembly open to all citizens and attended by several thousand. A council of 500 citizens, chosen by lot, set the agenda for the assembly meeting. The council's role was to define policy options. The Greek term for the council (*boule*) refers directly to its deliberative function (*bouleuein/bouleuesthai*, "to take counsel, deliberate"), and it is quite certain that formal votes were taken in the council. By the time the assembly met, three primary options – flee, fight on land, fight at sea – had emerged. Because the agenda for the assembly was announced in advance, ordinary citizens had the opportunity to deliberate among themselves before the decisive meeting, at which a vote of the citizenry would decide how the state would respond to an existential threat.

Although Athens was used to fighting its Greek neighbors, invasion by the Persian empire was an exceptional circumstance. Because decision rules cannot specify in advance relevant domains of expertise for exceptional circumstances, and because the decisive assembly vote would be directly on the options, citizens shared responsibility not only for judging experts, but also for establishing relevant domains in which expertise was thought to be of value and for aggregating domain-specific expertise into an option choice. The procedural task of identifying relevant domains and experts is accomplished in the first instance through deliberation and voting in the council, but all citizens in assembly must judge experts and calculate aggregates of domain-specific expertise. There is substantial variance among citizens in respect to individual capability in performing these tasks. Table 7.1 sets out a hypothetical distribution of capabilities among a sample population of 25 citizens. A minority of the citizens in this sample falls below the presumed point (0.5 on a scale of 0–1) at which his vote will make a positive contribution in each task. Yet, because the mean competence level in each column is above 0.5, we can appeal to a variant of the Condorcet Jury

---

[25] These other forms of relevant expertise aggregation are detailed in Ober 2013a.

Table 7.1 *Hypothetical distribution of voters on procedural tasks*

Voter	1 Recognize parts	2 Identify experts	3 Weight parts	4 Calculate aggregate	5 Judge experts	Average
A	0.85	0.45	0.55	0.6	0.3	0.542
B	0.8	0.85	0.45	0.65	0.4	0.617
C	0.75	0.8	0.4	0.45	0.85	0.642
D	0.7	0.75	0.4	0.4	0.35	0.500
E	0.45	0.4	0.8	0.85	0.75	0.642
F	0.6	0.35	0.35	0.8	0.7	0.546
G	0.55	0.6	0.7	0.75	0.65	0.646
H	0.5	0.35	0.65	0.45	0.6	0.504
I	0.45	0.5	0.6	0.65	0.55	0.546
J	0.4	0.45	0.55	0.6	0.5	0.500
K	0.35	0.4	0.5	0.55	0.45	0.454
L	0.3	0.35	0.45	0.5	0.4	0.404
M	0.25	0.3	0.5	0.45	0.35	0.375
N	0.3	0.25	0.55	0.4	0.5	0.408
O	0.35	0.5	0.6	0.5	0.25	0.450
P	0.4	0.55	0.3	0.45	0.3	0.433
Q	0.65	0.4	0.4	0.25	0.75	0.496
R	0.5	0.55	0.35	0.3	0.4	0.425
S	0.55	0.5	0.55	0.35	0.45	0.488
T	0.6	0.55	0.45	0.4	0.5	0.504
U	0.65	0.45	0.5	0.45	0.55	0.521
V	0.45	0.65	0.55	0.5	0.6	0.554
W	0.45	0.4	0.6	0.55	0.65	0.538
X	0.45	0.75	0.65	0.6	0.3	0.563
Y	0.85	0.8	0.35	0.45	0.75	0.663
Average	0.53	0.52	0.51	0.52	0.51	0.52
Below 0.5	12	12	10	12	11	9

Notes: 0–1 scale of competence (likeliness to judge correctly) in each category.

Theorem (Grofman et al. 1983; List and Goodin 2001) to suggest that the collectivity will do adequately well in each task. As the number of voters increases (from 500 councilors to thousands of assemblymen), the likelihood of a spread among vote counts adequate to yield a best choice among options likewise increases.[26]

The council takes up the issue of the Persian invasion in meetings that are less time-constrained than the subsequent decisive meeting of the assembly. The deliberation begins by determining the relevant domains of expertise.

[26] Of course, per standard Condorcet reasoning, if the average competence were below 0.5, the increase in size would degrade likelihood of identifying the best option.

Based on their experience in deliberating on other issues, the councilors have a good sense of the distribution of capabilities among their membership – that is, they have got something like Table 7.1 in their heads.[27] Because they seek the best choice and the stakes are high, the councilmen allow councilors A, B, C, D, and Y, who are rightly (Table 7.1, column 1) thought most capable at setting relevant domains, to take the lead in these deliberations. Councilman A gains majority support for the importance of the attitude of the gods and thus the morale of the populace.[28] This becomes one of the domains in which expert advice will be sought. Councilmen B, C, D, and Y make successful arguments on behalf of other domains: Persia's strategic goals, Athenian mobilization capacity, attitudes and capacities of Athens's allies, and potential threats to Athenian unity. The selection of relevant domains ends when no majority favors adding another domain.[29]

The council's deliberations and votes establish the relative importance of the domains and determine the domain experts who will offer testimony. As the experts' recommendations are discussed, the views of C, E, F, Q, and Y – who are known to be especially astute judges of experts (Table 7.1, column 5), are especially influential. In the course of iterated deliberation and voting, the three primary options (flee, fight on land, fight at sea) emerge and are tested against the opinions of domain experts whose views are sought by the council. The process leads the council to rank the "fight-at-sea" option first.[30]

---

[27] It may seem unrealistic to expect each councilor to have an adequate sense of the capabilities of 499 fellow councilors. But much of the actual deliberative work of the council was carried out by ten representative teams of 50 men (Ober 2008a: 142–155). It seems quite plausible that each councilor had in his head a more or less accurate "REA capability table" of his 49 teammates.

[28] The gods' will was revealed, cryptically, in responses to Athenian queries to Apollo's oracle at Delphi regarding policy options. Gods, and the value of oracles, were taken by most Greeks to be facts about the world. These were not (we would say) brute facts about nature, but they were salient social facts (Searle 1995) that would have considerable bearing on behavior.

[29] The sequence of deliberation and voting are hypothetical, and the domains are inferred from the wording of the Decree, but the Athenian council did regularly hear expert testimony (e.g., from generals) on various aspects of major issues: Rhodes 1985: 42–46. Although we lack evidence for formal votes to establish relevant domains, voting by domains was certainly known in Athens, notably when the assembly annually voted to reauthorize or revise each part of the law code: MacDowell 1975: 66–69. Aristotle, *Rhetoric* 1.1359b34–1360a12 divides the general legislative domain of "war and peace" into four specific domains, on which military experts would be expected to speak: (1) national military capacity, current and potential; (2) past relations with and military developments in rival states; (3) relative strength of rival states; (4) outcomes of previous conflicts.

[30] That the council's recommendation was adopted in the final vote is suggested by the formula of enactment employed in the Decree: "resolved by the council and the demos." Decrees passed without a recommendation from the council typically used the formula "resolved by the demos": Hansen 1999: 139–140.

With the options identified and ranked, a meeting of the full citizen assembly was called and the results of the council's deliberative/voting process reported. The assembly then carried out its own deliberations, thus potentially allowing domains of expertise ignored by the council to be considered. Herodotus reports (7.142) that "many opinions" were offered, with prominent citizens supporting different options. Expert testimony was offered for and against each option – Herodotus reports that certain oracle interpreters (*chresmologoi*) argued that the gods disfavored the option of fighting at sea. Although the Athenians were strongly committed to the value of free speech, if we are to judge by later (fourth century BCE) practice, those regarded as nonexpert in the relevant domain under discussion were not given a full hearing; the time constraints did not allow the luxury of attending to uninformed opinion.[31]

The winning option in the final, voting, stage is the one that best takes into account the most relevant domains and the most credible experts. Because the final vote is directly on the options, each individual citizen is responsible for calculating for himself the relative importance of the several domains (Table 7.1, column 3), as well as judging the experts in each domain (column 2). Some citizens will undoubtedly overweight a relatively trivial domain. Yet the assumption that there is an adequate aggregate competence in the procedural task of calculation does not place an impossible cognitive burden upon the citizens. Their burden is, in any event, lighter than that taken on by voters on public referenda in modern liberal democracies, for whom ranking of domain-relevance and certification of domain experts are not provided in advance by a deliberative body.

In 481 BCE, the fight-at-sea option, put into the form of a proposal by Themistocles (recorded in the inscribed Decree), eventually carried the day. Themistocles's own reputation as a trustworthy leader and as an expert in naval affairs certainly played a role in the choice. Yet Herodotus and the Decree suggest that those favoring the fight-at-sea option took up several heavily weighted domains of expertise: The attitude of the gods was, according to Herodotus (7.143), addressed by Themistocles's convincing reinterpretation of the key oracle. Persian strategic goals, plans for Athenian naval mobilization, the attitudes and capacities of Greek allies, and provisions for securing unity by recalling exiled citizens were addressed in detail in the Decree. Because the final vote was conducted by estimating the number of raised hands, rather than by counting ballots, the vote, even when

---

[31] Nonexperts in relevant domains shouted down: Plato, *Protagoras* 319b–c. For discussions of the role of experts in legislation, and the response by democratic audiences to experts in later fifth- and fourth-century Athens, see Ober 1989: 314–327; Kallet-Marx 1994.

nonunanimous, could be observed by the assembly as a "unified whole" (Schwartzberg 2010). Indeed, as Mirko Canevaro (forthcoming) has now shown, many, perhaps most, votes in Greek democratic assemblies were unanimous, or nearly so. The goal was consensus on a best course of action, not victory of a narrow majority. Herodotus and the Decree describe the decision as that of the people of Athens, not of a majority faction. The assembly's vote in favor of fighting at sea was understood as a direct expression of the demos's collective judgment on a matter of grave common interest. The Decree was implemented on the following day, as generals began allotting commanders, marines, and rowers to Athenian warships.

Given the impossibility of specifying counterfactuals, we cannot know whether the Athenian assembly chose the best option, but fighting at sea certainly appears, ex post, better than the other options. The decision, as Herodotus emphasizes, affected the course of Greek history in ways that were overall positive for the Athenians. Herodotus states (7.139) that the Athenian decision to fight at sea determined the outcome of the war and that after winning the Battle of Salamis, democratic Athens went on to become the preeminent state of the Greek world. Herodotus elsewhere pointed out (5.97.2–3) that decisions of the Athenian assembly sometimes led to bad outcomes. Yet, over time, the Athenians' capacity to organize useful knowledge through democratic processes of judgment, and thereby to make relatively good policy choices, helped to make Athens an exceptionally influential, secure, and prosperous city-state (Ober 2008a).

7.7 AGGREGATING EXPERTISE AT SCALE

Ancient Athens, with a total population of perhaps a quarter-million, was tiny compared to most modern states. That small scale is certainly one reason that the relevant expertise aggregation approach worked well for Athens as its primary form of legislating by direct votes of the citizen body. The REA approach might, however, be adapted to the purposes of a much larger democratic state, one in which legislation is ordinarily made by representatives. The basic approach of preliminary deliberation on domains and experts by a smaller agenda-setting body as advisory to a larger legislative body could readily be adopted by a system of political representation. But is REA also scalable for a directly democratic legislative process – for example a system employing occasional public referenda? The large-scale citizen referendum does not have an especially good reputation among social scientists, who rightly point out that the very high costs of gaining the information necessary to cast a responsible vote are not paid by most citizens.

As a result, referenda may not reliably produce policy that tracks majority preferences, much less that secures the common interest (Achen and Bartels 2016: Chapter 3). The design of the REA process, described above, might alleviate that problem.

As noted above (Section 3.1), basic democracy must answer the question of why a rational individual would choose to pay the high costs of responsible citizenship. The REA process aims to achieve epistemically satisfactory outcomes *without* imposing on individual citizens an unrealistically high cognitive burden, or a level of effort that would preclude pursuing other socially valued projects. The case study described above suggests that in ancient Athens something like an REA process in fact produced the desired outcome without imposing excessive costs. The question is whether the process is scalable, and thus potentially suited to a large modern state.

Hypothetically, at least, the REA process might be adapted to a contemporary system of public decision making by citizen referendum.[32] Suppose that, after a ballot measure to be voted on directly by the citizenry has been proposed and certified through an established process of initiation, a representative citizen council is selected by democratic process (say, sortition by random selection). Through a process of deliberation and voting similar to that described in the Athenian example, the citizen council establishes a set of domains of expertise relevant to the issue, hears expert testimony in each domain, and identifies and then rank-orders two or more options. The results of the council's work (including domain weighting and vote tallies on each option, by domain) are published in advance of the popular vote on the issue.

The published results are intended to provide voters with valuable and readily processed information about the judgments of a cross-section of their fellow citizens (Hawthorne und.: 40–53). Some voters might take the time to review the council's narrative of its hearings, votes, and deliberations. Yet simply by checking the relevance-weighted domains by which the council voted, a voter can decide how well the council's choice and ranking of domains tracks her own sense of these matters. The vote in each domain tells her how the various options fared domain-by-domain, based on the councilors' judgment of expert testimony. She knows which option would be chosen, and what the final scores for each option would be, if the decision were made on the basis of the aggregated domain-votes of the councilors. And she can take all of this into consideration in her own

---

[32] Some American states, notably Oregon, do employ official Citizen Review Boards to provide guidance to voters on referenda; see discussion in Mendez 2016: Chapter 4.

option choice, in light of her views on the competence of the councilors and any other information to which she cares to attend. REA resembles real-world experiments incorporating deliberation into democratic decision making (Warren and Pearse 2008), but it arguably provides more information directly useful to voters at a substantially lower information-procurement cost to each voter.[33]

This cursory account of a democratic approach to expertise aggregation necessarily leaves much unspecified – notably the details of arguments by which domains, options, and experts are identified and ranked in a process of iterated deliberation and voting. The point of the exercise is to suggest that a very large citizenry is, in theory, capable of making use of valuable expertise when deciding directly on matters of great importance and common interest. Moreover it can do so a reasonable cost and without sacrificing the core democratic commitment to participation or the conditions of freedom, equality, and dignity.

The REA approach assumes a certain level of competence across the citizen population in the political skills of specifying options, experts, domains, and ranking. It also assumes a level of common knowledge regarding political processes; an ability and willingness to learn through experience how to distinguish highly skilled from unskilled practitioners; and a general agreement that some democratic decisions are rightly regarded as matters for aggregated judgment rather than aggregated preferences. Whether those assumptions are valid for a given population will depend on the distribution and subsequent social development of (in Aristotelian terms) practical wisdom. The argument of Chapter 5, concerning natural human capacities, supports a presumption that the distribution of the potential for developing practical wisdom is adequate. My discussion of civic education points to how that potential could be cultivated in a systematic way by a democratic society sufficiently concerned with its own perpetuation.

The approach to legislation that I have sketched in this chapter is not meant to be the *primary* decision method for a large, modern state. It is not suited to the many decisions that must be made based primarily on majority preferences. For any large, modern state, it is assumed to be supplementary to something resembling familiar competitive systems (whether parliamentary or presidential) of democratic political representation. But

---

[33] Alternatively, the council's job could be limited to setting relevant domains and options, and independent citizen panels could be appointed to hear expert testimony and vote on options in each domain. This would limit opportunities for strategic behavior by the councilors, but would also limit the voters' experience of one another, and thus their knowledge of each other's capabilities.

even assuming that the direct involvement of citizens in matters of judgment on issues of common interest remains no more than an occasional supplement to government by representatives, it is, based on the argument for revocable delegated authority offered above, an *essential* supplement: Democracy must, by definition, avoid elite capture. Representatives are likely, in almost any democracy, to be in various ways elite. While elites may compete, there remains the danger that elite representatives will coordinate to promote elite interests against the common interest of the demos. If representatives are to be prevented from using their position to capture the political system, they cannot be allowed a monopoly on the legislative process.[34]

Basic democracy's institutional solution to the threat of elite capture is for the citizens to have ready at hand the option of governing the state directly, not only in their own name but also by their own choices. Even if used only rarely, the existence of a credible direct-democracy alternative forces elite representatives to attend closely to common interests, in their own interest as privileged political actors, in order to minimize the likelihood that the citizenry will avail itself of the direct alternative. The people's interest in keeping the alternative credible gives citizens good reason to educate themselves, but also to reward representatives who legislate in the common interest with an eye to elegant simplicity, and to punish those who do not.

The system I have described as relevant expertise aggregation is offered as one possible design solution to the problem of enabling a capable demos to assume direct responsibility for legislation in a large, modern state. It is modeled on the Athenian experience of direct democracy. Athenian decision-making processes were demonstrably fallible and REA would, likewise, be a fallible method of policy making. There is no reason to think that, assuming there is a best choice among feasible options, an REA process would invariably identify an option set that includes the best option or would select the best option if it were included in the set. But, unless and until some infallible method of making policy is devised, fallibility ought not to preclude consideration of a decision method.

Direct democracy, as an occasional expedient, does not have to clear the bar of consistently governing as well as the best-functioning representative system. So long as it can substantially outperform random choice, and at least equal the performance of a well-functioning autocracy, it will have fulfilled the functional requirements of a basic democracy. If the direct

---

[34] I discuss these issues, in reference to classical Athens, in Ober 1989.

alternative is likely to produce very inferior policy, then preventing elite capture by revoking decision authority comes at a high cost, even if it is used only rarely. But insofar as the direct alternative is genuinely epistemic, and thereby capable of producing innovative and valuable policy, it may be counted as providing a potential benefit over and above its value in preserving the end of nontyranny. Whether an occasional resort to directly democratic government in a real-world democracy would be a net benefit, in terms of welfare and security outcomes, if citizens had the best possible education, is not easily answered. The empirical evidence on modern referenda cannot answer that question given the limited civic education offered by modern democracies.

The preceding chapters sketched the primary rules of a system of basic democracy, the civic education of its citizens, the values it supports, and a few of the institutions that might be devised to sustain it. In the concluding chapter I seek to move from the specifics of the history of democracy in ancient Athens and the thought experiment of Demopolis to a general theory of democracy.

CHAPTER 8

A Theory of Democracy

A realistic normative and positive political theory of democracy should do at least two things: First, it should explain how, despite the advantages autocrats enjoy in command and control, democratic states have historically done comparatively well in providing security and welfare. Next, it should highlight the kind of laws, norms, and habitual behavior to which democratic citizens ought to aspire if they are best to promote their own joint and several flourishing. The prominence of liberal values in contemporary political theory, and of liberal institutions in modern constitutional systems, has concentrated the attention of theorists on the contribution of liberalism to democracy's success and to its aspirations. The goal of this book has been to isolate and illuminate the contribution of collective and limited self-government by citizens in the realization of those ends.

8.1 THEORY AND PRACTICE

Basic democracy, as illustrated by the thought experiment of Demopolis, is a solution to the puzzle of how, within a competitive ecology of states, a large and diverse body of people might create a stable political order that is at once secure, prosperous, and nonautocratic. The solution is a set of rules facilitating collective and limited self-governance by well-motivated and capable citizens – individuals with reasons to cooperate in political action and the skills to make their actions count. Both in theory and in historical practice, as illustrated by the history of classical Athens, democracy can, under the right conditions, meet what I called "Hobbes's challenge," the claim that any secure and prosperous state requires a third-party enforcer in the guise of a lawless sovereign.

Basic democracy solves the collective action problem that lies at the heart of Hobbes's challenge by providing individual citizens, who share a preference for nontyranny and have a common interest in security and prosperity, with good reasons to believe that participation costs are shared by their fellow citizens. Because those costs are also construed as benefits, and because democracy can offer high honors to the ambitious, while restraining disruptive forms of self-aggrandizement, democracy addresses problems of psychological motivation that Hobbes raised in *Leviathan* but failed fully to resolve. It provides citizens with the tools, in the form of procedural mechanisms and behavioral habits, that enable them to respond effectively, as individuals and as a demos, to the challenging and mutable world in which they live.

Because citizens who are able and ready to coordinate against violators are mutually protected against exploitation by the arrogant and powerful, they rationally invest in human capital and share what they know when it may be of value in the pursuit of their common interests. Gains in the stock of knowledge and its effective uses counterbalance the relatively high operating costs of collective self-governance. Epistemic depth and diversity create a comparative advantage relative to autocratic states. The upshot is a regime of limited self-government that provides internal and external security and adequate levels of welfare for an extensive and socially diverse population within a bounded territory. That regime places substantial but not onerous responsibilities of political participation upon citizens. Basic democracy creates adaptive institutions and promotes commitment to political liberty, political equality, and civic dignity, sustaining conditions that in turn enable and preserve the secure, prosperous, and nontyrannical regime.

Basic democracy reliably provides citizens with the democratic good of freely exercising their constitutive human capacities of employing reason and communication to the most significant social ends. They do so through deliberating and making decisions about important matters relevant to their joint and several well-being. Because a basic democracy recognizes political participation as a both a responsibility and a good in itself, it pushes in the direction of civic inclusivity. It requires justification for exclusion of long-term residents of the state territory from the status of citizen. At the same time it requires that citizens be adequately educated in the ends for which the democratic state exists, and in the public means necessary to secure those ends. Because all long-term residents are presumptively potential citizens, the state must educate all of its residents.

A basic democracy may delegate authority for day-to-day government to representatives. It must devise mechanisms that enable the citizens to avail themselves of expertise. But the demos must also remain vigilant against the threat of elite capture of the state. The citizens themselves must be capable of governing in case representatives violate the trust placed in them by the demos. In order to fulfill his or her participatory role in the democratic system, each citizen must have access to education and adequate welfare. Although basic democracy does not, in and of itself, generate a justice-based distributive principle (comparable to, for example, the difference principle of Rawls 1971), it must provide a baseline of welfare and education for citizens and for potential citizens.

Basic democracy sustains the conditions of political liberty, political equality, and civic dignity. It does so reliably, whether or not these conditions are valued by the citizens as ends in themselves, because democracy functionally requires these conditions if it is to sustain nontyranny while producing benefits of social cooperation sufficiently abundant to address existential threats. In the place of autocratic social coordination based on hierarchy, centralized command and control, and ideological mystification, basic democracy substitutes coordinated collective action of highly motivated and rationally self-interested citizens. It does so by employing well-publicized rules (laws and norms) as focal points for the mobilization of citizens in defense of the civic dignity that is the precondition of each citizen having the secure high standing essential for full participation. Dignity in turn helps to moderate competing distributive justice demands arising from freedom and equality, and thus preserves a self-reinforcing social equilibrium.

Basic democracy is legitimate in that it can justify to citizens and potential citizens, through civic education, why they ought to obey democratically enacted rules and why the participatory costs of citizenship ought to be paid by each citizen. Democracy can develop institutional mechanisms and associated behavioral habits that make possible the identification, aggregation, and mobilization of expertise while keeping the threat of elite capture at bay. This enables citizens to judge reasonably well among a variety of policy options relevant to common interests. Authority delegated to representatives remains conditional and revocable, which in turn provides representatives with incentives not to violate their trust. Democracy can, in theory, reliably provide the ends of security, prosperity, and nontyranny for which the state exists, and can provide the first two ends at least as well as can a well-functioning autocracy.

Democracy is not easily realized in practice. A political regime that conformed (within the historically contingent frame) to the ideal type of basic democracy as illustrated by Demopolis was sustained for some six human generations in classical Athens (Ober 2008a, 2012). Athens provides the best-documented example of a long-lasting and high-performing democracy unaffected by early-modern or contemporary liberalism. Although the

Athenians imposed constitutional limits on their own legislative authority, theirs was a direct democracy, without need of elected representatives. Athens was, however, by the standards of modernity, a very small state. For basic democracy to be possible under the conditions of modernity, it must be scalable. Representative institutions address the problem of scale, but create new opportunities for elite capture of government.

The difficulty of implementing democracy is compounded by value pluralism: Hobbes was not being tendentious, even though he was wrong, when he asserted that limited self-government by citizens (along with other forms of limited government) would be incapable of sustaining prosperity and security. It is not surprising that democracy, despite its deep history as the normal form of small-scale human social organization before the development of agriculture and the rise of large states, has been only rarely achieved in the recorded history of complex societies. Although democracy is today a near-universal aspiration, there is also a near-universal sense that it is inadequately realized. Various failed experiments with democratization in the twentieth and twenty-first centuries demonstrate that it is no simple matter to implement citizen self-government.

The intertwined history of republicanism and liberalism in Europe and America (Kalyvas and Katznelson 2008), a history which was, by the nineteenth century, further enmeshed with self-consciously democratic theory and practice, makes it more difficult to identify basic democracy in modernity. No modern regime fully exemplifies the ideal type. But at least some modern regimes may reasonably be characterized as collective and limited self-government by citizens, through their accountable representatives. Candidate examples include (but certainly are not limited to) the US in the Jacksonian era of in the early nineteenth century and in the civil rights era of the mid twentieth century; British parliamentary democracy of the later nineteenth century; European social democracies of the mid twentieth century; and the highly pluralistic democracy of modern India.

What of basic democracy today? In contemporary liberal-democratic states, the resort to popular referenda and citizen-sponsored legislative initiatives in both local and national jurisdictions is often associated with pushback by citizens against what is perceived as overreaching by agents of an unaccountable government. The role of independent agencies and representatives can be justified in contemporary liberalism, and is consistent with the idea that the democratic authority of the people is readily and appropriately separated from government. But among the concerns that drive populist politics and/or the resort to directly democratic mechanisms in modern states is a widespread conviction that government is illegitimately dominated by elites and technocrats, who rule in their own interest and against the interests of ordinary people.

Legislative referenda and citizen initiatives seem symptomatic of the antityrannical impulse that creates reverse dominance hierarchy in face-to-face foraging communities and gave rise to democratic government in ancient Athens. In imaginary Demopolis the citizens are capable of governing, and so the occasional resort to direct democracy does not degrade state performance. But the stunted civic education offered by real modern states may be unequal to the task of producing a capable demos. In the absence of adequate civic education, citizens lack the motivation and the skills necessary to govern themselves. In that case, the antityrannical impulse facilitates populism and/or facilitates elite capture, as demogogues and moneyed interests frame the political debate. It fosters unstable perversions of democracy, as opportunistic politicians channel antityrannical sentiment into paranoia and warped nostalgia for a mythic age of national unity and civic virtue. In a worst-case scenario the incoherent interventions of an incapable demos could end in a Hobbesian state of nature. The fear of undesirable outcomes like these has contributed to the rejection of citizen self-government by liberal theorists and political scientists. This book defends democracy by showing how a demos could become capable of governing: how citizens could rule themselves as a collectivity under demanding yet realistically achievable conditions.

8.2 SO WHAT?

Sir Moses Finley, an influential twentieth-century Cambridge historian of Greek and Roman antiquity, reputedly used to insist that authors of complex arguments about arcane topics explain the significance of their work with questions that that could be summed up in two words: "So what?"[1] I imagine this laconic query as encapsulating a more extended challenge in this form:

> Suppose we, as critical but potentially sympathetic readers with a sincere interest in the topic of your book, are willing to stipulate that everything you have claimed so far is true. Why should the result be of interest to us? What have we learned? How do your conclusions change the way we ought to be thinking about some matter of genuine importance?

[1] Finley's method is elucidated in his published works, e.g., Finley 1975, 1985.

A "so what challenge" to the theory of democracy before liberalism might be motivated by the fact that the practice of democracy was re-established only in the late eighteenth and nineteenth centuries, in conjunction with what might be called the "liberal suite" of institutional design principles – including representation, balance of governmental powers, federalism, and the conception of the sovereignty of the people as separate from any given agency of government. Those design principles were developed within a framework of liberal ideas and values, and they arguably have been crucial to the development and persistence of democratic regimes in large, modern societies. So why bother with a theory that seemingly strips from democracy the conditions of its modern possibility and leans on a small-scale ancient example as proof of its feasibility?

I claimed in the first chapter that distinguishing democracy as such from liberal democracy *makes sense* both analytically (insofar as democracy and liberalism are different things) and historically (insofar as democracy antedates liberalism). But clearing the bar of making sense does not answer the so what question. The remainder of this concluding chapter asks what practical value a theory of democracy before liberalism might have for the implementation and design of contemporary liberal and nonliberal political regimes. Along the way it compares the theory of democracy I have developed in the previous chapters with other contemporary political theories of democracy.

8.3 TOO ILLIBERAL OR TOO LIBERAL?

As I sought to show in the previous chapters, basic democracy – in the foundational sense of a set of rules for sustaining security, prosperity, and non-tyranny – is a genuine political phenomenon. But basic democracy is not readily observed in the contemporary world. This is because regimes come with a superstructure of rules concerned with values; in liberal-democratic regimes, the relevant values typically include commitments to personal autonomy, universal human rights, distributive justice, and state-level religious neutrality. The superstructure may be the point of the regime, just as the above-ground superstructure is the point of a building. But, so I have argued, without a secure political foundation, the regime, like a building, will not stand.

In response to the so what challenge, I propose that basic democracy will be a candidate for a theory of substantial interest if it has the potential to provide a foundation on which either liberal or nonliberal superstructures of rules and norms may be constructed. Moreover, that foundation ought, potentially, to allow for the superstructure to be substantially revised, or even torn down and built anew. It ought to enable that sort of change to occur without destroying the political basis of the state's persistence, under a system of government that reliably preserves the basic ends for which the state exists and on which the citizens can agree. This political robustness at the base allows for high levels of value pluralism among the state's residents, for ongoing disagreement, and for frank and open contestation regarding the moral ends that ought and ought not to be pursued by the state. But it also allows for a baseline of agreement, enabling coordination among citizens.

If it is to support either liberal or nonliberal institutions and norms, the democratic foundation must not be, itself, inherently liberal or illiberal. This means that I must be able to refute two sets of objections, neither of which is, on the face of it, implausible. We may think of these objections as the Scylla of "too illiberal to sustain liberalism" and the Charybdis of "too liberal to sustain nonliberal norms." The passage between whirlpool and shoals may seem dauntingly narrow.

The first objection is that in the absence of liberalism democracy is inherently illiberal. A political regime is, I suppose, inherently illiberal if in order to exist it requires illiberal conditions – institutions, norms, and behavioral habits. Illiberal conditions may, for our purposes, be defined as those conditions that would be regarded as ethically impermissible by a contemporary liberal or would be legally forbidden in a contemporary liberal constitutional regime. Of course, there is range of views within contemporary liberalism about what is ethically permissible and what ought to be legally forbidden. But presumably any regime must be regarded as illiberal if it depends for its existence on slavery, on a discriminatory state religion, or on political institutions that violate ordinary conceptions of human rights.

Ancient Athens, along with other Greek states, supported slavery, had a state religion, and practiced ostracism. Athens was, in these relevant ways, an illiberal society. The question remains whether Athenian democracy, as a political regime, depended on these (or other) illiberal conditions for its existence. It is often supposed that the answer must be yes. Some liberal political theorists have responded to their nonliberal (or less liberal) interlocutors by accusing them of "polis nostalgia" and by characterizing ancient democracy as inherently illiberal.[2]

---

[2] Holmes 1979 (with particular reference to the work of Leo Strauss and Hannah Arendt); Waldron 1992.

There is no doubt that ancient Greek democracies were in fact *not* liberal in various relevant ways, even if we stay within the ambit of the community of citizens. In addition to the obvious facts of slavery and denial of political participation rights to women and most long-term foreign residents, to which we return below, Athens had a law forbidding impiety. Citizens could be, and were (infamously, in the case of Socrates) tried and punished for failing to meet community standards of piety. Moreover, the Athenian institution of ostracism meant that a citizen could be expelled from the community without a trial, indeed without being formally accused of legally actionable wrong-doing, simply because a plurality of his fellow citizens were troubled by his presence.

If Demopolis, as a model of a basic democracy that can be imagined as existing in modernity, must be committed to those sorts of rules (or to slavery, or monopoly of participation rights by native males) in the sense that such rules are necessary conditions of its existence, then it is, in fact, fundamentally *illiberal* in the incompatibility sense, rather than being merely *nonliberal* in the sense of lacking liberal features. If that is the case, it fails one important "so what" test. There is not much reason to think that a *necessarily* illiberal political regime is likely to be of great interest to people now and around here, when "around here" is defined as the developed western world. In any event, if I cannot answer the "necessarily illiberal" version of the "so what" question, I will not have advanced much beyond earlier, strictly historical, work on democracy before liberalism.

The second objection that, if sustained, would render my project relatively uninteresting, is that, under the large-state conditions of modernity, liberal conditions (institutions, norms, behaviors) are necessary for democracy. That is to say that now and around here – with "around here" in this case being the whole world – there *can be* no democracy without liberalism. If that is right, then, if it is not simply a category error, nonliberal democracy, whether or not it is illiberal (in the sense noted above), is one of two things, neither of which is of great interest to political theory: Either it is a historical curiosity, the irreproducible product of conditions uniquely typical of a bygone age. Or it is a fantasy, the product of wishful projection on the part of nonliberal theorists.

If nonliberal democracy is impossible under the conditions of modernity, then any modern population unwilling or unable to embrace liberalism is ipso facto denied the chance of living under its own democratic regime. In order to pass the second, "necessarily liberal," so what test, a basic democracy (one that is not sustained by the special circumstances of

Greek antiquity) must be able to accommodate a nonliberal regime, meaning that I must be able so show that (outside antiquity) democracy is not inherently liberal.[3]

If basic democracy were, in fact, necessarily liberal, the Demopolis thought experiment (supposing it is regarded as plausible) would, at best, have produced a thin theory of liberal democracy. In light of the range of rich, deep, and sophisticated theories of liberal democracy currently on offer, a thin new variant is not likely to be of much interest to people now and around here, when "around here" is the developed west. Moreover, it is not likely to be of any interest to people now and *not* "around here." By that, I mean the many people in other parts of the world who *are* strongly attracted to the idea of a government predicated on nontyranny but *are not* attracted to liberalism (Section 8.5). Some of those people might, under the right conditions, be willing to pay the costs of participatory citizenship. But *ex hypothesi* they reject value neutrality and/or some other essential piece of the contemporary liberal package.

The practice of ancient democracy was, per above, not liberal in various ways. But might ancient democracy also have been in salient ways liberal? Certain institutional features of democracy in classical Athens do bear a family resemblance to some aspects of liberalism.[4] While civic dignity is not predicated on universal human rights, it can, so I have argued elsewhere, be understood as a set of "quasi-rights" (Ober 2000 = 2005a: Chapter 5). Political liberty and political equality, which, as I have claimed, were indispensable for Athenian democracy, are familiar cornerstones of liberal political theory. The development in the direction of a stronger version of rule of law, the background Athenian commitment to impartiality in respect to judicial judgment, and the openness of certain Athenian institutions, in the sense of granting access to citizens and noncitizens alike, are consistent with conceiving of the government of ancient Athens as manifesting features consistent with liberal values.

Basic democracy will not be of much interest to a group seeking a form of nonliberal and nontyrannical order if these seemingly liberal features of Athenian democracy point to a necessary commitment on the part of a

---

[3] Müller 2016 argues that "illiberal democracy" is a category error, but his target is the understanding of democracy as majority tyranny advocated by democratic agonists and by autocrats who style themselves democrats.

[4] Cf. Balot 2016, who suggests that I have, in earlier work, presented classical era Greek democracy as, in important ways, resembling liberal democracy. For earlier accounts of "liberal ancient Athens," see Havelock 1957; Jones 1964.

basic democracy to value neutrality. If basic democracy turns out to require (in Rawls's terms) that comprehensive commitments to a particular version of the human good are excluded from the realm of public reason, if basic democracy forbids the establishment of a state religion, then it will certainly be too liberal for the purposes of some traditionally religious societies whose residents might seek a nontyrannical political order.

By reformulating the two objections as questions, I suppose that it is possible to move basic democracy beyond candidacy for the status of a political theory of substantial interest. Basic democracy can legitimately claim to be an interesting theory, and thereby answer the "so what" challenge, if it can offer a satisfactory answer to a query on the part of each of the two imagined groups of people alluded to above: The first group says, "We seek to build a secure and prosperous liberal society; how do we go about providing it with a stable foundation?" The second group says, "We seek to build a secure, prosperous, nontyrannical, society that is consistent with our shared traditional religious convictions; to what institutions and behavioral habits must we commit ourselves in order to achieve that goal?"

If the theory has good enough answers for the people in each of those groups, the "so what" question is answered, first, because the people posing those questions are not at all difficult to imagine in the world in which we find ourselves, here and now. That is, there really are people in the real world seeking to stabilize liberal societies and there are other people seeking to create nontyrannical, nonliberal societies.

The "so what" question is answered, next, because democratic theory does not currently have satisfactory answers for the people in either imagined group: Contemporary liberal political theory tends to say to the liberals seeking a stable order: "Get your liberal values right, you will find that stable democratic institutions follow." If the argument I have made in the previous chapters, to the effect that democracy *does*, and liberalism does *not*, have an equilibrium solution in a realistic, large, and socially diverse population of self-interested individuals, that answer is not satisfactory. To the nonliberals seeking nontyranny, the answer of current liberal theory is, "Get the right democratic institutions. Those institutions do bring with them a commitment to certain liberal values, but that ought not to trouble you." But if that commitment *does* deeply trouble them, then contemporary liberal-democratic theory has nothing to say to those unwilling to adapt their existing core values to the fundamental premises of liberalism.

Contemporary nonliberal political theory, for example agonistic pluralism, addresses questions that are elided or ignored in liberal theory. But agonistic democratic theory is not aimed at addressing the issues of stability and institution-building that are at the center of the questions posed by the people in my two imagined groups.[5]

Finally, the "so what" challenge is answered if it can be shown that understanding democracy before liberalism has real-world policy implications. A good deal of human misery has attended twenty-first-century policies of "democracy promotion," notably in the Middle East. Those policies were arguably based on a muddled set of ideas about democracy. American and allied policy makers engaged in democracy promotion, however good (or bad) their intentions toward the people in foreign countries may have been, appear to have had little sense of a distinction between democracy and liberalism, or of the conditions necessary for sustaining citizen self-governance, or of the demands that democracy makes on citizens.[6]

If we think that democratic theory ought to have, but does not yet have, answers for the questions posed by people seeking a secure foundation for a liberal regime, *and* for people seeking a nonliberal and nontyrannical regime, *and* for policy makers who must decide how to respond to people holding those sorts of hopes and ambitions, then the theory of basic democracy ought to be of substantial interest even if it can offer only preliminary answers. In the final two sections of this chapter I address certain concerns that I suppose would be raised by people in each of the groups imagined above, if and when they were told, "basic democracy can help you to solve your problem."

First, the liberals who have been told that they can build a sustainable liberal regime on the foundation of a basic democracy will be worried that a basic democracy's rules will build fundamentally illiberal conditions into the constitutional framework, both at the level of the society as a whole, and at the level of the community of citizens. If this is the case, basic democracy cannot provide a preliberal foundation for a liberal state.

---

[5] A sampling of contemporary democratic theory that pushes back against parts of the moralism of Rawlsian and Habermasian strains of political liberalism includes "realists" (Philp 2007; Geuss 2008; Galston 2010; Floyd 2011; Waldron 2013 with response by Estlund 2014); agonists (Honig 1993, 2001; Laclau and Mouffe 2001; Mouffe 2000, 2005). Wolin 1994, 1996 offers a specifically anti-institutionalist understanding of democracy, aimed at criticizing and potentially subverting systems of power, rather than creating or sustaining a stable system of government.

[6] Schmidt and Williams 2008: 199–204 identify "democracy promotion": as one of the four primary features of the Bush Doctrine that underpinned US foreign policy in Iraq and elsewhere in the early twenty-first century. They note (202) that from the viewpoint of a realist approach to foreign policy, "the grand project of *spreading democracy to the Middle East on the basis of alleged universal liberal principles* [emphasis added] is simply the latest example of a moralistic and crusading spirit in American foreign policy." Carothers 2007 offers a critical review of American attempts at democracy-building during the George W. Bush administration.

Next, the traditionalists seeking a nonliberal and nontyrannical regime, are worried that collective self-governance by citizens will require accepting the liberal idea that the regime must be committed to neutrality in respect to religion. If those worries can be allayed, for liberals and nonliberals alike, then I suppose the "so what" question has been laid to rest – even though filling out the theory of democracy, in ways that might address other possible concerns of both liberals and nonliberals, remains incomplete.[7]

8.4 A FOUNDATION FOR A LIBERAL REGIME?

We may test basic democracy as a potential foundation for a liberal regime, addressing the worry about whether limited government is possible outside of a preexisting liberal framework, by asking two questions: First, in the realm of theory: Is there anything in the democratic constitution designed by the imagined Founders of Demopolis that would render it unsuitable as a foundation on which a liberal constitutional superstructure could be erected? Next, in the realm of history: Were the illiberal features of the Athenian political regime essential to fulfilling the ends of nontyranny, prosperity, and security?

In response to the first question, it is certainly *not* the case that Demopolis's constitutional order will support *every* variant of liberalism represented in contemporary mainstream political and ethical theory. Given its concern for secure borders and relatively stringent requirements (sketched in the previous chapters in terms of civic education) for the exercise of participatory citizenship, Demopolis is a *state*, in what I take to be the conventional sense of the term.[8] It is not a suitable foundation for any version of cosmopolitan liberal order that regards state-based restrictions on immigration and rights of citizenship as inherently illegitimate. Some liberal-democratic theorists have argued for a strongly cosmopolitan world order, and against the legitimacy of national border controls or restrictions on grants of citizenship.[9] Moreover, given that prosperity is among the ends

---

[7] Of course each group will probably also have *other* concerns – but the goal here is to show that the rough theory of basic democracy offered here is interesting enough to warrant further consideration by the groups in question, not to show that all possible concerns that it raises have been, or could be, definitively laid to rest.

[8] The definition of the state, and whether the Greek polis is (as I suppose) rightly considered a state, is discussed by Rhodes 1995; Berent 1996, 2000, 2006; Hansen 2002. Because I suppose that the Greek polis is rightly understood as a state, I do not suppose that expecting ordinary citizens to participate in enforcement of rules drops Demopolis into the category of "acephaplous, stateless society."

[9] State control of borders illegitimate in light of the demands of global justice: Carens 1987; Archibugi 2012; Abizahdeh 2012.

for which Demopolis exists, it will not answer the demands of global justice theorists who require "down-leveling" wealth transfers from affluent to impoverished countries, such that all persons of the world end up at roughly the same, relatively low (by the current standards of developed countries), state of material existence.[10]

Cosmopolitan and global justice arguments have, however, been answered, within liberal-democratic theory, by political theorists who have made a case for the legitimacy of the state with at least some authority to control access to its territory and membership, and that ranks local welfare above global welfare. These "liberal statist" arguments are explicitly *liberal* in that they do not rest on claims about special rights arising from nationalism or a historically shared culture. Insofar as the arguments offered by the liberal statists have purchase, it is not, therefore, obvious on the face of it that Demopolis's restrictions on immigration and citizenship, or greater concern for local than for universal prosperity, render it, ipso facto, fundamentally illiberal.[11]

Demopolis will not be a suitable basis for any variant of liberalism that conceives of the demands of within-country distributive justice in terms of the strongest forms of either social equality or personal freedom (Section 6.8). The regulating function of civic dignity requires a substantial level of social services for citizens and thus requires a level of taxation sufficient to support those services. Those requirements are likely to conflict with the justice demands of variants of liberalism that merge with market libertarianism. But civic dignity also limits Demopolis's level of material goods redistribution in ways that will fail to satisfy the requirements of versions of liberalism that merge with state socialism.

These restrictions on the range of liberalism that can readily be supported by basic democracy leave available, however, a very substantial set of liberal social arrangements. These range, I suppose, from the sort of virtue-centered civism advocated by Michael Sandel (1998), to the democratic republicanism of the recent work of Philip Pettit (2013), to the utilitarian representative democracy preferred by J. S. Mill (1861), to the experimental pragmatism of John Dewey (1917), to the anti-elitist "Machiavellian democracy" of John McCormick (2011), to the decent regime of Rawls's

---

[10] Brock and Moellendorf 2005 offers essays pro and con cosmopolitan global justice; Pogge 2008 is an influential statement of the position that justice demands a strong form of global wealth redistribution.

[11] Liberal state theorists: Blake 2003; Stilz 2009, 2011; Scheuerman 2012, responding to cosmopolitan liberals (above) and to nationalism theorists, notably Miller 2000, and shared-culture theorists, notably Kymlicka 1995. Note that the legitimacy of Demopolis is *not* predicated on claims arising from nationalism or a past history of shared culture.

Law of Peoples (1999), to the overlapping consensus of Rawls's *Political Liberalism* (1996), to the deontological justice-centered regime chosen behind the veil of ignorance in Rawls's *Theory of Justice* (1971).[12] If none of these regimes looks, on the face of it, much like Demopolis, it is because what I have called the value-based superstructure has profoundly altered the regime's appearance, and obscures the basic democratic infrastructure.

The civic education that makes it possible for citizens in Demopolis to carry out the responsibilities of citizenship in a capable manner is unsuited to variants of liberalism predicated on a very strong conception of individual autonomy and therefore on strict state neutrality among the ends individuals might choose to pursue. Demopolis's civic education promotes a political preference for nontyranny. It may urge the value of exercising human capacities for sociability, reason, and communication at the highest levels of decision making. It seeks to create a certain character – insofar as character is defined as certain habitual behaviors (notably, defense of those threatened with indignity) based on commonly held beliefs (the badness of inflicted humiliation and infantilization).

On the other hand, Demopolis's civic education is nonideological in the sense of being reality based (grounded in the evidence of history and natural and social science) and revisable in light of new scientific findings. Although it cannot accommodate religious convictions forbidding political participation, it does not otherwise promote any particular attitude toward a divine order. Finally, civic education is nonmandatory, in that there are (albeit costly) opt-out options, both in terms of choosing to be a resident noncitizen (with whatever disabilities that may entail) or to exit the community. Prominent liberal theorists, committed to the general principle of personal autonomy, have defended the right and responsibility of a liberal state to enforce mandatory standards in public education, when necessary overriding the religious convictions of parents. It seems plausible to suppose that a range of variants of liberalism would be accommodated within the scope of the kind of civic education required of citizens by a basic democracy.[13]

---

[12] Basic democracy does not, on the face of it, conflict with a range of liberal redistributive programs, ranging from, for example, Tomasi 2012 on the right to Rawls 2001 on the left. It is not, on the face of it, compatible with, on the libertarian side, Nozick 1974 or, on the socialist side, Cohen 2008.

[13] Shklar 1989: 33 argues that "no liberal state can ever have an educative government that aims at creating certain kinds of character and enforces its own beliefs." Demopolis does aim at creating citizens with certain behavioral habits, but it does not *enforce* its own beliefs, so it is not clear that it is "didactic in intent in that exclusive and inherently authoritarian way." Liberalism and mandatory public education: Gutmann 1999; Macedo 2000; Reich 2002, with literature cited.

Meanwhile, a liberal may be reassured by basic democracy's reliance on the conditions of political liberty, political equality, and civic dignity. While these are thinner conceptions of liberty, equality, and dignity than the liberal will want, they are securely entrenched as necessary conditions, and are available as first steps toward thicker value-laden conceptions. While neither value neutrality (other than specified above) nor human rights are demanded by basic democracy, neither are they blocked by it.

When we move to the realm of history, we see that, while citizenship was a clearly defined status within Athenian society, Athens did not create caste-like conditions in which the lives of all noncitizens were sharply separated from and systematically inferior to the lives of citizens. Recent scholarship on Athenian social history has emphasized the many ways in which lives of citizens and noncitizens were interdependent and interwoven in practice. While citizenship did provide privileged access to certain property rights (notably the right to own land), as well as unique access to voting and officeholding, citizens and noncitizens participated on essentially equal footing in many aspects of commercial, religious, and associational life. Athenian civil law protected noncitizens in various ways. On the whole, access to public institutions tended to become more open over the course of Athenian democratic history.[14]

There is no reason to think that extending citizenship rights to most long-term free residents of Athenian territory would have compromised the security or prosperity of the ancient Athenian polis. As we have seen (Section 2.1), Athens extended citizenship to all those who fell within the limits of the ancient Greek imaginative frame, but the Greek cultural imagination concerning who could be a citizen limited full participation rights to native males and some privileged foreigners. It would be peculiar to think that Athenian security or prosperity depended upon the restriction of citizenship to adult males. Quite to the contrary, there are reasons to think that, had the Athenians been able to think outside the box of their cultural imagination of citizenship, the performance of the state would have been enhanced by extending political participation rights to native women and to those resident foreigners eager and willing to take on the responsibilities of participatory citizenship. The causal arrow from epistemic diversity within the citizenry to effective policy, posited in Section 7.4, suggests that such inclusion would have promoted Athens's state capacity.[15]

---

[14] On intertwined lives of citizens and noncitizens, see the essays collected in Taylor and Vlassopoulos 2015. More open access over time: Ober 2010.

[15] The plan to give women participation rights, in Aristophanes's comedy *Assemblywomen*, is predicated on the assumption that women would be better than men at devising policies aimed at security

The economic contribution of ancient slavery to Greek society is, on the other hand, a vexed issue. Would a counterfactual Athens that had abolished slavery and enfranchised former slaves after the Peloponnesian War (for example), have been more or less secure and prosperous than real-world Athens over the next 80 years?[16] The argument that the leisure necessary for civic participation was made possible entirely, or even primarily, by exploitation of slaves is weak.[17] The labor inputs of slaves were of obvious value to the state, but it does not seem beyond the realm of possibility that Athens could have attracted an adequate supply of free laborers without the expedient of purchasing slaves. Given that the wages of at least some slaves were equal to wages of free citizens and resident aliens who were engaged in similar occupations, it is not obvious that slavery in and of itself (as opposed to the labor inputs of noncitizen residents, free and slave) added massively to the overall material prosperity of the community.[18] Public slaves, serving as expert secretaries, provided some forms of bureaucratic expertise that were very valuable to the state. But it is possible to imagine that free persons (whether citizens – some of whom did serve as secretaries to offices, or resident aliens) could have provided similarly valuable expertise.[19]

It is, nonetheless, possible to argue that these free labor alternatives would not have provided adequate labor inputs and so, without resort to the expedient of unfree labor, Athens would have failed to provide the three ends of security, prosperity, and nontyranny within the competitive environment of the Greek states.[20] But in this instance, at least, history is not dispositive: Now and around here, in the developed parts of the modern world, machines are our slaves – in that they do much of the productive and burdensome work that would otherwise have to be done by humans, and

and prosperity. While this is a comedy, it captures the idea that the Athenians, by restricting political participation to men, were missing out on a resource that could have benefited the state.

[16] A proposal to enfranchise all noncitizens, including slaves, who had supported the democratic side in the recent civil was passed by the Athenian assembly but was nullified by a legal challenge: [Aristotle] *Constitution of Athens* 40.2. This would not have amounted to the abolition of slavery but might be imagined as a step in that direction. Aristotle *Politics* 1.1255a–b suggests that some theorists, with whom he fundamentally disagreed, objected to all slavery as inherently unnatural. Monoson 2011: 272 characterizes the ancient critics of slavery alluded to by Aristotle as abolitionists.

[17] See Wood 1988, who deflates the claim that there is a necessary relationship between slavery and the provision of citizens' leisure.

[18] Slave labor and economics: Scheidel 2008; E. Cohen 1992. Manumission: Zelnick-Abramovitz 2005, 2009; Akrigg 2015; Kamen 2017.

[19] Ismard 2015 argues that the Athenian civic culture of democracy was defended by "outsourcing" the need for expertise in various areas necessary to government to public slaves. But on expertise within (as well as beyond) the citizen body, see Pyzyk 2015.

[20] Osborne 1995, for example, claims that democratic Athens did in fact depend on slave labor for its continued existence. Scheidel 2008 offers an overview of the question of the degree to which ancient economies fundamentally depended on slavery.

they do it at a lower cost. Nonfree, slave or slave-like human labor remains prevalent (if officially illegal) in many modern societies, including modern liberal democracies. But under the technological conditions of modernity, it is implausible to say that any sort of democratic regime, liberal or non-liberal, *requires* slavery for its continued security and prosperity.

Turning to conditions within the community of citizens: There is no reason to suppose that laws mandating religious piety, or allowing for institutions like ostracism, are essential to the functioning of a basic democracy. In the case of Athens, the law forbidding impiety did not, in fact, define piety, leaving it to the majority vote of the citizen jury in each specific case to choose between the accounts of piety offered by defendant and prosecutor. I have argued elsewhere (Ober 2016) that personal responsibility for the public effects of one's own public speech was a central aspect of the Athenian conception of free speech. The conviction of Socrates in 399 BCE is at least in part explained by the belief among his fellow citizens that Socrates was criminally unwilling to take responsibility for the likely (if unintended) effects his own speech. While "assuming personal and legal responsibility for the effects of public speech" does not figure among the central commitments of liberalism, neither is it, on the face of it, illiberal.[21] The ostracism law remained on the books through the democratic era, but no ostracism was held after ca. 415 BCE. Since Athenian democracy lasted long after ostracism was actually employed, ostracism was clearly not a necessary condition of Athens's democracy.[22]

As I have argued in more detail elsewhere, although Athens never became a liberal state, certain rules established by citizens extended (at least in principle) significant "rights-like" legal immunities to Athens-resident noncitizens: to women, foreigners, and even to slaves. Moreover, as a historical trend, especially in the generations after the Peloponnesian War, the state tended increasingly to publicly recognize and promote the religious interests of non-Athenian and non-Greek minority populations (through grants of public land for religious sanctuaries), and to extend more opportunities for access to legal dispute resolution (at least in certain spheres) to noncitizens.[23]

---

[21] As the standard free speech limit case example of "shouting fire in a crowded theater" readily demonstrates. Williams 1993: Chapter 3 shows that there was no tight connection between intention and responsibility in ancient Greek conceptions of personal responsibility for outcomes, and argues that in this, as in other sorts of ethical reasoning, the Greeks got it more or less right.

[22] Ostracism: Ober 2015b: 174–175, with literature cited. There is little reason to think that the "shadow" of potential ostracism was doing any work by the fourth century BCE.

[23] Ober 2008a: 249–253; but cf. ibid., 258–263 for the limited "horizons of fairness" in classical Athens.

8.5 A NONLIBERAL, NONTYRANNICAL REGIME?

The second question, above, was posed by a hypothetical group of religious traditionalists. They seek a prosperous and secure form of nontyranny, but reject state-level value neutrality in respect to religion, and perhaps other core tenets of liberalism. Basic democracy is obviously unsuited to any community whose comprehensive beliefs *require* autocratic political authority. A religious community will not be able to make use of basic democracy as a form of government if their shared views entail granting a politically unaccountable individual or group final decision authority over centrally important matters of public policy (e.g., veto power over decisions made in a democratic assembly, or unaccountable legislative authority), on the basis of those persons' (putative) special relationship to a divine order. On the other hand, a religious community *lacking* the requirement that an individual or small group must hold ultimate and unaccountable authority over government *could* in principle choose to implement a basic democracy. Such a community might establish and entrench a state religion. It might be intolerant of other forms of religious expression. Citizenship might require religious conformity. Such a community would not be liberal, but it would not, ipso facto, be blocked from adopting a regime of basic democracy.

Freedom of political speech and association, along with political equality for citizens, remain essential conditions in a nonliberal basic democracy. Citizens must be free to imagine and advocate new institutional forms, and their collective judgment (as expressed, for example, in voting, whether for representatives or directly on legislation) must determine the community's policy on important matters of common interest. But the political forms of freedom and equality that are essential to basic democracy do not necessarily extend to robust forms of "freedom of conscience," or to toleration of religious beliefs believed by the community to be false. Autonomy, as it is understood in liberal moral theory, may be quite foreign to the value system of the religious community in question.

Likewise, the form of religion entrenched by a nonliberal-democratic state might be hierarchical, according special social status to some individuals and doing so on the basis of features (e.g., ancestry or "calling") that are extraneous to civic dignity. So long as the religious hierarchy accords citizens equal high standing in their public role as citizens, so long as they are not subjected to humiliation or infantilization in the course of participating in public action relevant to the collective self-governance of their community, social hierarchy need not be an impediment to the development of democracy. The civic dignity essential to basic democracy is what one experiences in one's life as a citizen; it protects against arbitrary acts by government officials and powerful individuals, but it does not guarantee equal standing within a community of faith.

Citizenship itself might be constitutionally restricted on the basis of conditions that would be regarded as extraneous to political participation by a liberal regime, e.g., gender or birthright. While basic democracy benefits from an epistemically diverse citizen body, it does not require diversity across all parameters that are taken as essential bases of equality in contemporary liberal societies. On the other hand, as we have seen, the political stability, and thus the security requirement of basic democracy, requires that all people who are culturally imagined as potential citizens have the opportunity to seek citizenship via undertaking the requisite civic education. In modernity, it is increasingly difficult for any society to claim that native, adult women cannot be locally unimagined as citizens. Likewise, the restriction of citizenship to those who can claim it as their birthright is increasingly difficult for democratic states to justify. Without a plausible justification, statutory restriction will tend to destabilize the society, thus threatening the end of security.

Basic democracy necessarily guarantees quite an extensive set of civic rights for citizens. It may, also for prudential reasons, guarantee certain civil rights to noncitizens – in the first instance to those whose lives are interdependently bound up with the lives of citizens. In the historical case of Athens, the practice of democracy, the experience of civic dignity by the citizens, the inherent danger to social order posed by arrogant expressions of superiority by the strong, and the recognition of the benefits (economic and otherwise) reaped by the community from the presence in the community of nonnatives, led to the extension of important legal immunities and protections to persons outside the citizenry. But a society adopting basic democracy may elect not to legislate the promotion, or even the active protection, of universal human rights. A nonliberal democracy may, therefore, reject the premise that rights are inherent in all persons on account of some prepolitical feature of the world – whether it is nature, reason, or divine dispensation.[24]

Basic democracy is, therefore, available as a *theoretical* option for a hypothetical community of persons in search of a nontyrannical and yet

---

[24] Like many other societies, ancient Greek cultural norms specified (in the guise of divine mandates) decent treatment of strangers. Inter-Greek wars were fought under a vague set of agreed-upon rules of engagement (Ober 1996: Chapter 5). But these cultural norms did not rise to the level of anything like "human rights." Whether there was a conception of "natural rights" in late-classical Greek thought is debated: Mitsis 1999; Cooper 1999: 427–448.

nonliberal form of social order. It remains an open question whether it is a *practical* option for any contemporary real-world religious community. The required conditions of civic participation, political liberty, political equality, and civic dignity place limits on the scope of religious authority. Moreover, the tendency of democracy to generate institutional innovation in response to the challenges presented by a mutable environment may prove threatening to established religion.

Finally, a contemporary basic democracy that restricted citizenship to, say, native-born male believers, would need to compete, not only against well-ordered autocratic states, but against democratic states with more diverse citizen bodies. I suggested in Section 7.4 that the aggregation of useful knowledge (expert and otherwise) dispersed across an epistemically diverse citizenship offers democracy a competitive advantage against non-democratic states. Any democracy that chose to restrict citizenship along the lines suggested above would forgo a substantial part of the potentially useful knowledge possessed by the wider community, and thereby surrender one part of the democratic advantage.

Looking down the game tree, considering the historical record of classical Athens, and confronting the consequences of adopting a basic democracy, the hypothetical group seeking a nontyrannical and nonliberal form of social order might decide that the costs were too high. Or, having attempted to create democratic institutions that would simultaneously sustain prosperity, security, and a nonliberal social order, they might find that the design problem was insoluble. The point of this section has not been to suggest that it would be *easy* to implement a nonliberal basic democracy under the conditions of modernity, only that the option is not blocked ex ante as a conceptual possibility.

The goal of this book has been to define a basic form of democracy, to specify the conditions necessary for its existence, and to list the goods that it provides, in theory and historical practice. I have tried to show that it is possible to do so before introducing the normative and institutional apparatus of liberalism – or of any other moralized system of value. Basic democracy will not provide all of the things that most people ask of a modern government. But it answers a central question posed by political philosophy, before and after liberalism: How might we, whoever we are, better live our lives, together?

Democracy after Liberalism

This book set out to offer a theory of democracy as collective self-government by citizens. It sought to highlight the positive value to individuals of engaging in political participation, of civic dignity as being held worthy of participation, and of a civic education that prepares citizens for participation. In the Preface I described my theory as guardedly optimistic. But, like a famous article by Judith Shklar (1989: "The Liberalism of Fear"), this book was written in the shadow of fear. My fear is that contemporary liberalism lacks the resources necessary to take on the most pressing political, economic, and environmental problems of our times. If the institutions of liberalism prove unequal to the challenges posed by those and other highly salient issues, then, in a readily imaginable scenario, citizens of developed countries may choose (with whatever level of regret) to jettison relevant features of contemporary liberalism. What happens then?

If liberalism and self-government are so entangled that they must stand or fall together, what happens is that democracy will collapse. The new regime will be some form of autocracy. If, however, the argument offered in the previous chapters goes through, then a basic democratic framework could remain intact after certain features of contemporary liberalism have been lost. If the basic democratic frame stands, and if I am right about the conditions that are required to sustain it, then there is a decent (if hardly ideal) nonliberal alternative to insecurity, immiseration, and tyranny. If, as I have claimed, basic democracy is *not* majoritarian tyranny, and therefore is not a political option available to illiberal populists, then democrats have a ready response when, in a postliberal world, opportunists seek to appropriate the term "democracy" for autocratic purposes. Meanwhile, liberal democrats may have an alternative to counsels of unmitigated despair, a despair that might otherwise seem to be as justified as it is deep.

The challenges confronted by liberal democracies in the first decades of the twenty-first century are profound. Indeed they are existential. As I write these words, we are a quarter-century past the post–Soviet Union wave of democratization and a decade past the rise and fall of the President George W. Bush–era doctrine of American-led imperial democratization. Autocratic government has been successfully merged with capitalism and nationalism in China and Russia. America is challenged by political polarization, racial strife, and the rise of virulent forms of technopopulism that seek to rebrand liberalism as a viciously self-indulgent "political correctness." Liberal regimes in Europe are in the throes of a protracted fiscal crisis, a long economic recession, and a burgeoning migration and refugee crisis. Nonstate terrorism, inspired by apocalyptic ideologies communicated across global networks, offers a stark threat to values of toleration and to liberal state and international institutions.

Many parts of the world have seen a resurgence of exclusionary nationalism as a political ideology that is openly advocated by political leaders. That ideology has proved compelling. Many people, on the left and right alike, now deploy "liberalism" as a term of abuse. Liberalism is widely associated with elitism, globalism, and predatory capitalism on the one hand, and with complacent cosmopolitanism, a divisive adulation of diversity for its own sake, and the wholesale abandonment of traditional values on the other. Liberalism is, moreover, often contrasted (by liberals and their opponents) with a vision of people's government whose goal is ethno-national self-determination and whose primary mechanism is the popular referendum. I write in the aftermath of the British referendum of June 2016, in which a majority of voters in the UK chose to leave the European Union. That British referendum was followed by the election, five months later, of an American President whose nationalist-populist campaign centered on fierce hostility to liberalism.[1]

The growth of a politics grounded in parochial nationalism in many parts of the world, including those countries that were once at the vanguard of liberal internationalism, puts intense pressure on the liberal side of democratic liberalism. States and federations in much of the developed world are now confronting the difficult question of whether they are willing to put their own prosperity and security at risk in order to honor the principles of universal human rights canonized in the United Nations Universal Declaration of Human Rights, and in state constitutions. Increasingly, the answer seems to be, "no." In a series of measures passed in late 2015 to

---

[1] It is worth noting that, while the "leave" vote in the British referendum won a majority of the total votes cast (51.9 percent), Donald Trump failed to win even a plurality of the votes in the 2016 American presidential election. The total of votes cast by citizens was, however, constitutionally irrelevant because Trump won the majority of the votes in the Electoral College, an institution designed by the liberal framers of the American Constitution to avoid directly democratic decision making.

mid-2016, the parliament of Sweden – a country with an especially strong modern history of honoring the rights of refugees – sharply restricted the opportunity of refugees to enter Sweden and for asylum seekers to obtain Swedish residency permits.

The question of the trade-off between protecting local security and prosperity, as opposed to honoring commitments arising from universal human rights, is now at the center of the contemporary public policy table. The trend seemingly indicated by the new Swedish refugee policy, the British referendum vote, and Donald Trump's election may prove ephemeral. But it may not. It is not obvious that, in the twenty-first century, electorates will consistently support policies that sustain universal human rights if those policies are seen to come with high costs to local security or welfare.

Both Donald Trump's presidential campaign and the British "Leave" campaign emphasized national self-determination and demonized immigrants. In the run up to the British referendum, intellectuals on the left found strange bedfellows in xenophobes on the right; both urged British citizens to get out of the European Union in the name of democracy. In the 2016 American presidential campaign, critics of the status quo on both left and right denounced bankers and government insiders alike as self-serving elitists, out of touch with ordinary citizens. Meanwhile, in an editorial in the *New York Times*, the leader of far-right French National Front Party, Marine Le Pen, celebrated the British decision to exit the European Union as "the people's first real victory." She predicted that, "the People's Spring is now inevitable." Leaders of resurgent ultra-nationalist parties across Europe lauded Trump's election as the revolutionary emergence of a new era, in Le Pen's words, "the end of the twentieth century." None of this necessarily means that liberal democracies are in a death spiral. But recent developments do suggest that it is far from inevitable that policy predicated on the principles of contemporary liberalism will be the future norm in either the developing or the developed world.[2]

Liberal theorists might respond to the current situation by turning away from democracy in disgust or despair, by advocating epistocracy – urging that public authority be placed in the presumably capable hands of an educated elite (Brennan 2016). That solution is unrealistic: Like Plato before them, twenty-first century epistocrats lack any feasible plan for convincing

---

[2] Left intellectuals for Brexit: Richard Tuck, "The Left Case for Brexit" www.dissentmagazine.org/online_articles/left-case-brexit (accessed June 28, 2016). Marine Le Pen editorial: www.nytimes.com/2016/06/28/opinion/marine-le-pen-after-brexit-the-peoples-spring-is-inevitable.html (accessed June 28, 2016). European ultra-nationalists celebrate Trump's election: www.nytimes.com/2016/11/12/world/europe/donald-trump-marine-le-pen.html (accessed November 11, 2016).

an ignorant democratic majority to submit peacefully to the rule of a putatively wise minority. But even if liberal epistocrats did somehow convince
citizens to abandon collective self-government, the arguments presented in
this book suggest that those (former) citizens would have made a mistake.
Not only would certain conditions of their own flourishing be forfeit, but
liberal epistocracy would be inherently unstable. Liberalism, or so I have
argued, requires a democratic foundation if it is to be stable over time in a
population of even partially self-interested individuals.

This book will not have given much comfort to liberals who regard
human rights as absolute. But it is meant to show that basic democracy
reliably preserves political conditions that track some part of the set of relations that liberals seek to defend as rights. It also provides arguments for
liberal democrats who oppose nationalistic populists seeking to hide xeno-
phobic policies behind a democratic veil. Liberals are right to point out
that basic democracy might fail to prevent the rise of a populist despot and
could devolve into autocracy. But despots can take power only when citizen self-government is reduced to a simple form of majoritarian tyranny.
This book has shown that basic democracy, before liberalism, is not that.

Democracy is recaptured from the arsenal of populist nationalists, as a
political regime if not as a brand name, when it is recognized that the conditions necessary for citizens actually to govern themselves include free speech
and association, political equality, and civic dignity. Those conditions are
denigrated by populist-nationalist opportunists, but may be embraced, if
for different reasons, by liberal and nonliberal citizens alike. A theory of
basic democracy measures out a common high ground of nontyranny conjoined with security and prosperity. I believe that is a ground on which a
broad political coalition could be mustered. And if that is right, then basic
democracy points to a political way forward in a postliberal world. Perhaps,
as I hope, liberal democracy will surmount its current challenges. But insofar as the emergence of a postliberal world, now and around here, is a real
possibility, it is the duty of democratic theorists to prepare for it. If, as I
have argued, basic democracy both supports human flourishing and could
be a focal point for a broad-based political coalition, the kind of realistic
democratic theory I have attempted in these pages need not be conceived
in a spirit of despair. Indeed it can be written with a measure of hope.

Bibliography

Abizahdeh, Arash. 2012. "On the Demos and Its Kin: Nationalism, Democracy, and the Boundary Problem." *American Political Science Review* 106: 867–882.

Acemoglu, Daron, and James A. Robinson. 2006. *Economic Origins of Dictatorship and Democracy*. New York: Cambridge University Press.

——— 2016. "Paths to Inclusive Political Institutions." Pp. 3–50 in *Economic History of Warfare and State Formation*, edited by J. Eloranta et al. Singapore: Springer.

Acemoglu, Daron, Suresh Naidu, Pascual Restrepo, and James A. Robinson. 2014. *Democracy Does Cause Growth*. Cambridge, Mass.: National Bureau of Economic Research.

Achen, Christopher H., and Larry M. Bartels. 2016. *Democracy for Realists: Why Elections Do Not Produce Responsive Government*. Princeton, N.J.: Princeton University Press.

Akrigg, Ben. 2015. "Metics in Athens." Pp. 155–176 in *Communities and Networks in the Ancient Greek World*, edited by Claire Taylor and Kostas Vlassopoulos. Oxford: Oxford University Press.

Allen, Danielle. 2004. *Talking to Strangers: Anxieties of Citizenship since Brown v. Board of Education*. Chicago: University of Chicago Press.

Amar, Akhil Reed. 2005. *America's Constitution: A Biography*. New York: Random House.

Anderson, Elizabeth. 1999. "What Is the Point of Equality?" *Ethics* 109: 287–337.

——— 2006. "The Epistemology of Democracy." *Episteme: Journal of Social Epistemology* 3(1): 8–22.

——— 2007. "How Should Egalitarians Cope with Market Risks?" *Theoretical Inquiries in Law* 9: 61–92.

Anderson, Greg. 2009. "The Personality of the Greek State." *Journal of Hellenic Studies* 129: 1–22.

Archibugi, Daniele, Mathias Koenig-Archibugi, and Raffaele Marchetti, eds. 2012. *Global Democracy: Normative and Empirical Perspectives*. Cambridge: Cambridge University Press.

Austin, J. L. 1975. *How to Do Things with Words*. Cambridge, Mass.: Harvard University Press.

Badian, E. 2000. "Back to Kleisthenic Chronology." Pp. 447–464 in *Polis and Politics [Festschrift Hansen]*, edited by P. Flensted-Jensen, T. H. Nielsen, and L. Rubinstein. Copenhagen: Museum Tusculanum Press.

Balot, Ryan K. 2014. *Courage in the Democratic Polis: Ideology and Critique in Classical Athens*. Oxford: Oxford University Press.

2016. "Recollecting Athens." *Polis* 33: 92–129.

Barber, Benjamin R. 1984. *Strong Democracy: Participatory Politics for a New Age*. Berkeley: University of California Press.

Beaumont, Elizabeth. 2014. *The Civic Constitution: Civic Visions and Struggles in the Path toward Constitutional Democracy*. Oxford: Oxford University Press.

Bell, Duncan. 2014. "What Is Liberalism?" *Political Theory* 42(6): 682–715.

Berent, Moshe. 1996. "Hobbes and the 'Greek Tongues.'" *History of Political Thought* 17: 36–59.

2000. "Anthropology and the Classics: War, Violence and the Stateless Polis." *Classical Quarterly* 50: 257–289.

2006. "The Stateless Polis: A Reply to Critics." *Social Evolution & History* 5(1): 140–162.

Berlin, Isaiah. 1969. *Four Essays on Liberty*. Oxford: Oxford University Press.

Blake, Michael. 2003. "Immigration." Pp. 224–237 in *The Blackwell Companion to Applied Ethics*, edited by R. G. Frey and Christopher Wellman. London: Blackwell.

Bobonich, Christopher. 2002. *Plato's Utopia Recast: His Later Ethics and Politics*. Oxford: Oxford University Press.

Boehm, Christopher. 1999. *Hierarchy in the Forest: The Evolution of Egalitarian Behavior*. Cambridge, Mass.: Harvard University Press.

2012a. *Moral Origins: Social Selection and the Evolution of Virtue, Altruism, and Shame*. New York: Basic Books.

2012b. "Prehistory." Pp. 29–39 in *The Edinburgh Companion to the History of Democracy*, edited by Benjamin Isakhan and Stephen Stockwell. Edinburgh: Edinburgh University Press.

Boix, Carles. 2003. *Democracy and Redistribution*. Cambridge: Cambridge University Press.

2015. *Political Order and Inequality: Their Foundations and Their Consequences for Human Welfare*. Cambridge: Cambridge University Press.

Bovens, Luc, and Wlodek Rabinowicz. 2006. "Democratic Answers to Complex Questions – An Epistemic Perspective." *Synthese* 150: 131–153.

Bradshaw, John. 2013. *Cat Sense: How the New Feline Science Can Make You a Better Friend to Your Pet*. New York: Basic Books.

Bratman, Michael E. 1999. *Faces of Intention: Selected Essays on Intention and Agency*. Cambridge: Cambridge University Press.

2014. *Shared Agency: A Planning Theory of Acting Together*. Oxford: Oxford University Press.

Brennan, Geoffrey, and Philip Pettit. 2004. *The Economy of Esteem: An Essay on Civil and Political Society*. Oxford: Oxford University Press.

Brennan, Jason. 2016. *Against Democracy*. Princeton, N.J.: Princeton University Press.

Brettschneider, Corey Lang. 2007. *Democratic Rights: The Substance of Self-Government*. Princeton, N.J.: Princeton University Press.

Brock, Gillian, and Darrel Moellendorf, eds. 2005. *Current Debates in Global Justice*. Berlin: Springer.

Burn, Sean Meghan. 2009. "A Situational Model of Sexual Assault Prevention through Bystander Intervention." *Sex Roles* 60: 779–792.

Callander, Steven. 2011. "Searching for Good Policies." *American Political Science Review* 105(4): 643–662.

Canevaro, Mirko. 2015. "Making and Changing Laws in Ancient Athens." In *The Oxford Handbook of Ancient Greek Law*, edited by Edward M. Harris and Mirko Canevaro. Oxford: Oxford University Press. doi:10.1093/oxfordhb/9780199599257.013.4

——— Forthcoming. "Majority Rule vs. Consensus: The Practice of Democratic Deliberation in the Greek Poleis." In *Ancient Greek History and Contemporary Social Science*, edited by Mirko Canevaro, Andrew Erskine, Benjamin Gray, and Josiah Ober. Edinburgh: Edinburgh University Press.

Caplan, Bryan. 2007. *The Myth of the Rational Voter*. Princeton, N.J.: Princeton University Press.

Carawan, Edwin. 2013. *The Athenian Amnesty and Reconstructing the Law*. New York: Oxford University Press.

Carens, Joseph H. 1987. "Aliens and Citizens: The Case for Open Borders." *Review of Politics* 49: 251–273.

——— 2005. "On Belonging: What We Owe People Who Stay." *Boston Review* 30(3–4): 16–19.

Carothers, Thomas. 2007. *US Democracy Promotion during and after Bush*. Washington, D.C.: Carnegie Endowment for International Peace.

Cartledge, Paul. 2016. *Democracy: A Life*. Oxford: Oxford University Press.

Carugati, Federica. 2015. "In Law We Trust (Each Other): Legal Institutions, Democratic Stability and Economic Development in Classical Athens." PhD diss., Classics, Stanford University, Stanford, Calif.

Carugati, Federica, Josiah Ober, and Barry Weingast. 2016. "Development and Political Theory in Classical Athens." *Polis: The Journal for Ancient Greek Political Thought* 33: 71–91.

——— 2017. "Is Development Uniquely Modern?" *Unpublished manuscript.*

Chapman, Emilee. 2016. "Voting Matters: A Critical Examination and Defense of Democracy's Central Practice." PhD diss., Politics, Princeton University, Princeton, N.J.

Christiano, Thomas. 1996. *The Rule of the Many: Fundamental Issues in Democratic Theory*. Boulder, Colo.: Westview Press.

——— 2008. *The Constitution of Equality: Democratic Authority and Its Limits*. Oxford: Oxford University Press.

Chwe, Michael Suk-Young. 2013. *Jane Austen, Game Theorist*. Princeton, N.J.: Princeton University Press.

Cohen, Edward E. 1992. *Athenian Economy and Society: A Banking Perspective*. Princeton, N.J.: Princeton University Press.

Cohen, G. A. 2008. *Rescuing Justice and Equality*. Cambridge, Mass.: Harvard University Press.

Cohen, Joshua. 1986. "An Epistemic Conception of Democracy." *Ethics* 97 (1): 26–38.

——. 1996. "Procedure and Substance in Deliberative Democracy." Pp. 94–119 in *Democracy and Difference: Contesting the Boundaries of the Political*, edited by Seyla Benhabib. Princeton, N.J.: Princeton University Press.

——. 1997. "The Arc of the Moral Universe." *Philosophy and Public Affairs* 26(2): 91–134.

Cooper, John M. 1999. *Reason and Emotion: Essays on Ancient Moral Psychology and Ethical Theory*. Princeton, N.J.: Princeton University Press.

Cox, Gary, Douglass C. North, and Barry R. Weingast. 2012. "The Violence Trap: A Political-Economic Approach to the Problems of Development." *Working paper*.

Cronin, Thomas E. 1989. *Direct Democracy: The Politics of Initiative, Referendum, and Recall*. Cambridge, Mass.: Harvard University Press.

Dabla-Norris, Era, et al. 2015. "Causes and Consequences of Income Inequality: A Global Perspective." International Monetary Fund. www.imf.org/external/pubs/ft/sdn/2015/sdn1513.pdf.

Dahl, Robert Alan. 1989. *Democracy and Its Critics*. New Haven, Conn.: Yale University Press.

——. 2015. *On Democracy*. New Haven, Conn.: Yale University Press.

Dahl, Robert Alan, and Edward R. Tufte. 1973. *Size and Democracy*. Stanford, Calif.: Stanford University Press.

Darwall, Stephen. 2006. *The Second-Person Standpoint: Morality, Respect, and Accountability*. Cambridge, Mass.: Harvard University Press.

Dewey, John. 1917. *Democracy and Education: An Introduction to the Philosophy of Education*. New York: Macmillan.

Domingo Gygax, Marc. 2016. *Benefaction and Rewards in the Ancient Greek City: The Origins of Euergetism*. Cambridge: Cambridge University Press.

Donlan, Walter. 1970. "Changes and Shifts in the Meaning of *Demos* in the Literature of the Archaic Period." *Parola Del Passato* 135: 381–395.

Doucouliagos, Hristos, and Mehmet Ali Ulubaşoğlu. 2008. "Democracy and Economic Growth: A Meta-Analysis." *American Journal of Political Science* 52(1): 61–83.

Dryzek, John S., and Christian List. 2003. "Social Choice Theory and Deliberative Democracy: A Reconciliation." *British Journal of Political Science* 33(1): 1–28.

Ellerman, David. 2015. "Does Classical Liberalism Imply Democracy?" *Ethics and Global Politics* 8. doi:10.3402/egp.v8.29310.

Ellison, Ralph. 1952. *Invisible Man*. New York: Random House.

Elster, Jon. 2011. "Deliberation, Cycles, and Misrepresentation." *Working paper*.

Ericsson, K. Anders. 2006. "The Influence of Experience and Deliberate Practice on the Development of Superior Expert Performance." Pp. 683–703 in *The Cambridge Handbook of Expertise and Expert Performance*, edited by K. Anders Ericsson et al. Cambridge: Cambridge University Press.

Ericsson, K. Anders, et al., eds. 2006. *The Cambridge Handbook of Expertise and Expert Performance*. Cambridge: Cambridge University Press.

Espejo, Paulina Ochoa. 2011. *The Time of Popular Sovereignty: Process and the Democratic State*. State College: Penn State University Press.

Estlund, David M. 2003. "Why Not Epistocracy?" Pp. 53–69 in *Desire, Identity and Existence: Essays in Honor of T. M. Penner*. Berrima, NSW: Academic Printing and Publishing.

2008. *Democratic Authority: A Philosophical Framework*. Princeton, N.J.: Princeton University Press.

2014. "Utopophobia." *Philosophy and Public Affairs* 42: 113–134.

Finley, M. I. 1975. *The Use and Abuse of History*. London: Chatto and Windus.

1985. *Ancient History: Evidence and Models*. London: Chatto and Windus.

Fischer, Frank. 2009. *Democracy and Expertise: Reorienting Policy Inquiry*. Oxford: Oxford University Press.

Fisher, Nick, and Hans Van Wees, eds. 2015. *Aristocracy in Antiquity: Redefining Greek and Roman Elites*. Cardiff: Classical Press of Wales.

Floyd, Jonathan, and Marc Stears, eds. 2011. *Political Philosophy versus History? Contextualism and Real Politics in Contemporary Political Thought*. Cambridge: Cambridge University Press.

Foisneau, Luc. 2016. *Hobbes: La vie inquiète*. Paris: Gallimard.

Forsdyke, Sara. 2005. *Exile, Ostracism, and Democracy: The Politics of Expulsion in Ancient Greece*. Princeton, N.J.: Princeton University Press.

Frank, Jason. 2010. *Constituent Moments: Enacting the People in Postrevolutionary America*. Durham, N.C.: Duke University Press.

Frankfurt, Harry. 1987. "Equality as a Moral Ideal." *Ethics* 98: 21–43.

Frey, Bruno S., and Alois Stutzer. 2000. "Happiness, Economy and Institutions." *The Economic Journal* 110: 918–938.

2002. *Happiness and Economics: How the Economy and Institutions Affect Human Well-Being*. Princeton, N.J.: Princeton University Press.

Fukuyama, Francis. 2011. *The Origins of Political Order: From Prehuman Times to the French Revolution*. New York: Farrar, Straus, and Giroux.

2014. *Political Order and Political Decay: From the Industrial Revolution to the Globalization of Democracy*. New York: Farrar, Straus, and Giroux.

Fung, Archon. 2004. *Empowered Participation: Reinventing Urban Democracy*. Princeton, N.J.: Princeton University Press.

2015. "Putting the Public Back into Governance: The Challenges of Citizen Participation and Its Future." *Public Administration Review* 75(4): 513–522.

Furstein, Michael. 2008. "Epistemic Democracy and the Social Character of Knowledge." *Episteme: Journal of Social Epistemology* 5(1): 74–93.

Gallie, W. B. 1955. "Essentially Contested Concepts." *Proceedings of the Aristotelian Society* 56: 167–198.

Galston, William. 2010. "Realism in Political Theory." *European Journal of Political Theory* 9: 385–411.

Garsten, Bryan. 2009. *Saving Persuasion: A Defense of Rhetoric and Judgment*. Cambridge, Mass.: Harvard University Press.

2011. "The Rhetoric Revival in Political Theory." *Annual Reviews in Political Science* 14(1): 159–180.

Gaus, Gerald. 2014. "Liberalism." In *Stanford Encyclopedia of Philosophy*. https://plato.stanford.edu/entries/liberalism/.

Geuss, Raymond. 2008. *Philosophy and Real Politics*. Princeton, N.J.: Princeton University Press.

Gidycz, Christine A., Lindsay M. Orchowski, and Alan D. Berkowitz. 2011. "Preventing Sexual Aggression Among College Men: An Evaluation of a Social Norms and Bystander Intervention Program." *Violence against Women* 17(6): 720–742.

Goodin, Robert E. 2007. "Enfranchising All Affected Interests, and Its Alternatives." *Philosophy and Public Affairs* 35(1): 40–68.

Gowder, Paul. 2016. *The Rule of Law in the Real World*. Cambridge: Cambridge University Press.

Green, Jeffrey Edward. 2015. "Political Theory as Both Philosophy and History: A Defense against Methodological Militancy." *Annual Reviews in Political Science* 18: 425–441.

Greif, Avner and David D. Laitin. 2004. "A theory of endogenous institutional change." *American Political Science Review*. 98:633-652.

Grieb, Volker. 2008. *Hellenistische Demokratie. Politische Organisation und Struktur in freien griechischen Poleis nach Alexander dem Grossen*. Stuttgart: Steiner.

Grofman, Bernard, Guillermo Owen, and Scott L. Feld. 1983. "Thirteen Theorems in Search of the Truth." *Theory and Decision* 15: 261–278.

Gutmann, Amy. 1980. *Liberal Equality*. Cambridge: Cambridge University Press.
  1999. *Democratic Education*. Princeton, N.J.: Princeton University Press.

Gutmann, Amy, and Dennis F. Thompson. 1996. *Democracy and Disagreement*. Cambridge, Mass.: Belknap Press of Harvard University Press.

Habermas, Jürgen. 1996. *Between Facts and Norms: Contributions to a Discourse Theory of Law and Democracy*. Cambridge, Mass.: MIT Press.

Hainmueller, Jens, and Dominik Hangartner. 2013. "Who Gets a Swiss Passport? A Natural Experiment in Immigrant Discrimination." *American Political Science Review* 107(1): 159–187.

Hamon, Patrice. 2010. "Démocraties grecques après Alexandre. À propos de trois ouvrages." *Topoi* 16: 389–424.

Hampton, Jean. 1988. *Hobbes and the Social Contract Tradition*. Cambridge: Cambridge University Press.

Hansen, Mogens Herman. 1986. "The Origin of the Term *Demokratia*." *Liverpool Classical Monthly* 11: 35–36.
  1987. *The Athenian Assembly in the Age of Demosthenes*. Oxford: B. Blackwell.
  1996. "The Ancient Athenian and the Modern Liberal View of Liberty as a Democratic Ideal." Pp. 91–104 in *Dêmokratia*, edited by J. Ober and C. W. Hedrick. Princeton, N.J.: Princeton University Press.
  1999. *The Athenian Democracy in the Age of Demosthenes: Structure, Principles and Ideology*. Norman: University of Oklahoma Press.
  2002. "Was the Polis a State or a Stateless Society?" Pp. 17–47 in *Even More Studies in the Ancient Greek Polis: Papers from the Copenhagen Polis Centre 6*, edited by Thomas Heine Nielsen. Stuttgart: F. Steiner.

Harari, Yuval Noah. 2015. *Sapiens: A Brief History of Humankind*. New York: Harper.

Hardin, Russell. 1999. *Liberalism, Constitutionalism, and Democracy*. Oxford: Oxford University Press.

Havelock, Eric Alfred. 1957. *The Liberal Temper in Greek Politics*. New Haven, Conn.: Yale University Press.

Hawthorne, James. Und. "Voting in Search of the Public Good: The Probabilistic Logic of Majority Judgments." *Working paper*.

Hedrick, Charles W., Jr. 2004. "The American Ephebe: The Ephebic Oath, US Education and Nationalism." *Classical World* 97: 384–407.

Hobbes, Thomas. 1991 [1651].*Leviathan*. Edited by Richard Tuck. Cambridge: Cambridge University Press.

Hoekstra, Kinch. 2007. "A Lion in the House: Hobbes and Democracy." Pp. 191–218 in *Rethinking the Foundations of Modern Political Thought*, edited by Annabel Brett and James Tully. Cambridge: Cambridge University Press.

2017. "Thomas Hobbes and the Creation of Order." *Unpublished manuscript.*

Holmes, Stephen T. 1979. "Aristippus in and out of Athens." *American Political Science Review* 73: 113–128.

Honig, Bonnie. 1993. *Political Theory and the Displacement of Politics*. Ithaca, N.Y.: Cornell University Press.

2001. *Democracy and the Foreigner*. Princeton, N.J.: Princeton University Press.

Huntington, Samuel P. 1968. *The Clash of Civilizations and the Remaking of World Order*. New York: Simon and Schuster.

Iori, Luca. 2015. *Thucydides Anglicus: Gli Eight Bookes di Thomas Hobbes e la Ricezione Inglese delle Storie di Tucidide (1450–1642)*. Rome: Edizioni di Storia e Letteratura.

Ismard, Paulin. 2015. *La démocratie contre les experts: Les esclaves publics en grèce ancienne*. Paris: Seuil.

Jones, A. H. M. 1964. *Athenian Democracy*. Oxford: Blackwell.

Kahneman, Daniel. 2011. *Thinking, Fast and Slow*. New York: Farrar, Straus, and Giroux.

Kallet-Marx, Lisa. 1994. "Money Talks: Rhetor, Demos, and Resources of the Athenian Empire." Pp. 227–252 in *Ritual, Finance, Politics: Athenian Democratic Accounts Presented to David Lewis*, edited by Robin Osborne and Simon Hornblower. Oxford: Clarendon Press.

Kalyvas, Andreas, and Ira Katznelson. 2008. *Liberal Beginnings: Making a Republic for the Moderns*. Cambridge: Cambridge University Press.

Kamen, Deborah. 2017. "Manumission in Ancient Greece: Modes, Meanings, and Metaphors." *Unpublished manuscript.*

Kant, Immanuel. 1991. *Political Writings*. Cambridge: Cambridge University Press.

Kateb, George. 2006. *Patriotism and Other Mistakes*. New Haven, Conn.: Yale University Press.

Kaufmann, Bruno, and M. Dane Waters. 2004. *Direct Democracy in Europe: A Comprehensive Reference Guide to the Initiative and Referendum Process in Europe*. Durham, N.C.: Carolina Academic Press.

Kennedy, George A. 1963. *The Art of Persuasion in Greece*. Princeton, N.J.: Princeton University Press.

Kraut, Richard. 2007. *What Is Good and Why: The Ethics of Well-Being*. Cambridge, Mass.: Harvard University Press.

Kuran, Timur. 1991. "Now Out of Never: The Element of Surprise in the East European Revolution of 1989." *World Politics* 44(1): 7–48.

———. 1995. *Private Truths, Public Lies: The Social Consequences of Preference Falsification*. Cambridge, Mass.: Harvard University Press.

Kymlicka, Will. 1995. *Multicultural Citizenship: A Liberal Theory of Minority Rights*. Oxford: Oxford University Press.

Laclau, Ernesto, and Chantal Mouffe. 2001. *Hegemony and Socialist Strategy: Towards a Radical Democratic Politics*. London: Verso.

Laird, J. 1942. "Hobbes on Aristotle's 'Politics.'" *Proceedings of the Aristotelian Society* 43: 1–20.

Lakoff, George, and Mark Johnson. 2003. *Metaphors We Live By*. Chicago: University of Chicago Press.

Lambert, S. D. 2011. "What Was the Point of Inscribed Honorific Decrees in Classical Athens?" Pp. 193–214 in *Sociable Man: Essays on Ancient Greek Social Behaviour in Honour of Nick Fisher*, edited by S. D. Lambert, N. R. E. Fisher, and Douglas L. Cairns. Swansea: Classical Press of Wales.

Landemore, Hélène. 2012. *Democratic Reason: Politics, Collective Intelligence, and the Rule of the Many*. Princeton, N.J.: Princeton University Press.

Landemore, Hélène, and Jon Elster, eds. 2012. *Collective Wisdom: Principles and Mechanisms*. Cambridge: Cambridge University Press.

Lane, Melissa S. 2013. "Claims to Rule: The Case of the Multitude." Pp. 247–274 in *Cambridge Companion to Aristotle's Politics*, edited by Marguerite Deslauriers and Pierre Destrée. Cambridge: Cambridge University Press.

———. 2016. "Popular Sovereignty as Control of Officeholders: Aristotle on Greek Democracy." Pp. 52–71 in *Popular Sovereignty in Historical Perspective*, edited by Richard Bourke and Quentin. Skinner. Cambridge: Cambridge University Press.

Liddell, Henry George, Robert Scott, and Henry Stuart Jones. 1968. *A Greek-English Lexicon*. Oxford: Clarendon Press.

List, Christian. 2005. "Group Knowledge and Group Rationality: A Judgment Aggregation Perspective." *Episteme: Journal of Social Epistemology* 2(1): 25–38.

———. 2011. "The Logical Space of Democracy." *Philosophy and Public Affairs* 39: 262–297.

List, Christian, and Robert E. Goodin. 2001. "Epistemic Democracy: Generalizing the Condorcet Jury Theorem." *Journal of Political Philosophy* 9(3): 277–306.

List, Christian, and Philip Pettit. 2011. *Group Agency: The Possibility, Design, and Status of Corporate Agents*. Oxford: Oxford University Press.

Lloyd-Jones, Hugh. 1971. *The Justice of Zeus*. Berkeley: University of California Press.

Locke, John. 1988 [1690]. *Two Treatises of Government*. Edited by Peter Laslett. Cambridge: Cambridge University Press.

Ma, John. 2013. "Review of Mann and Scholz '*Demokratie*' *im Hellenismus.*" *Sehepunkte. Rezensionsjournal für Geschichtswissenschaften* 13(7/8). www .sehepunkte.de/2013/07/21837.html.

Macdowell, Douglas M. 1975. "Law-Making at Athens in the Fourth Century B.C." *Journal of Hellenic Studies* 95: 62–74.

Macedo, Stephen. 2000. *Diversity and Distrust: Civic Education in a Multicultural Democracy.* Cambridge, Mass.: Harvard University Press.

Macedo, Stephen, et al., eds. 2005. *Democracy at Risk: How Political Choices Undermine Citizen Participation, and What We Can Do about It.* Washington, D.C.: Brookings Institution Press.

Manin, Bernard. 1997. *The Principles of Representative Government.* Cambridge: Cambridge University Press.

Manville, B., and J. Ober. 2003. "Beyond Empowerment: Building a Company of Citizens." *Harvard Business Review* 81(1): 48–51.

Marmot, M. G. 2004. *Status Syndrome: How Your Social Standing Directly Affects Your Health and Life Expectancy.* London: Bloomsbury.

McCormick, John P. 2011. *Machiavellian Democracy.* Cambridge: Cambridge University Press.

McQueen, Alison. 2017. "Salutary Fear? Hans Morgenthau and the Politics of Existential Crisis." *American Political Thought* 6:78-105.

Meckstroth, Christopher. 2015. *The Struggle for Democracy: Paradoxes of Progress and the Politics of Change.* New York: Oxford University Press.

Mendez, Ariel T. 2016. "Equal Opportunity for Political Influence in Democratic Problem-Solving." PhD diss., Political Science, Stanford University, Stanford, Calif.

Milanovic, Branko. 2011. *The Haves and the Have-Nots: A Brief and Idiosyncratic History of Global Inequality.* New York: Basic Books.

Milanovic, Branko, Peter H. Lindert, and Jeffrey G. Williamson. 2011. "Pre-Industrial Inequality." *The Economic Journal* 121(551): 255–272.

Mill, John Stuart. 1861. *Considerations on Representative Government.* London: Parker, Son, and Bourn.

Miller, David. 2000. *Citizenship and National Identity.* Cambridge: Polity Press/Blackwell.

Missiou, Anna. 2011. *Literacy and Democracy in Fifth-Century Athens.* Cambridge: Cambridge University Press.

Mitsis, Philip. 1999. "The Stoic Origin of Natural Rights." Pp. 153–177 in *Topics in Stoic Philosophy*, edited by K. Ierodiakonou. Oxford: Oxford University Press.

Monoson, S. Sara. 2011. "Recollecting Aristotle: American Proslavery Thought and the Argument of *Politics* I." Pp. 247–271 in *Ancient Slavery and Abolition: From Hobbes to Hollywood*, edited by Edith Hall, Richard Alston, and Justine Mcconnell. New York: Oxford University Press.

Morris, Ian. 2010. *Why the West Rules – for Now: The Patterns of History and What They Reveal about the Future.* New York: Farrar, Strauss, and Giroux.

———. 2014. *War! What Is It Good For? Conflict and the Progress of Civilization from Primates to Robots.* New York: Farrar, Straus, and Giroux.

Mossé, Claude. 1979. "Comment s'élabore un mythe politique: Solon, 'père fondateur' de la démocratie athénienne." *Annales (ESC)* 34: 425–437.

Mouffe, Chantal. 2000. *The Democratic Paradox*. London: Verso.

2005. *On the Political*. London: Routledge.

Müller, Jan-Werner. 2011. *Contesting Democracy: Political Ideas in Twentieth-Century Europe*. New Haven, Conn.: Yale University Press.

2016. *What Is Populism?* Philadelphia: University of Pennsylvania Press.

Murray, Oswyn. 1990. "Cities of Reason." Pp. 1–25 in *The Greek City: From Homer to Alexander*, edited by Oswyn Murray and S. R. F. Price. Oxford: Oxford University Press.

Nagel, Thomas. 1974. "What Is It Like to Be a Bat?" *Philosophical Review* 83: 435–450.

North, Douglass Cecil, John Joseph Wallis, and Barry R. Weingast. 2009. *Violence and Social Orders: A Conceptual Framework for Interpreting Recorded Human History*. Cambridge: Cambridge University Press.

Nozick, Robert. 1974. *Anarchy, State, and Utopia*. New York: Basic Books.

Nussbaum, Martha Craven. 2011. *Creating Capabilities: The Human Development Approach*. Cambridge, Mass.: Belknap Press of Harvard University Press.

Ober, Josiah. 1989. *Mass and Elite in Democratic Athens: Rhetoric, Ideology, and the Power of the People*. Princeton, N.J.: Princeton University Press.

1996. *The Athenian Revolution: Essays on Ancient Greek Democracy and Political Theory*. Princeton, N.J.: Princeton University Press.

1998. *Political Dissent in Democratic Athens: Intellectual Critics of Popular Rule*. Princeton, N.J.: Princeton University Press.

2000. "Quasi-Rights: Participatory Citizenship and Negative Liberties in Democratic Athens." *Social Philosophy and Policy* 17(1): 27–61.

2001. "The Debate over Civic Education in Classical Athens." Pp. 273–305 in *Education in Greek and Roman Antiquity*, edited by Yun Lee Too. Leiden, Netherlands: Brill.

2003. "Conditions for Athenian Democracy." Pp. 2–21 in *The Making and Unmaking of Democracy: Lessons from History and World Politics*, edited by Theodore K. Rabb and Ezra N. Suleiman. New York: Routledge.

2005a. *Athenian Legacies: Essays in the Politics of Going on Together*. Princeton, N.J.: Princeton University Press.

2005b. "Law and Political Theory." Pp. 394–411 in *Cambridge Companion to Ancient Greek Law*, edited by Michael Gagarin and David Cohen. Cambridge: Cambridge University Press.

2007a. "'I Besieged That Man': Democracy's Revolutionary Start." Pp. 83–104 in *The Origins of Democracy in Ancient Greece*, edited by Kurt Raaflaub, Josiah Ober, and Robert W. Wallace. Berkeley: University of California Press.

2007b. "Natural Capacities and Democracy as a Good-in-Itself." *Philosophical Studies* 132: 59–73.

2008a. *Democracy and Knowledge: Innovation and Learning in Classical Athens*. Princeton, N.J.: Princeton University Press.

2008b. "The Original Meaning of Democracy: Capacity to Do Things, Not Majority Rule." *Constellations* 15(1): 3–9.

2009. "Public Action and Rational Choice in Classical Greek Political Theory." Pp. 70–84 in *A Companion to Ancient Political Thought*, edited by Ryan K. Balot. Oxford: Blackwell.

2010. "The Instrumental Value of Others and Institutional Change: An Athenian Case Study." Pp. 156–178 in *Valuing Others in Classical Antiquity*, edited by Ineke Sluiter and Ralph Rosen. Leiden, Netherlands: Brill.

2012. "Democracy's Dignity." *American Political Science Review* 106(4): 827–846.

2013a. "Democracy's Wisdom: An Aristotelian Middle Way for Collective Judgment." *American Political Science Review* 107(1): 104–122.

2013b. "Political Animals Revisited." *Good Society* 22: 201–214.

2014. "Democratic Rhetoric: How Should the State Speak?" *Brooklyn Law Journal* 79: 1015–1022.

2015a. "Nature, History, and Aristotle's Best Possible Regime." Pp. 224–243 in *Aristotle's "Politics": A Critical Guide*, edited by T. Lockwood and T. Samaras. Cambridge: Cambridge University Press.

2015b. *The Rise and Fall of Classical Greece*. Princeton, N.J.: Princeton University Press.

2015c. "Political Knowledge and Right-Sizing Government." *Critical Review* 27(3): 362–374.

2016. "The Trial of Socrates as a Political Trial." Pp. 65–87 in *Political Trials: Interdisciplinary Perspectives*, edited by J. Meierhenrich and D. O. Pendas. Cambridge: Cambridge University Press.

2017a. "Inequality in Late-Classical Democratic Athens: Evidence and Models." Pp. 125–147 in *Democracy and Open Economy World Order*, edited by G. C. Bitros and N. C. Kyriazis. New York: Springer.

2017b. "Equality, Legitimacy, Interests, and Preferences: Historical Notes on Quadratic Voting in a Political Context." *Public Choice*. doi:10.1007/s11127-017-0409-0.

Ober, Josiah, and Charles W. Hedrick, eds. 1996. *Dêmokratia: A Conversation on Democracies, Ancient and Modern*. Princeton, N.J.: Princeton University Press.

Ober, Josiah, and Tomer Perry. 2014. "Thucydides as a Prospect Theorist." *Polis* 31: 206–232.

Olson, Mancur. 1965. *The Logic of Collective Action: Public Goods and the Theory of Groups*. Cambridge, Mass.: Harvard University Press.

Osborne, Robin. 1995. "The Economics and Politics of Slavery at Athens." Pp. 27–43 in *The Greek World*, edited by Anton Powell. London: Routledge.

Ostrom, Elinor. 1990. *Governing the Commons: The Evolution of Institutions for Collective Action*. Cambridge: Cambridge University Press.

Page, Scott E. 2007. *The Difference: How the Power of Diversity Creates Better Groups, Firms, Schools, and Societies*. Princeton, N.J.: Princeton University Press.

Paine, Thomas. 1995 [1792]. *"Rights of Man," "Common Sense," and Other Writings.* Oxford: Oxford University Press.

Pateman, Carole. 1970. *Participation and Democratic Theory.* London: Cambridge University Press.

Patterson, Cynthia. 2005. "Athenian Citizenship Law." Pp. 267–289 in *The Cambridge Companion to Ancient Greek Law,* edited by Michael Gagarin and David Cohen. Cambridge: Cambridge University Press.

Pettit, Philip. 2004. "Depoliticizing Democracy." *Ratio Juris* 17(1): 52–65.

2013. *On the People's Terms: A Republican Theory and Model of Democracy.* Cambridge: Cambridge University Press.

2014. *Just Freedom: A Moral Compass for a Complex World.* New York: W. W. Norton.

Philp, Mark. 2007. *Political Conduct.* Cambridge, Mass.: Harvard University Press.

Pitkin, Hanna Fenichel. 1967. *The Concept of Representation.* Berkeley: University of California Press.

Pogge, Thomas W. 2008. *World Poverty and Human Rights.* Cambridge: Polity.

Posner, Eric A., and E. Glen Weyl. 2015. "Voting Squared: Quadratic Voting in Democratic Politics." *Vanderbilt Law Review* 68(2): 441–500.

Poteete, A., M. Janssen, and Elinor Ostrom. 2011. *Working Together: Collective Action, the Commons, and Multiple Methods in Practice.* Princeton, N.J.: Princeton University Press.

Pyzyk, Mark. 2015. "Economies of Expertise: Knowledge and Skill Transfer in Classical Greece." PhD diss., Classics, Stanford University, Stanford, Calif.

Raaflaub, Kurt. 1996. "Equalities and Inequalities in Athenian Democracy." Pp. 139–174 in *Dēmokratia: A Conversation on Democracies, Ancient and Modern,* edited by Josiah Ober and Charles W. Hedrick. Princeton, N.J.: Princeton University Press.

Rawls, John. 1971. *A Theory of Justice.* Cambridge, Mass.: Harvard University Press.

1996. *Political Liberalism.* New York: Columbia University Press.

1999. *The Law of Peoples.* Cambridge, Mass.: Harvard University Press.

2001. *Justice as Fairness: A Restatement.* Cambridge, Mass.: Harvard University Press.

Raz, Joseph. 1986. *The Morality of Freedom.* Oxford: Oxford University Press.

Reich, Robert B. 2002. *Bridging Liberalism and Multiculturalism in American Education.* Chicago: University of Chicago Press.

Reiter, Dan, and Allan C. Stam. 2002. *Democracies at War.* Princeton, N.J.: Princeton University Press.

Rhodes, P. J. 1981. *A Commentary on the Aristotelian Athenaion Politeia.* Oxford: Oxford University Press.

1985. *The Athenian Boulê.* Oxford: Clarendon Press.

1995. "The 'Acephalous' Polis?" *Historia* 44: 153–167.

Riker, William H. 1982. *Liberalism against Populism: A Confrontation between the Theory of Democracy and the Theory of Social Choice.* San Francisco: W. H. Freeman.

Roberts, Jennifer Tolbert. 1994. *Athens on Trial: The Antidemocratic Tradition in Western Thought.* Princeton, N.J.: Princeton University Press.

Robinson, Eric W. 1997. *The First Democracies: Early Popular Government outside Athens.* Stuttgart: F. Steiner.

2011. *Democracy beyond Athens: Popular Government in the Greek Classical Age.* Cambridge: Cambridge University Press.

Rosanvallon, Pierre. 2006. *Democracy Past and Future.* New York: Columbia University Press.

Runciman, David. 2013. *The Confidence Trap: A History of Democracy in Crisis from World War I to the Present.* Princeton, N.J.: Princeton University Press.

2017. "Political Theory and Real Politics in the Age of the Internet." *Journal of Political Philosophy* 25(1): 3–21.

Sandel, Michael J. 1998. *Liberalism and the Limits of Justice.* Cambridge: Cambridge University Press.

Sapolsky, Robert M. 2004. "Social Status and Health in Humans and Other Animals." *Annual Reviews in Anthropology* 33: 393–418.

2005. "The Influence of Social Hierarchy on Primate Health." *Science* 308: 448–652.

Saxonhouse, Arlene. 2006. *Free Speech and Democracy in Ancient Athens.* Cambridge: Cambridge University Press.

Scheidel, Walter. 2008. "The Comparative Economies of Slavery in the Greco-Roman World." Pp. 105–126 in *Slave Systems: Ancient and Modern,* edited by Enrico Dal Lago and Constantina Katsari. Cambridge: Cambridge University Press.

2010. "Real Wages in Early Economies: Evidence for Living Standards from 1800 BCE to 1300 CE." *Journal of the Social and Economic History of the Orient* 53: 425–462.

2017. *The Great Leveler. Violence and the Global History of Inequality from the Stone Age to the Present.* Princeton, N.J.: Princeton University Press.

Schelling, Thomas C. 1980 [1960]. *The Strategy of Conflict.* Cambridge, Mass.: Harvard University Press.

Scheuerman, William. 2012. "Global Democracy and the Antistatist Fallacy." *Working paper.*

Schmidt, Brian C., and Michael C. Williams. 2008. "The Bush Doctrine and the Iraq War: Neoconservatives versus Realists." *Security Studies* 17: 191–220.

Schmitt, Carl. 2004. *Legality and Legitimacy.* Translated by Jeffrey Seitzer. Durham, N.C.: Duke University Press.

2007. *The Concept of the Political.* Chicago: University of Chicago Press.

Schumpeter, Joseph Alois. 1947. *Capitalism, Socialism, and Democracy.* New York: Harper.

Schwartzberg, Melissa. 2010. "Shouts, Murmurs and Votes: Acclamation and Aggregation in Ancient Greece." *Journal of Political Philosophy* 18(4): 448–468.

Scott, James C. 1998. *Seeing Like a State: How Certain Schemes to Improve the Human Condition Have Failed.* New Haven, Conn.: Yale University Press.

Searle, John R. 1995. *The Construction of Social Reality.* New York: Free Press.

Seeley, Thomas D. 2010. *Honeybee Democracy.* Princeton, N.J.: Princeton University Press.

Sen, Amartya. 1993. "Capability and Well-Being." Pp. 30–53 in *The Quality of Life: Studies in Development Economics*, edited by Martha Nussbaum and Amartya Sen. Oxford: Oxford University Press.

Shapiro, Ian. 2016. *Politics against Domination*. Cambridge, Mass.: Harvard University Press.

Shear, Julia L. 2011. *Polis and Revolution: Responding to Oligarchy in Classical Athens*. Cambridge: Cambridge University Press.

Shearman, David J. C., and Joseph Wayne Smith. 2007. *The Climate Change Challenge and the Failure of Democracy*. Westport, Conn.: Praeger.

Shklar, Judith N. 1989. "The Liberalism of Fear." Pp. 21–38 in *Liberalism and the Moral Life*, edited by Nancy L. Rosenblum. Cambridge, Mass.: Harvard University Press.

Simon, Herbert Alexander. 1955. "A Behavioral Model of Rational Choice." *Quarterly Journal of Economics* 65: 99–118.

Singer, Peter. 1993. *Practical Ethics*. Cambridge: Cambridge University Press.

Skinner, Quentin. 1998. *Liberty before Liberalism*. Cambridge: Cambridge University Press.

——— 2007. "Surveying the Foundations: A Retrospect and Reassessment." Pp. 236–261 in *Rethinking the Foundations of Modern Political Thought*, edited by Annabel Brett and James Tully. Cambridge: Cambridge University Press.

——— 2008. *Hobbes and Republican Liberty*. Cambridge: Cambridge University Press.

Smith, Adam. 1981 [1776]. *An Inquiry into the Nature and Causes of the Wealth of Nations*. Vol. 1. Indianapolis, Ind.: Liberty Fund.

Somin, Ilya. 2013. *Democracy and Political Ignorance: Why Smaller Government Is Smarter*. Stanford, Calif.: Stanford University Press.

Song, Sarah. 2017. "Immigration and the Limits of Democracy." *Unpublished manuscript*.

Starr, Paul. 2007. *Freedom's Power: The True Force of Liberalism*. New York: Perseus.

Stilz, Anna. 2009. *Liberal Loyalty: Freedom, Obligation, and the State*. Princeton, N.J.: Princeton University Press.

——— 2011. "Nations, States, and Territory." *Ethics* 121: 572–601.

——— 2013. "Occupancy Rights and the Wrong of Removal." *Philosophy and Public Affairs* 41: 324–356.

Stone, Peter. 2015. "Hobbes' Problem." *Good Society* 24(1): 1–14.

Sunstein, Cass R. 2013. *Simpler: The Future of Government*. New York: Simon and Schuster.

Tarnopolsky, Christina H. 2010. *Prudes, Perverts, and Tyrants: Plato's Gorgias and the Politics of Shame*. Princeton, N.J.: Princeton University Press.

Taylor, Charles. 1994. *Multiculturalism: Examining the Politics of Recognition*. Princeton, N.J.: Princeton University Press.

Taylor, Claire, and Kostas Vlassopoulos, eds. 2015. *Communities and Networks in the Ancient Greek World*. Oxford: Oxford University Press.

Teegarden, David. 2014. *Death to Tyrants! Ancient Greek Democracy and the Struggle against Tyranny*. Princeton, N.J.: Princeton University Press.

Thaler, Richard H. 2015. *Misbehaving: The Making of Behavioral Economics*. New York: W. W. Norton.

Thompson, Dennis F. 1976. *John Stuart Mill and Representative Government*. Princeton, N.J.: Princeton University Press.

Tiersch, Claudia, ed. 2016. *Die athenische Demokratie im 4. Jahrhundert: Zwischen Modernisierung und Tradition*. Stuttgart: Franz Steiner.

Tomasi, John. 2012. *Free Market Fairness*. Princeton, N.J.: Princeton University Press.

Tuck, Richard. 2007. "Hobbes and Democracy." Pp. 171–190 in *Rethinking the Foundations of Modern Political Thought*, edited by Annabel Brett and James Tully. Cambridge: Cambridge University Press.

2008. *Free Riding*. Cambridge, Mass.: Harvard University Press.

2016. *The Sleeping Sovereign: The Invention of Modern Democracy*. Cambridge: Cambridge University Press.

Turchin, Peter. 2015. *Ultrasociety: How 10,000 Years of War Made Humans the Greatest Cooperators on Earth*. Storrs, Conn.: Beresta Books.

Urbinati, Nadia. 2006. *Representative Democracy: Principles and Genealogy*. Chicago: University of Chicago Press.

2012. "Competing for Liberty: The Republican Critique of Democracy." *American Political Science Review* 106(3): 607–621.

Valentini, Laura. 2012. "Ideal vs. Non-ideal Theory: A Conceptual Map." *Philosophy Compass* 7/9: 654–664.

Vermeule, Adrian. 2007. *Mechanisms of Democracy: Institutional Design Writ Small*. New York: Oxford University Press.

Waldron, Jeremy. 1992. "Minority Cultures and the Cosmopolitan Alternative." *University of Michigan Journal of Law Reform* 25: 751–793.

2013. "*Political* Political Theory: An Inaugural Lecture." *Journal of Political Philosophy* 21(1): 1–23.

Wallis, John Joseph. 2008. "The Concept of Systematic Corruption in American Political and Economic History." Pp. 23–62 in *Corruption and Reform: Lessons from America's Economic History*, edited by Edward L. Glaeser and Claudia Goldin. Chicago: University of Chicago Press.

Warren, Mark, and Hilary Pearse, eds. 2008. *Designing Deliberative Democracy: The British Columbia Citizens' Assembly*. Cambridge: Cambridge University Press.

Weingast, Barry R. 1997. "The Political Foundations of Democracy and the Rule of Law." *American Political Science Review* 91: 245–263.

Westbrook, Raymond. 1995. "Social Justice in the Ancient Near East." *Contributions in Political Science* 354: 149–164.

Whelan, Frederick G. 1983. "Prologue: Democratic Theory and the Boundary Problem." *Nomos* 25: 13–47.

Whitehead, David. 1993. "Cardinal Virtues: The Language of Public Approbation in Democratic Athens." *Classica et Mediaevalia* 44: 37–75.

Williams, Bernard. 1993. *Shame and Necessity*. Berkeley: University of California Press.

2005. *In the Beginning Was the Deed: Realism and Moralism in Political Argument.* Princeton, N.J.: Princeton University Press.

2006. *Philosophy as a Humanistic Discipline.* Princeton, N.J.: Princeton University Press.

Wolin, Sheldon S. 1994. "Norm and Form: The Constitutionalizing of Democracy." Pp. 29–58 in *Athenian Political Thought and the Reconstruction of American Democracy*, edited by J. Peter Euben, John Wallach, and Josiah Ober. Ithaca, N.Y.: Cornell University Press.

1996. "Fugitive Democracy." Pp. 31–45 in *Democracy and Difference: Contesting the Boundaries of the Political*, edited by Seyla Benhabib. Princeton, N.J.: Princeton University Press.

Wood, Ellen Meiksins. 1988. *Peasant-Citizen and Slave: The Foundations of Athenian Democracy.* London: Verso.

Yates, J. Frank, and Michael D. Tschirhart. 2006. "Decision-Making Expertise." Pp. 421–438 in *The Cambridge Handbook of Expertise and Expert Performance*, edited by K. Anders Ericsson et al. Cambridge: Cambridge University Press.

Zakaria, Fareed. 1997. "The Rise of Illiberal Democracy." *Foreign Affairs* 76(6): 23–43.

2003. *The Future of Freedom: Illiberal Democracy at Home and Abroad.* New York: W. W. Norton.

Zelnick-Abramovitz, Rachel. 2005. *Not Wholly Free: The Concept of Manumission and the Status of Manumitted Slaves in the Ancient Greek World.* Leiden, Netherlands: Brill.

2009. "Freed Slaves, Their Status and State Control in Ancient Greece." *European Review of History* 16(3): 303–318.

Index